Linux Mint Essentials

A practical guide to Linux Mint for the novice to the professional

Jay LaCroix

BIRMINGHAM - MUMBAI

Linux Mint Essentials

First published: May 2014

Production Reference: 1150514

Published by Packt Publishing Ltd.
Livery Place
35 Livery Street
Birmingham B3 2PB, UK.

ISBN 978-1-78216-815-7

www.packtpub.com

Cover Image by Ravaji Babu (ravaji_babu@outlook.com)

Credits

Author

Jay LaCroix

Reviewers

Vinay Balraj

Abhilash Hebbar

Scott Newlon

Michael D. Prothero

Commissioning Editor

Grant Mizen

Acquisition Editor

James Jones

Content Development Editor

Dayan Hyames

Technical Editor

Menza Mathew

Copy Editors

Janbal Dharmaraj

Deepa Nambiar

Karuna Narayanan

Project Coordinator

Swati Kumari

Proofreaders

Simran Bhogal

Maria Gould

Paul Hindle

Indexers

Monica Ajmera Mehta

Priya Subramani

Production Coordinator

Kyle Albuquerque

Cover Work

Kyle Albuquerque

About the Author

Jay LaCroix is a Linux Administrator with over 12 years of experience and nine certifications. He is a technologist who enjoys all things tech, including (but not limited to) hardware, software, servers, networking, and development. When Jay is not buried in a plethora of computer books, he enjoys photography, music, gaming, and writing. Jay is passionate about open source software, especially Linux, and its long-term adoption.

Jay is also the proud author of the self-published Sci-Fi novel, *Escape to Planet 55*.

> To my dad, Bill; my sons, Alan and Johnny; my brother, Gordon; my sisters, Cheri, April, and Christina; as well as their children; my dear friends, Krys and Jim; and all of the men and women who spend countless hours volunteering their time to make open source the best software on Earth.

About the Reviewers

Vinay Balraj is a mechanical engineer by profession and is currently pursuing his masters. He, like most open source programmers, is a hobbyist software developer and is well versed in the areas of Windows, Android, UNIX, Linux, Mac, and some other operating systems. He is also well known for his ability as an advanced cross-platform user and developer, contributing in many areas for improvements on computer software.

He balances life as a graduate student and as a software developer and also guides three batches of engineering students in their final year research.

Vinay started his career as a software developer, as a hobby, and now seeks other enthusiasts just like him who wouldn't mind spending time to make things better and learn more.

I would like to thank my mother for her patience and putting up with me sitting at the computer for long hours, perfecting the document. Without her patience, it would not have been possible. I would also like to thank Swati for her timely efforts and superb co-ordination in bringing out this wonderful book, and, of course, Google for being one of the most wonderful teachers in every aspect.

Abhilash Hebbar is a young and aspiring software professional with a passion for open source technologies. He got attracted to the world of open source and Linux by the various campus events held at his college, Sri Jayachamarajendra College of Engineering. During his college days, he worked on creating a Linux distribution, which was not a success. This gave him a great exposure to the ins and outs of Linux and open source technologies.

He has worked on building cloud applications and APIs on top of open source stacks, such as Node.js, Python, Java, Ruby on Rails, and so on. He is currently working as Head of Engineering in Openly. The company provides consultation and software development services on cloud applications.

Thanks to my family, friends, and colleagues for their suggestions and the time they have put in to help me review this book.

Scott Newlon is an enthusiastic ambassador of technology and an avid autodidact. He has built his own computers, way back when computers comprised of giant monitors and floppy disks. Technology was his hobby for years when he was working as a furniture delivery driver and freight logistics manager. This hobby later turned to passion and led him to pursue a degree in Computer Science and a new career in IT when he was in his late 30s.

Scott started working as a university technical support specialist. He helped others adopt newer technology by embarking on several support projects for non-profit organizations, including PACES, a conductive education facility for differently abled youth in Sheffield, England, where he helped them establish their first online resources for their clients' families. Scott went on from the support realm to network and project management for a large national corporation in Montana.

In 2007, Scott began using LINUX. He finds LINUX empowering and educational because of its universal accessibility in terms of usage and available information. He began with Fedora, openSUSE, and Ubuntu and landed on Linux Mint 7 (Gloria) as his distro of choice when it was released in 2009. Another aspect of LINUX that has resonated for Scott was the user community through which he educated himself, including mintCast, a podcast by the Linux Mint community for all users of Linux, covering general Linux news and events and the open source space.

When the hosts put a call out for replacements, three years ago, Scott jumped in and along with his co-host, Rob Hawkins, has been a force in honing and developing the podcast, which was named as one of the top five Linux podcasts by the Linux Format magazine.

Scott now lives with his wife in Durham, NC, and works as an IT project manager for a large data management firm in the healthcare industry. *Linux Mint Essentials* is his first book.

I would like to thank my wonderful wife, Adrienne, for all her support and understanding as I have fed my ever-growing appetite for all things open source. Without your patience, I would not be where I am today.

Michael D. Prothero retired after serving 21 years in the US military to join the honorable ranks of teachers and still continues to serve his nation. His love for learning has aided him in obtaining an MS degree in Information Systems, a BS degree in Education and Computer Science, and an AS degree in Electronics. His love for sharing what he has learned has earned him the respect of his family, students, colleagues, and employers.

Michael is serving as an IT Instructor for ECPI University in Charlotte, NC. He conducts various courses on computer security and network infrastructure, as well as programming and operating systems.

This was the first book that he has worked on; however, he is eager to continue.

I would like to thank all of my students who patiently allow me to share my knowledge with them and are polite enough to share their experiences and knowledge with me. I believe that everyone has something to contribute.

www.PacktPub.com

Support files, eBooks, discount offers and more

You might want to visit www.PacktPub.com for support files and downloads related to your book.

Did you know that Packt offers eBook versions of every book published, with PDF and ePub files available? You can upgrade to the eBook version at www.PacktPub.com and as a print book customer, you are entitled to a discount on the eBook copy. Get in touch with us at service@packtpub.com for more details.

At www.PacktPub.com, you can also read a collection of free technical articles, sign up for a range of free newsletters and receive exclusive discounts and offers on Packt books and eBooks.

http://PacktLib.PacktPub.com

Do you need instant solutions to your IT questions? PacktLib is Packt's online "digital book library. Here, you can access, read and search across Packt's entire library of books.

Why Subscribe?
- Fully searchable across every book published by Packt
- Copy and paste, print and bookmark content
- On demand and accessible via web browser

Free Access for Packt account holders

If you have an account with Packt at www.PacktPub.com, you can use this to access PacktLib today and view nine entirely free books. Simply use your login credentials for immediate access.

Table of Contents

Preface

Welcome to the world of Linux Mint! With this book as your guide, you'll explore this exciting Linux distribution from its installation all the way to its administration and maintenance. Geared toward the Linux novice, this book will build skills that will not only help you use Linux Mint for your day-to-day computing tasks, but also build a foundation on which you can expand your knowledge. Whether you simply want to benefit from a bird's-eye view of Linux Mint or get started on the road to becoming a Linux admin, this book will help you get there. Along the way, we'll work through how to complete day-to-day tasks such as creating/managing files and documents, and we'll also work on configuring our Mint installation, managing packages, connecting to networks, increasing security, adding/removing users, troubleshooting, and more!

What this book covers

Chapter 1, Meet Linux Mint, discusses what Linux Mint is and what sets it apart from other distributions. We'll also talk about some reasons you'd want to choose Linux in the first place.

Chapter 2, Creating Boot Media and Installing Linux Mint, will walk you through the process of installing Linux Mint on your computer. Several methods of installation, such as bootable DVD and bootable flash drive, are covered in this book, and you'll also learn about some of the best practices for the installation of Linux Mint, including tips on partitioning your hard disk.

Chapter 3, Getting Acquainted with Cinnamon, discusses Cinnamon, a fresh and exciting desktop environment (a graphical user interface) that is taking the Linux community by storm. In this chapter, we'll tackle this interface head-on.

Chapter 4, An Introduction to the Terminal, will explain how to navigate the filesystem, execute commands, search for files, and even work through an introduction to scripting. Although using a Terminal is not required in order to use Mint, learning the basics of the terminal will further empower your skills.

Chapter 5, Utilizing Storage and Media, discusses how to work through the examples of accessing various types of media in Mint. The examples shown in this chapter include formatting and mounting removable storage, along with analyzing disk usage, burning CDs and DVDs, and utilizing Mint's USB Image Writer.

Chapter 6, Installing and Removing Software, discusses how to work through the examples of installing and removing software on our Mint installation, as it features a large repository of free software packages. Also, several different methods of software management will be covered, with examples of both graphical programs and terminal commands.

Chapter 7, Enjoying Multimedia on Mint, is all about enjoying multimedia on Mint. This chapter covers features such as listening to MP3s, ripping audio CDs, editing audio tags, watching DVDs, and more!

Chapter 8, Managing Users and Permissions, talks about users and permissions. You'll learn how to create/remove users and groups, as well as how to configure user access to administrative commands with sudo.

Chapter 9, Connecting to Networks, is all about networking. Concepts such as wired and wireless networking will be covered, as well as accessing your machine via SSH and also how to share files.

Chapter 10, Securing Linux Mint, will work on hardening our Linux Mint system with concepts such as choosing strong passwords, encrypting your home folder, blocking access to specific websites, and even backing up and restoring important data.

Chapter 11, Advanced Administration Techniques, will cover advanced concepts for managing your installation. In this chapter, setting up cron jobs, moving to new Mint releases and killing processes, and monitoring resources will be covered.

Chapter 12, Troubleshooting Linux Mint, concludes our journey with Mint by providing certain tips and tricks for what to do when things go wrong. In this chapter, you'll learn about dealing with problems such as booting issues, audio and networking woes, as well as how to access system logs for troubleshooting.

Appendix A, *Reinstalling Mint while Retaining Data*, discusses a technique on how to move from one release of Linux Mint to another, as Linux doesn't really feature a direct utility for you to do this.

Appendix B, *Using the MATE edition of Linux Mint*, discusses another edition of Linux Mint, MATE. In this appendix, we'll explore the various specific features of the MATE edition, which runs better on older hardware.

Appendix C, *Using the KDE edition of Linux Mint*, discusses another popular desktop environment, and Mint features it as the default desktop edition. In our final appendix, we'll explore the KDE Mint flavor.

What you need for this book

In order to work through the examples within this book, you'll need a computer with at least the following specs:

- 10 GB hard drive space (30 GB or higher recommended)
- 512 MB system RAM (1 GB or higher recommended)
- 1.0 GHz Processor (1.6 GHz dual-core or higher recommended)
- Video card with 128 MB video RAM
- DVD drive or 2 GB or higher flash drive (to create installation media)

Given the lightweight nature of Linux, you can certainly run Mint on lesser resources, of course. The better your system's resources are, the faster and more efficient your experience will be.

Who this book is for

This book is geared primarily toward the Linux novice. Perhaps you've heard of Linux and are curious about it, or you just want to experience a new way of computing. In this book, we'll start our Linux exploration from the ground up using Linux Mint as our guide, so someone who is just starting out with Linux (or even someone who has never used it before) would see the maximum benefit. This book is also great for those who want an overall guide to Linux Mint, as we'll be covering all the core concepts required to make the most out of this exciting distribution.

Conventions

In this book, you will find a number of styles of text that distinguish between different kinds of information. The following are some examples of these styles, and an explanation of their meaning.

Code words in text, database table names, folder names, filenames, file extensions, pathnames, dummy URLs, user input, and Twitter handles are shown as follows: "In addition, feel free to join the `#linuxmint-help` IRC chat room and speak to other users there as well."

Any command-line input or output is written as follows:

```
ls -l /dev/disk/by-uuid
```

New terms and **important words** are shown in bold. Words that you see on the screen, in menus or dialog boxes for example, appear in the text like this: "Clicking on the **Apply** button will save your settings."

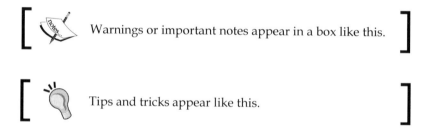

Warnings or important notes appear in a box like this.

Tips and tricks appear like this.

Any terminal output is written as follows:

```
# cat /var/log/syslog
```

Reader feedback

Feedback from our readers is always welcome. Let us know what you think about this book—what you liked or may have disliked. Reader feedback is important for us to develop titles that you really get the most out of.

To send us general feedback, simply send an e-mail to `feedback@packtpub.com`, and mention the book title via the subject of your message.

If there is a topic that you have expertise in and you are interested in either writing or contributing to a book, see our author guide on `www.packtpub.com/authors`.

Customer support

Now that you are the proud owner of a Packt book, we have a number of things to help you to get the most from your purchase.

Errata

Although we have taken every care to ensure the accuracy of our content, mistakes do happen. If you find a mistake in one of our books—maybe a mistake in the text or the code—we would be grateful if you would report this to us. By doing so, you can save other readers from frustration and help us improve subsequent versions of this book. If you find any errata, please report them by visiting http://www.packtpub.com/submit-errata, selecting your book, clicking on the **errata submission form** link, and entering the details of your errata. Once your errata are verified, your submission will be accepted and the errata will be uploaded on our website, or added to any list of existing errata, under the Errata section of that title. Any existing errata can be viewed by selecting your title from http://www.packtpub.com/support.

Piracy

Piracy of copyright material on the Internet is an ongoing problem across all media. At Packt, we take the protection of our copyright and licenses very seriously. If you come across any illegal copies of our works, in any form, on the Internet, please provide us with the location address or website name immediately so that we can pursue a remedy.

Please contact us at copyright@packtpub.com with a link to the suspected pirated material.

We appreciate your help in protecting our authors, and our ability to bring you valuable content.

Questions

You can contact us at questions@packtpub.com if you are having a problem with any aspect of the book, and we will do our best to address it.

1
Meet Linux Mint

Welcome to *Linux Mint Essentials*; your exciting journey into the world of Linux Mint starts here. There's no better place to start your adventure than Mint. Its user friendly nature along with its scalability caters to both beginners and power users alike; the out-of-the-box Mint includes everything you need to work and play. In this book, you'll discover how to master this amazing distribution from the initial installation all the way to maintaining and troubleshooting it. We'll start with an in-depth look at how to complete the installation, and then we'll proceed through each of Mint's core technologies to help boost your knowledge. Along the way, we'll work on some fun activities to put your new knowledge to use.

Before we get started though, it's very important that you understand the core concepts behind Mint and what makes it so great. In this chapter, we'll explore key concepts such as the Linux kernel, what a distribution is, and some reasons why Linux Mint is so awesome. If you are already aware of these concepts (or you're itching to get your feet wet), skip ahead to *Chapter 2, Creating Boot Media and Installing Linux Mint,* where we'll set up our very own Linux Mint installation.

In this chapter, we will cover the following topics:

- What is Linux?
- The difference between Linux and a distribution of Linux
- What makes Mint such a great distribution?
- Sign up for forum and community accounts

While getting accustomed to Linux, there's most likely a great deal of things that you'll want to learn. Mint comes equipped to help you handle most tasks, such as checking e-mail, working with files, editing documents, and sharing files. We'll tackle most of the common use cases in this book to help you become productive with Mint.

Linux isn't only about getting work done. Whether you enjoy listening to music, watching videos, or just having fun with your leisure time, we'll cover those concepts as well. In fact, *Chapter 7, Enjoying Multimedia on Mint* is dedicated to consuming multimedia, and I may throw in a Linux game or two for good measure.

As we reach the end of our journey, we'll go over concepts of how to maintain our installation as well as how to troubleshoot it. Most of the troubleshooting and maintenance tasks in Mint aren't distribution specific, so you'll learn some real-world skills that you can take with you to other platforms.

Why choose Linux?

It may surprise some to discover that they use Linux every day, even if they don't realize it. If you checked your e-mail today or posted a social networking status update, you've used Linux. Since Linux servers make up a large portion of servers on the Internet, chances are you interacted with a site or service hosted on a Linux server and you probably do so every day. If you own a smart TV, chances are it's powered by a stripped-down version of the Linux kernel. In fact, if you are reading this book on an e-reader, the device was most likely built on top of Linux. And even if you purchased a print copy, the point of sale software used to facilitate your purchase of the book quite possibly ran on Linux. Linux is everywhere! And on the desktop, it's a powerful alternative to proprietary operating systems.

To be fair, most computer users don't care which operating system is installed on their computer or what underlying software the websites they visit runs on. When someone purchases a computer and powers it on for the first time, they are typically presented with a license agreement; they type in their desired user name, and then they're ready to connect to the Internet so they can check their Facebook account and watch cat videos. Even though there are several different operating systems that one can install on a computer, most of the users aren't aware that there is a choice. When a typical user thinks of an operating system, they immediately think of Windows since it's what the majority of PCs ship with. When an Apple user thinks about a Mac, the OSX operating system is largely assumed. This is why when two people have an argument regarding Mac versus PC, they are actually arguing over which operating system is superior since Windows isn't the only operating system available for the PC, much like the fact that OSX isn't the only operating system you can install on a Mac. They aren't aware that there is a choice other than what comes preinstalled from the factory.

While Linux isn't technically an operating system (we'll discuss more on this later), it represents another choice for installation on your computer. Linux comes in many flavors (also known as "distributions"), each catering toward a specific purpose, and some of which aim to be a full-featured replacement for proprietary operating systems such as Windows or OSX on your PC or Mac. And many of them do a very good job, with distributions such as Mint and Ubuntu leading the pack.

Why use Linux in place of what came with your computer? The answer to that question varies depending on who is asking it. Some may be frustrated over the multitude of Windows viruses in the wild. While no operating system or kernel is completely immune to viruses, there is no question that Linux is the more secure choice when compared to Windows as it suffers far fewer intrusions and viruses. The reason why Linux is more secure is open to debate. Some believe this is due to its lack of popularity on the desktop, while others believe that its security is inherent.

Regardless of the reason, using Linux on your desktop or laptop is a very fulfilling (and liberating) experience. While there is no one "best" operating system (as each has its own purpose for existence), Linux distributions such as Mint give you more control over your computer than you may have thought possible. The modular nature of Linux distributions allow you to easily swap out components you don't like and swap in those that you do, for example, if you're not fond of the file manager that ships with Mint, remove it and install a different one instead. In fact, if you decide that you don't enjoy the user interface (desktop environment), install another one as there are many to choose from. The possibilities in customizing your own environment are limitless. Also, the proven stability and security of Linux are welcoming aspects as well. Installing Linux can open your eyes to a whole new world. Linux Mint is a great gateway into this world as it is a wonderful example of a user friendly Linux distribution done right.

What is a distribution?

So, with all that talk about Linux, what exactly is a **distribution**? First, it's important to understand that Linux is not an operating system, though you'll often hear of it being referred to as such, solely out of convenience. Linux actually just refers to the kernel, which is the core of the operating system. A distribution of Linux is equivalent to an operating system as you may understand it from a Windows or OSX perspective. To put it simply, a distribution (also known as **distro**) is a suite of applications bundled along with the Linux kernel that make up an operating system, which suits a particular purpose or targets a specific type of user. There are distributions in all shapes and sizes. Some target absolute beginners, others target power users, and some even target specific individual tasks such as performing network security testing, cloning hard drives, and even removing viruses or recovering data from Windows machines.

Perhaps the most daunting task for a newcomer is to determine which Linux distribution to start with. In fact, there are literally over 100 distributions to choose from, such as Ubuntu, Debian, Arch, Fedora, and OpenSUSE; so which one of these should you pick? Each distribution targets a specific audience; so, it is important to choose a distribution that will match your experience level or the task that you wish to accomplish. Not only is Mint one of the most user-friendly distributions available, it also scales to advanced users as well. This means that you can use Mint to hone your initial Linux skills, and also continue using it as you graduate to become an advanced or expert user. As your skills grow, you'll find yourself discovering more and more neat ways to tweak it, since Mint is also one of the most customizable distributions available.

Mint's primary focus is to be a full-featured replacement for the Windows or Mac OSX operating systems. Mint comes bundled with various software and utilities to allow you to be productive right away; for example, Firefox is bundled with the distribution, which will allow you to instantly browse the web; LibreOffice is installed to facilitate the opening and creation of office documents and spreadsheets; Pidgin is included to send instant messages on networks such as Yahoo Messenger, AOL Instant Messenger, and others, and you even have your choice of one of four different **graphical user interfaces** (**GUIs**) for the overall desktop. In a nutshell, Mint is a complete operating environment right out of the box. Best of all, it's free—there are no licensing fees. In fact, it's perfectly legal to make copies of the Mint installation media and pass it along to friends; unlike proprietary operating systems, this is actually encouraged.

Free means Freedom. When compared to closed source operating systems such as Windows and OSX, there is quite a bit more flexibility with how a free Linux distribution such as Mint can be used and distributed. With Mint, you'll never need a product key or a proprietary license agreement. You can download and install Mint without paying a dime, though donations certainly help keep the project going. In the case of Windows, you often have to pay a licensing fee of over $100 for each major release. And even if you do pay for it, you're only allowed to install it on a single computer. After installation, you'll have to activate the product via the Internet or a toll-free phone number to verify that the product is only installed on one machine. In the case of OSX, it is actually against the licensing agreement to install it on anything other than a Mac.

When it comes to most Linux distributions, you do not have to activate the software, nor are there any restrictions in the form of agreements that dictate which type of machine you install it on. If you can find a way to install Linux on a game console, a tablet, or even a toaster, you'll get more power. In fact, when a new version of the distribution is released, which in the case of Mint, happens every 6-8 months, you can download the new version immediately also for free.

Linux Mint's ability to be free is due to various open source licenses that govern its software; for example, Firefox, which comes bundled with the distribution, is released under the Mozilla Public License, while the Linux kernel is released under the **GPL (GNU Public License)** Version 2. Proprietary elements, such as proprietary drivers, that are required to make some hardware work and closed source multimedia technologies are not free software, but are included with Mint wherever required to make some functionality work. More information regarding the GPL license can be found at `https://www.gnu.org/licenses/gpl.html`.

You may hear some negative feedback regarding the free nature of Linux, such as the claim that it being free means that it has less support, or that the fact that it being open source makes it more vulnerable to attack since crackers are able to look through the source code to attempt to discover how to break it. In actuality, neither could be further from the truth. First, there is certainly no shortage of support for Linux Mint and many other distributions. There is a large community in the form of chat rooms and message boards where volunteers are ready and eager to help if you run into an issue. Unlike Windows and OSX, their vendors (Microsoft and Apple respectively) charge for support, so their users end up using chat rooms and forums in much the same way.

Also, with regards to support, there are paid support firms that will provide technical support, as is the case with other operating systems. As for the security aspect, the fact that Linux is open source puts it under more scrutiny, which in turn makes it more secure. Many developers and enthusiasts will look through the source code quite often to attempt to locate vulnerabilities. Since the source code is open, anyone can check through it and look for anything of concern. In addition, the source code being available helps ensure that there are no proprietary back doors that malicious users, governments, or large corporations may place in order to carry out surveillance on users.

Is Linux hard to learn?

Quite often, I am asked whether or not Linux is hard to learn. The reputation Linux has of being hard to use and learn most likely stems from the early days when typical distributions actually were quite difficult to use. I remember a time when simply installing a video card driver required manually recompiling the kernel (which took many hours) and enabling support for media such as MP3s required multiple manual commands.

Nowadays, however, how difficult Linux is to learn and use is determined by which distribution you pick. If, for example, you're a beginner and you choose a distribution tailored for advanced users, you are likely to find yourself frustrated very quickly. In fact, there are distros available that make you do everything manually, such as choosing which version of the kernel to run and installing and configuring the desktop environment. This level of customizability is wonderful for advanced users who wish to build their own Linux system from the ground up, though it is more likely that beginners would be put off by it. General purpose distributions such as Mint are actually very easy to learn, and in some cases, some tasks in Mint are even easier to perform than in other operating systems.

The ease of use we enjoy with a number of Linux distributions is due in part to the advancements that Ubuntu has made in usability. Around the time when Windows Vista was released, a renaissance of sorts occurred in the Linux community. At that time, quite a few people were so outraged by Windows Vista that a lot more effort was put into making Ubuntu easier to use. It can be argued that the time period of Vista was the fastest growth in usability that Linux ever saw. Tasks that were once rites of passage (such as installing drivers and media codecs) became trivial. The exciting changes in Ubuntu during that time inspired other distributions to make similar changes. Nowadays, usage of Ubuntu is beginning to decline due to the fact that not everyone is pleased about its new user interface (Unity); however, there is no denying the positive impact it had on Linux usability. Being based on Ubuntu, Mint inherits many of those benefits, but also aims to improve on its proposed weaknesses. Due to its great reception, it eventually went on to surpass Ubuntu itself. Mint currently sits at the very top of the charts on `Distrowatch.com`, and with a good reason—it's an amazing distribution.

Distributions such as Mint are incredibly user friendly. Even the installation procedure is a cinch, and most can get through it by simply accepting the defaults. Installing new software is also straightforward as everything is included in software repositories and managed through a graphical application (we will explore software installation in *Chapter 6, Installing and Removing Software*). In fact, I recently acquired an HP printer that comes with a CD full of required software for Windows, but when connected to my Mint computer, it just worked. No installation of any software was required. Linux has never been easier!

What Mint does differently

There are many distributions available, each vying for your attention. So, why use Linux Mint and not some other distro such as Ubuntu or Fedora? The user-friendly nature of Linux Mint is certainly a good reason to use it. However, there is more to its value than just that. As the famous saying goes:

> *If I have seen further, it is by standing on the shoulders of giants.*

> — *Sir Isaac Newton*

Linux Mint, being based on Ubuntu, is certainly built on a giant. It takes the already solid foundation of Ubuntu, and improves on it by using a different user interface, adds custom tools, and includes various tweaks to make its media formats recognized right from the start.

A distribution being based on other distributions is a common occurrence in the Linux community, the reason being that it's much easier to build a distribution on an already existing foundation, since building your own base is quite time consuming (and expensive). By utilizing the existing foundation of Ubuntu, Mint benefits from the massive software repository that Ubuntu has at its disposal, without having to reinvent the wheel and recreate everything from the ground up. The development time saved by doing this allows the Linux Mint developers to focus on adding exciting features and tweaks to improve its ease of use. Given the fact that Ubuntu is open source, it's perfectly fine to use it as a base for a completely separate distribution. Unlike the proprietary software market, the developers of Mint aren't at risk of being sued for recycling the package base of another distribution. In fact, Ubuntu itself is built on the foundation of another distribution (Debian), and Mint is not the only distribution to use Ubuntu as a base.

As mentioned before, Mint utilizes a different user interface than Ubuntu. Ubuntu ships with the Unity interface, which (so far) has not been highly regarded by the majority of the Linux community. Unity split Ubuntu's user community in half as some people loved the new interface, though others were not so enthused and made their distaste well-known. Rather than adopt Unity during this transition, Mint opted for two primary environments instead, **Cinnamon** and **MATE**. Cinnamon is recommended for more modern computers, and MATE is useful for older computers that are lower in processing power and memory. MATE is also useful for those who prefer the older style of Linux environments, as it is a fork of **GNOME 2.x**.

Many people consider Cinnamon to be the default desktop environment in Linux Mint, but that is open to debate. The Mint developers have yet to declare either of them as the default. Mint actually ships five different versions (also known as spins) of its distribution. Four of them (Cinnamon, MATE, KDE, and Xfce) feature different user interfaces as the main difference, while the fifth is a completely different distribution that is based on Debian instead of Ubuntu, and is not covered in this book. Due to its popularity, Cinnamon is the closest thing to a default in Mint and as such, it is the recommended version to download to be able to follow along with this book. However, many of the topics and examples will work in the other spins as well. We will cover the Cinnamon desktop environment in *Chapter 3, Getting Acquainted with Cinnamon*.

Releases and support

Linux Mint typically releases new versions of the distribution every 7 months or so. Each new release features the newest available versions of all packages software (as available in the Ubuntu software repository) as well as new features. Each release is given a female name, which also ends with the letter "a", for example, Version 7 was codenamed "Gloria" and Version 15 was named "Olivia".

While Ubuntu itself releases new versions every 6 months on a strict schedule, Mint generally releases one month after each Ubuntu release, as long as it is ready and there are no bugs preventing the final release. In the case of Ubuntu, it's not uncommon for a new release to be published even if a few bugs remain. Very rarely is a release of Ubuntu held back for any reason. In the case of Mint, it's not uncommon for a release to be held back if it does not meet testing standards. For Mint, publishing a quality product is more important than releasing it on time.

Each release of Mint follows Ubuntu's support schedule. Support in terms of a distribution release generally refers to the period of time in which software updates will be made available. Like Ubuntu, each Mint release is supported for 9 months. After the 9 months expire, it will no longer receive updates and is then not recommended for general use.

In addition, some releases of Ubuntu are considered **Long Term Support** (**LTS**) releases, which are supported for 18 months. As a result, any version of Mint released using an LTS release of Ubuntu as a foundation is also considered an LTS release. LTS releases may feature software that is more out of date than other releases, but offer more stability.

Of course, there is nothing stopping someone from using an expired release. However, if you ask for assistance from the community and you are using an older version, you will probably be encouraged to upgrade to a supported release before troubleshooting will continue. If a bug report is submitted against an expired version of a distribution, chances are it will be immediately closed.

Whenever possible, it is recommended to use either the latest normal release or the latest LTS release. The installation and related best practices will be covered in the next chapter.

Mint-specific tools

Although the main difference between Linux Mint and Ubuntu is the user interface, various tools that you can use to customize your environment are included, and these are specific to Mint. Some of the more prominent additions include the following tools:

- **The Update Manager**: Most distributions include their own software to handle updates in some form or another, but Mint decided to write their own instead of reusing the update manager that ships with Ubuntu. Mint's version prioritizes updates that are less likely to break your system. Installing updates are discussed in more detail in *Chapter 6, Installing and Removing Software*.

- **The Backup Tool**: This is a simple backup program you can use to create simple backups. You can choose to simply copy files from one location to another, or create a compressed archive. In addition, you can also create a list of installed software for importing into a new Mint install. However, the Backup Tool does not include any synchronization features.

- **The Domain Blocker**: This tool allows you to block specific websites on your computer. This is primarily useful if your computer is shared, especially by young people, and you would like to control which websites can be accessed.

- **Firewall Configuration**: Most distributions these days ship with the iptables firewall, but it does not contain a GUI. Firewall Configuration is a tool that allows you to configure iptables with a GUI rather than relying on specific shell commands.

- **The Upload Manager**: This is a very simplistic tool, which you can use to upload files to online services, such as FTP. For advanced FTP tasks, an advanced client software such as FileZilla will offer more features.

- **Software Sources**: Included with Mint are a set of repositories, which are collections of software available online for download. The repositories included in Mint are by no means the only ones that are available to you. It's often the case that developers may create third-party repositories containing additional software that is able to extend Mint even further; for example, `Virtualbox.org` features a repository one can use to ensure the latest version of **VirtualBox** is available. Software Sources is a program that allows you to easily add or remove additional repositories. Software Sources and repositories will be covered in *Chapter 6, Installing and Removing Software*.

Interacting with the Linux Mint community

The size of its community is one of the most important factors to consider when choosing a distribution. If it has a small community, it doesn't matter how great the distribution is; finding support from fellow users would be difficult and would result in frustration. Thankfully, Linux Mint has a sizable community with volunteers ready to answer your questions. If you experience any issues, you can post a message in the forum, or even chat in real time over **IRC** (**XChat** is included in Mint to facilitate IRC chatting out of the box).

To request assistance via the official forum, navigate to `forums.linuxmint.com`.

For IRC chat, you can connect to `#linuxmint-help` (or `#linuxmint-chat` for chatting about Mint without requesting assistance). For more information on how to access IRC channels such as the ones provided for Mint, see `http://community.linuxmint.com/tutorial/view/12` for an overview of how to connect.

Before submitting requests for assistance in any Linux community, it's important to do your research first. Volunteers may feel as though you are taking their time for granted if you do not first try to find the answer on your own. Typically, it's recommended to perform a Google search for your problem to see if someone else had already posted a similar message and found a solution. Quite often, you'll find that your issue has already been addressed.

In addition to an official forum and IRC chat room, Mint also features a neat community page (`http://community.linuxmint.com`), as shown in the following screenshot, where you can submit ideas on how the developers can improve the distribution. Ideas are voted up or down by other members of the community. In addition, you can find the status of upcoming releases, post/read tutorials, and track which countries have the most Mint users.

The Linux Mint community home page

The forum for Linux Mint and its community page utilize two separate logins. Creating an account on one doesn't create an account on the other.

Creating community and forum accounts

In the next chapter, you'll create your very own installation of Linux Mint. However, before we move on, it's highly recommended that you register an account on the official forum so that you can immediately join discussions with other Mint users and request assistance should you need help with anything outside the scope of this book. The steps to do so are as follows:

1. Access the official Linux Mint forum by navigating your browser to `http://forums.linuxmint.com`.

2. In the upper right-hand corner, click on **Register**.

3. Read and understand the user agreement that is displayed and after you understand them, click on **I agree to these terms**.

4. Fill out the form; ensure you have selected the proper time zone and language for your location. In addition, you will need to confirm your e-mail account in order to finalize your account.

Although it's not required to follow along with the examples in this book, creating an account at the community site is recommended. To do so, perform the following steps:

1. Navigate your browser to `http://community.linuxmint.com`

2. Click on **Register**.

3. Fill out the form and again click on **Register**.

Meet the community

Now that you have a forum and community account, take a moment to set up your profile and introduce yourself to other Mint users. In addition, feel free to join the `#linuxmint-help` IRC chat room and speak to other users there as well. The user community is very welcoming.

Summary

Linux is certainly an exciting technology, but it is also a very diverse one. In this chapter, we demystified core concepts and worked through creating forum and community accounts. You've learned that Linux refers to a kernel (while it is not an operating system) and a Linux distribution is a collection of software bundled along with the Linux kernel that provides a complete operating environment. You've also learned some of the many benefits of choosing Linux over proprietary software such as Windows and Mac, which includes its modular nature, stability, security, as well as the fact that open source distributions are devoid of the frustrating restrictions and licensing that proprietary systems such as Windows and Mac contain.

Next, in *Chapter 2, Creating Boot Media and Installing Linux Mint*, we will dive in to creating installation media and installing Linux Mint onto a computer. We'll cover the various means of doing so, such as creating a bootable DVD (or a bootable USB stick if you don't have a DVD drive) as well as planning your hard disk layout.

2
Creating Boot Media and Installing Linux Mint

During the installation process, you'll need to make various decisions about how to configure your system. These decisions might include determining your partitioning scheme and deciding whether or not to encrypt your home folder. Linux Mint, like most distributions, offers several ways in which you can configure it during installation. Mint can be installed on your hard drive by replacing the operating system that came with your computer, or it can be installed alongside existing operating systems or even on USB flash drives and virtual machines. In fact, Linux Mint can be used from bootable media (such as a DVD or flash drive) without wiping your hard drive. In this chapter, we'll go through most of the common installation scenarios and best practices. By the end of this chapter, you'll have your very own Linux Mint installation that you'll use to follow along with the remainder of the book.

In this chapter, we will discuss the following topics:

- Which version to download
- The different methods of installing Linux Mint
- Creating a bootable DVD
- Creating a bootable USB flash drive
- Testing out your live media
- Planning your partitioning scheme
- The installation process
- To encrypt or not to encrypt

Which version to download

As mentioned in *Chapter 1*, *Meet Linux Mint*, there are several versions (or spins) of Linux Mint. The primary difference is that each version features a different primary user interface (Cinnamon, MATE, KDE, and Xfce), but the differences don't stop there. The preinstalled applications also differ a bit between them.

Before you decide which spin to download, the first decision you should make is whether or not to install the 32-bit or 64-bit version. As a general rule, you should choose the 64-bit version if you have 4 GB or more of RAM. Considering that almost all computers sold at the time of writing this book shipped with 4 GB or more of RAM, the majority of readers should download the 64-bit edition. If you have an older computer with less than 4 GB of RAM and you have no intention of upgrading beyond 4 GB later, go with the 32-bit version of Mint. The version you choose will not impact your ability to follow along with this book in any way whatsoever.

> The general accepted benefit of a 64-bit distribution is that it is able to support 4 GB or more of RAM. However, there is a work-around that supports more than 4 GB of RAM even in 32-bit distributions, though it is beyond the scope of this book. For now, just choose the 64-bit version unless you have an older machine.

After deciding on which architecture to download, the next decision is which spin to use. The recommended version of Mint to be downloaded in order to follow along with this book is the Cinnamon edition, which is the closest thing to a default that Mint has among its different spins. However, most of the chapters will still be compatible with the other versions. What follows is a brief description of the different editions of the Linux machine.

The Linux Mint KDE edition

The KDE edition features the **K Desktop Environment (KDE)** instead of Cinnamon. KDE is considered to be a more Windows-like environment, though it has evolved quite a bit over the years and has taken on a look and feel of its own. KDE is one of the most customizable user interfaces available for Linux, thus allowing the user so much control that some may find it intimidating. For example, you are able to customize the desktop by adding various widgets (**Plasmoids**) in any number of combinations to create a desktop that is truly unique. KDE at one point was considered bloated and slow, but nowadays, it runs well even on modest hardware.

The KDE edition features some applications, such as **Amarok** (the music player), **Dolphin** (the file manager), and **Ktorrent** (the BitTorrent client), that are not installed by default in other spins. The following screenshot shows the desktop of the KDE edition:

The desktop of the KDE edition

The Linux Mint Xfce edition

This edition features the Xfce desktop environment, which is geared primarily toward those with older hardware. The system resources needed to run the Xfce environment are less than any other version of Mint. Additionally, even those with powerful hardware may run the Xfce spin in order to benefit from as little software overhead as possible. The Xfce edition largely features the same software selection as other spins, but the **Thunar** file manager and the **Whisker** application's menu are the noticeable differences. The following screenshot shows the desktop of the Xfce edition:

The desktop of the Xfce edition

The Linux Mint MATE edition

The MATE edition (pronounced Mah-Tay) is similar to the Xfce edition in the sense that it's geared toward those with older systems or those that just want an environment that runs lighter, though it's not quite as light as the Xfce edition. The MATE desktop environment is a fork of the older GNOME 2 desktop and is for those who are not impressed with the newer GNOME 3 desktop. The MATE desktop environment appears functionally similar to the Cinnamon edition.

The Linux Mint Cinnamon edition

Linux Mint Cinnamon is the recommended edition for use with this book. In fact, the following chapter is dedicated to it. Cinnamon is a full-featured desktop environment that runs fast and is full of exciting features. Like the other versions, it includes everything you need to be productive right away. Cinnamon is a visually appealing environment that is easy to learn and use. For quite some time, Cinnamon has largely been exclusive to Mint, though this environment has since made its way to other distributions of Linux as well. Don't let my recommendation of the Cinnamon edition of Mint stop you from trying the other spins. One of the things that makes Linux so amazing is the number of choices it gives you. If you have the time, check out the other spins as well. One of the most important milestones for a new Linux user is discovering which desktop environment you prefer.

The different methods of installing Linux Mint

Most operating systems are typically installed on your primary hard disk, and that's pretty much your only option. Linux (including Mint) is much more flexible and offers more options to install and use any given distribution. In the case of Mint, it can also take over your entire hard disk just like any other OS, but the fun doesn't stop here. Mint can also be installed on a USB flash drive (either as boot media or even as a full-fledged installation), which then becomes an operating environment in your pocket that you can take with you and use on any PC. Mint can also be installed on a virtual machine or alongside another operating system, thus allowing you to select between them when your computer starts up.

In fact, Mint doesn't have to be installed at all. The installation media you'll create is useful for more than just installing the distribution; you can even run Mint from the DVD or USB flash drive itself without installing it. This is known as the live mode, and it contains an entire operating environment that you can use without installing it onto a hard disk. The main downside of a live environment is that none of your changes are saved unless you configure something called **persistence** (otherwise, everything runs from the disc and is stored in RAM). Also, there is a considerable lag in the launching of applications since the access times are much slower than those of a standard hard disk. However, one of the biggest benefits of a live environment is that it can be used as an emergency boot media, which will enable you to access computers that will not boot their primary operating system. So, a live DVD or flash drive is something you'll always want to have in case you experience problems.

If you choose to burn a Linux Mint image onto a blank DVD, you'll want to make it a practice to recreate the live media at least once a year. Recordable DVD media does not last forever, and the data will actually fade over time. This is not the case with commercially produced DVDs, such as movies and games, that are manufactured via a completely different process.

The first step in our Linux Mint adventure is to create bootable media from which we can run and then later install the distribution. The bootable media that we'll create will contain an entire live environment, so you'll be productive with Mint very soon. However, before you jump into the installation of Mint onto your hard drive, take some time to use the live environment and see how it works on your hardware. In the following two activities, we'll create our very own installation media.

Creating a bootable DVD

The current activity as well as the next one will walk you through the creation of your very own bootable media. This activity will walk you through the creation of a bootable DVD, and the next one will cover the creation of a bootable flash drive. However, you only need to complete one or the other (not both). Whether you should create a bootable DVD or flash drive depends on your needs, what you hope to accomplish, and what kind of hardware you have.

Live DVDs are very useful boot discs that will work on the majority of computers made in the last several years. However, optical drives are no longer a standard requirement on computers shipped today. While most computers still come with a DVD drive, more and more computers are being manufactured without them. For example, if you were to buy an Ultrabook, a live DVD would be useless to you because few (if any) Ultrabooks come with an optical drive. At the time of writing this book, Apple has discontinued optical drives on literally the entirety of their product line. The days of optical media are definitely numbered. If your machine doesn't contain an optical drive, your only choice is to create a bootable flash drive.

If your computer has a DVD drive, a live DVD would be a very useful tool for you to create. You can use it to run a full-featured Mint environment right from the DVD (which is exactly the same as an installed version but runs slower and doesn't retain changes). You can also keep it on hand in case one of your computers suffers a software defect that causes it not to boot, thus enabling you to perform the recovery in a pinch. If your computer doesn't include a DVD drive, then this activity is of no value to you and you should skip it.

To create a live DVD, perform the following steps:

1. Access the Linux Mint website (`http://www.linuxmint.com`) from any computer with an Internet connection and a DVD burner.

2. Click on the **Download** link and download the 64-bit Cinnamon version (unless you decided to go with a different spin).

3. In the list that appears, find the mirror nearest to you and click on it. The ISO image should start downloading.

4. After the ISO image finishes downloading, burn it to a DVD using the **Burn Image** option in your burner program. After some time, a bootable disc will be created.

5. Reboot your PC with the disc in the drive, and as the BIOS screen appears, press the key combination designated for the boot menu and select your DVD drive as the boot source.

6. Linux Mint will now boot into a fully functioning environment, complete with all of its applications.

 There are many different DVD-burning applications available for various operating systems, and it is beyond the scope of this book to go over all of them. Generally speaking, avoid the **Burn data DVD** option as it is not the one you're looking for and will not result in a bootable DVD. The option you're looking for is typically named **Burn Image**.

Creating a bootable USB flash drive

Creating a bootable USB flash drive has the same benefits as creating a bootable DVD plus one. You can create a bootable flash drive where the changes you make are retained (persistence), unlike a DVD, which is entirely read only. Thus, you can have an entire operating system that fits in your pocket and can be booted from any PC. Depending on the type of computer you have, creating a bootable flash drive may be your only option if you lack a DVD drive, as is becoming more and more common. It's recommended that you use a 2 GB flash drive or a larger one. If you want your resulting flash drive to allow you to save files and changes, try to go for 4 GB or larger if you can.

The steps to create a bootable flash drive from within the Windows operating system are as follows:

1. Access the `pendrivelinux.com` website in your browser.

2. Look for **Universal USB Installer** and download it. At the time of writing this book, the direct URL is `http://www.pendrivelinux.com/universal-usb-installer-easy-as-1-2-3/`.

3. Open the file that you downloaded and accept the license agreement.

4. Select the version of Linux Mint that you would like to download in the dropdown.

5. Check the **Download Link** box. If you've already downloaded Mint, you'll be able to browse to where you saved it.

6. Once the download is complete, click on the **Browse** button and select the ISO file.

7. Select your flash drive in the second dropdown. Double-check that you selected the correct drive so you don't format the wrong one and lose data.

8. Check the **Show all Drives** box on the right-hand side to format your flash drive.

9. Finally, adjust the slider at the bottom of the window to designate how much space you would like to reserve for persistence (if any).

10. After the process completes, you will have a bootable Linux Mint flash drive!

The following screenshot is the output of the preceding steps:

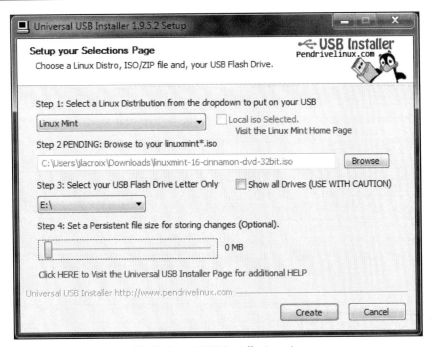

The Universal USB Installer in action

The amount of space you designate for persistence is the amount of space available for you to use within the live environment to save any changes. This is not a requirement, but it can definitely be handy. If you do not select any persistence at all, you're essentially creating read-only boot media.

Testing your live media

By now, I bet you're itching to create your very own Linux Mint installation. However, as mentioned earlier, it's important to test out any Linux distribution before installing it. One of the major benefits of live media is that it gives you a chance to see how well Mint will handle your specific computer. Take a moment to boot into the live environment and test out your hardware to ensure that everything works. For example, if you have a wireless card, make sure that you're able to connect to a wireless network. In addition, listen to audio and playback video (YouTube is a good test of the latter) to make sure the multimedia functions properly. If there are any other things that are important to you, test those too before installing them. In this way, you'll be able to discover any possible issues and identify fixes or work-arounds before you remove your existing operating system.

If you have any issues with Mint while using the live media, a quick Google search with relevant terms related to your problem will lead you to most answers. If not, log on to the Linux Mint forums and post a message about your issue. Make sure that you include relevant information considering the following aspects:

- The symptoms of the problem you're experiencing and what triggers it
- What you've done so far to try to resolve it yourself
- The exact model of the computer or hardware involved

While you're testing out the live environment, feel free to jump ahead to *Chapter 3*, *Getting Acquainted with Cinnamon*, to learn about the user interface, since running it in the live mode gives you a chance to kick the tires and play around with the interface. In this way, by the time you install Mint, you'll have already learned about the interface and how to customize it. It's important to think of the live environment as your own personal sandbox. Feel free to configure, change settings, and even try to break it if you want. If you mess it up, all you should have to do is reboot and everything will be back to normal.

 If you choose to create persistent USB media, you can revert any changes you've made by going through the second activity again, making sure to check the format checkbox. This will result in a fresh USB flash drive, but it will also wipe out any data you may have saved on the media.

Planning your partitioning scheme

When installing any distribution of Linux, it's important that we first plan out how we're going to partition the computer's hard disk. When you partition your hard drive, you're essentially creating artificial boundaries that split your disk into various sections. With Windows and Mac OS X, creating multiple partitions is not typical, though power users may favor this approach. Such users will often create a partition for the operating system, another partition for programs, another one for personal data, and so on. Mac and Windows computers are typically sold with a single partition, and most users will simply accept this as it is.

When it comes to Linux, partitioning is the norm and is a subject that is very commonly debated. As Linux users grow in their skills and knowledge, they will eventually come to prefer a specific partitioning scheme and in some cases, deem it superior to others. In actuality, there is no right or wrong approach to partitioning your disk. However, some partitioning schemes are better for certain tasks than others.

Including Mint, most distributions allow you to create a single partition and house the entire system within it. There's nothing wrong with this practice, and your Mint system would operate just as smoothly with a single partition as it would with ten. For a beginner, telling the distribution to take over the entire drive with a single partition is the easiest and fastest way through the installation process. However, the use of only a single partition would cause you to miss out on some important benefits, mainly the ability to retain your files and settings after a reinstallation of your distribution.

We will go over the filesystem in more detail in *Chapter 4, An Introduction to the Terminal*. However, for now, there are some key concepts to start with that will aid you in making an informed decision on how to lay out the partitions right from the beginning. For starters, when I refer to filesystem in this context, I am referring to the folder and subfolder structure of a typical Linux installation. There are various folders created in the Linux filesystem, each with their own purpose. The common directories that are important for our current task are outlined as follows. However, there are many more common directories that we'll learn about later:

- The / symbol: This symbolizes the beginning of the Linux filesystem. For Windows users, this is equivalent to `C:`. All folders in the Linux filesystem are subfolders of /. For example, the equivalent of `C:\MyFolder` in Windows would be `/MyFolder` in the Linux filesystem.

- The `/home` folder: The `/home` folder is where each user stores his or her personal files. Each user has a folder underneath `/home` named after their username. For example, if Sue's username is `swilliams`, her home folder would be `/home/swilliams`.

- The `/tmp` folder: Temporary files are stored in `/tmp`. This folder is not suitable for long term storage as the contents of the folder can and will be deleted. Some advanced users will mount `/tmp` in RAM to avoid having temp files written to the disk.

- The `/etc` folder: Though the `/etc` folder isn't typically given its own partition, this is where system-wide configuration files are stored. For example, configuration files relating to networking or running processes are stored here.

- The swap space: While the swap area is not a folder, this is an area of your hard disk used as RAM when your memory becomes full, similar to the paging file in Windows. Swap is designated with its own partition in Linux. Often, there is a great deal of debate on whether or not swap is still necessary nowadays, but it's recommended that you create it since it won't take up much space anyway.

Back to the subject of partitioning, when you create a partition on a Linux disk, it is mounted to a folder. For example, if you create a 60 GB partition and mount it to the /home folder, each time you navigate to /home, you are exiting your main partition and switching to that 60 GB partition. You wouldn't notice this because in the display the path would simply show /home, which makes the partition layout seem transparent. This is a benefit over operating systems such as Windows, which typically assign a drive letter to each partition. Instead of a drive letter, you assign a folder to a partition in Linux and it becomes part of the main filesystem tree. The first forward slash always represents the beginning of the filesystem, so you can read from /home that the folder is stored on the root of the filesystem or simply /.

The most common partitioning practice of Linux users is to create a separate partition for /home. With such a configuration, you can format and reinstall the distribution in the main root partition without erasing files and settings as long as you don't accidentally format the /home partition. This allows you to move from one version of the distribution to another while retaining all your data in the process. Otherwise, if you put everything into a single partition, you would have to manually back up all the files and settings prior to the installation of a new version. To help establish this point, consider the following scenario.

Joe has a 500 GB hard drive with 465 GB of usable space. He creates three partitions: the first partition is 40 GB; the second partition is 16GB; and the third partition he creates uses the remainder of the disk, which would be about 409 GB. Joe assigns the first partition to /. The second partition is dedicated to the swap area. Finally, he allocates the third partition to /home.

When Joe installs Linux Mint, the distribution is installed to the root partition or simply /. During the installation, he clarifies that he would like the 409 GB partition mounted under /home. Later, Joe decides to install a new version of Linux Mint. During the installation of the new version, he tells the installer that he would like to format / but *not* format the 409 GB partition, which belongs to /home. Since Joe chose not to format /home, all the files and settings he has stored there will remain intact even though he erased and reinstalled Linux Mint.

If Joe installed the distribution with a single partition instead, he would not have had this luxury. Since there would have been only a single partition, his only option would have been to reformat that partition, which would have erased everything on it. This means that he would have had to manually backup and restore his files. Dedicating a partition to /home is a major convenience that should not be overlooked.

When partitioning, it's recommended to allocate at least 30 GB to /. Linux Mint does not necessarily need 30 GB to be installed. In fact, the default installation may just take somewhere around 2 GB. As you use Mint, install programs, and run updates, you'll find that the installation will grow and take up more space. In most cases, 30 GB is more than enough to work with.

As for swap space, a good rule to follow is to create your swap partition of the same size as the amount of RAM your system has, plus an additional space of 1 GB. In practice, it's not uncommon to see Linux users omit the creation of a swap partition since RAM is extremely cheap, and the likelihood that you will run out of RAM while using your Linux installation is small on systems with the luxury of a lot of memory. However, it's important to point out that laptops utilize swap while hibernating (suspending to disk), so if you plan on using the hibernation feature, creating a swap partition is mandatory. Some programs may use swap space even when RAM isn't full, so omitting a swap partition is not recommended.

Finally, the /home partition should be the largest as that's where your personal data will be stored. If you have a large music or video collection, it's very easy to use quite a bit of space under /home. Although every Linux guru recommends different partitioning schemes, I recommend that you create the /home partition at the end with whatever space remains on your drive after the creation of other partitions. As an example, a partition layout on a 200 GB disk may look like the following:

- Partition 1 (30 GB) designated to /
- Partition 2 (8 GB) designated for the swap area
- Partition 3 (162 GB) designated for /home

If you have a very small hard drive, the creation of a separate partition for /home would not make sense. For example, I recommended that you create a root partition with a minimum of 30 GB space. This wouldn't be ideal if your entire disk was barely larger than that. If your entire disk is only something like 40 GB, you wouldn't have much space left after allocating 30 GB for /. If your disk is small, just use the **Erase disk and install Linux Mint** option during the installation as you wouldn't have enough space to work with otherwise.

The installation process

So far, you have learned the best practices related to partitioning and also come up with your own partitioning scheme. You may have even booted from your installation media to test drive the live environment using *Chapter 3, Getting Acquainted with Cinnamon*, as your guide. Now that you're completely armed and ready, it's time to install Linux Mint on your computer. If you haven't already done so, booting the live media is easy. To do so, perform the following steps:

1. Either insert a Linux Mint DVD or attach a Linux Mint flash drive to your computer, depending on the one you created.

   When you turn on your computer, a trigger will be displayed on the manufacturer logo screen that will mention something along the lines of accessing a boot menu. This trigger is different depending on which kind of computer you have. For example, Dell computers designate *F12* to access the boot menu, so this is what you would press on the Dell logo screen.

   You'll know that you've done it right if you see the Linux Mint logo. If your existing operating system appears instead, reboot and try again. On some computers, this startup screen flashes by very fast. So, you'll need to keep your eyes peeled, or else you'll miss the window of opportunity.

    With some computers, there may not be any text on the startup screen that identifies which key is used to access the boot menu. In fact, some computers don't even have a boot menu. If this is the case, you'll need to press the key designated to access your system's setup screen and configure either your optical drive or flash drive as the first thing the PC checks for in an operating system. Legacy computers may not understand booting from USB at all, thus making a DVD your only option.

2. After the live session starts, double-click on the **Install Linux Mint** icon, which is shown as follows:

The icon for the Linux Mint installer

3. Once you launch the installer and choose your language, you will come to a screen that looks like the following screenshot. In the following screenshot, as long as the **has at least 7.8 GB of available drive space** option is checked, you're clear for liftoff. While having an active Internet connection is handy, it's not required for installation.

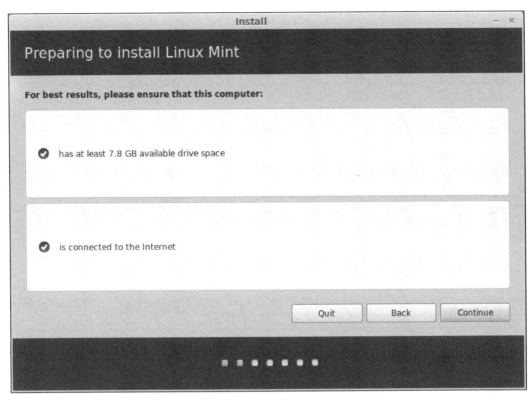

Preparing to install Linux Mint

4. The following screenshot shows the next screen, where you are shown various options to partition the computer's hard disk drive.

The first option is **Erase disk and install Linux Mint**. This will do exactly what it says—erase your entire hard disk and set up Linux Mint to occupy a single partition. On this screen, we'll choose **Something Else** so that we can set up the partitions manually. As mentioned earlier, if your disk is too small to warrant partitioning, choose **Erase disk and install Linux Mint** instead and then skip the section regarding partitioning that follows.

Other installation types such as **Encrypt the new Linux Mint installation for security** and **Use LVM with the new Linux Mint installation** are beyond the scope of this book.

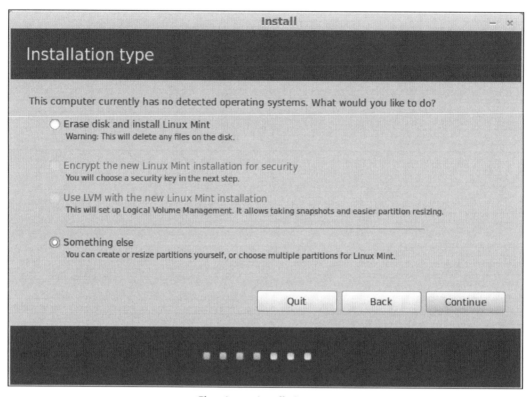

Choosing an installation type

5. In the next screen, you are shown your existing partition layout. Since we're removing the existing operating system, highlight each partition and click on the minus sign to delete them.

If you're using a brand new hard drive that has never been formatted, you won't see any partitions at all when you first get to this screen. It goes without saying that if you delete your existing partitions on this screen, you will lose all data stored in them. It's always important to make sure you have a good backup before installing a new operating system or Linux distribution even if you plan on retaining one or more existing partitions. One example might be the factory-restore partition, which most computers come with. If you were to delete such a partition, you would lose your ability to reinstall your original operating system if you decided to do so later.

6. Next, click on the plus sign to add a new partition. In our example, we'll create a partition for / to occupy 30 GB of space, a 4 GB swap area, and a /home partition that comprises the remaining space. On your system, adjust the partition sizes accordingly, as shown in the following screenshot:

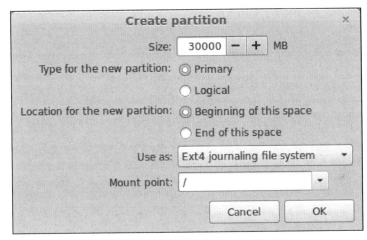

Configuring a partition during installation

7. Once you're done, your layout should look similar to the screenshot that follows. Please note that this particular system did not have a pre-existing restore partition.

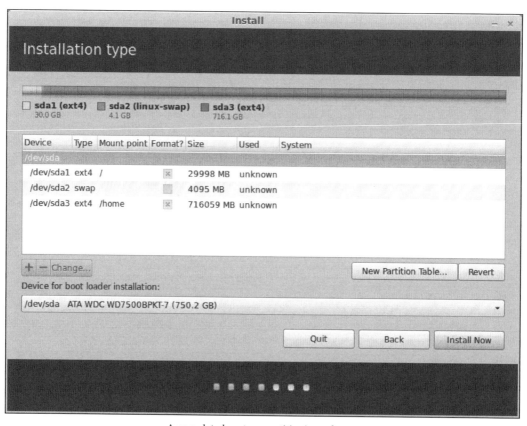

A completed custom partitioning scheme

8. After setting up your partition scheme, click on the **Install Now** button. The installation will commence immediately even though we have not completed all the steps yet. This is fine as we'll have plenty of time to complete them.

9. In the next screen, as shown in the following screenshot, we'll select our time zone. Click on the map with your mouse close to where you are located. It may be easier to type your region in the text box as pinpointing your exact location on the map can be tricky. In my example, I selected **Detroit** since that is the closest location on the list to where I live and then clicked on **Continue**.

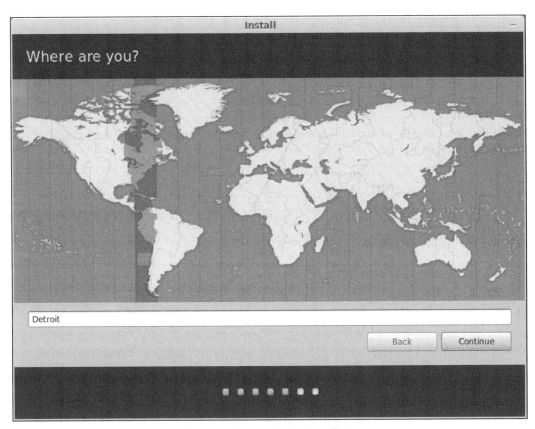

Choosing a location during installation

10. Next, it's time to choose your keyboard language. It defaults to **English (US)**, as shown in the following screenshot. So, change your keyboard layout accordingly should you need to do so. When you've chosen your keyboard layout, click on **Continue** to go to the next section.

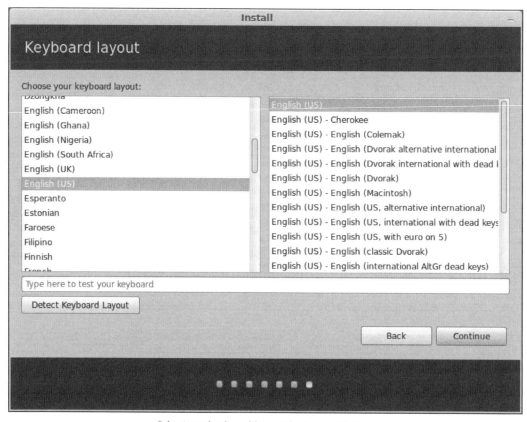

Selecting a keyboard layout during installation

11. Finally, we'll set up the main user account for the system for this chapter, as shown in the following screenshot. Unless you're setting up the computer for someone else, you'll input your user information here.

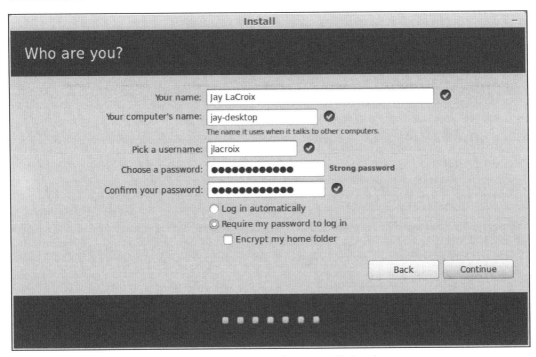

User account creation during installation

To encrypt or not to encrypt

While setting up your user account, you'll notice some additional options such as one that allows you to encrypt your home folder and another that will set up the system to automatically log you on without asking for your password. Your decisions on this screen have a major impact on the overall security of your data.

The first question is whether you should encrypt your home folder or not. If you do so, it would make it very difficult for a miscreant to gain access to your data if your device gets stolen. However, there is a significant trade-off. If you do encrypt your home folder, you'll defeat the entire purpose of having a separate /home partition in the first place. The reason for this is because it is very difficult to retain an encrypted home folder between one installation and another since a new installation would not contain a valid encryption key for the original home folder. Your choice here comes down to the classic battle between ease of use and security. If you decide to encrypt your home folder, your next Mint installation would have to be done from scratch when the next version is released. However, you would be better protected from data being accessed by an unauthorized person.

Similarly, it would certainly be convenient to have the system automatically log you in when it starts up. However, not needing a password would also make the process of accessing your data much easier for a miscreant. Make your choice wisely based on how confidential the information you plan to store on your machine is. A person who will only use the system to play games or check a social networking site may not care as much about security as someone keeping track of their company's accounting books.

Regardless of your decision, click on **Continue** to finish the installation. When it's done, a prompt will appear asking you to reboot. Do so, and the DVD will automatically eject, if you used one, and the system will reboot.

Summary

In this chapter, we went through the basics of what partitioning is and why you should consider setting up a separate /home partition. Bootable Linux Mint media was created on either a recordable DVD or flash drive. The installation process was also explained, and now you should have a fully operational Linux Mint system that we will use for the remainder of the book.

In the following chapter, we'll go through the Cinnamon user interface so you will know how to navigate your freshly installed Mint system. We'll cover aspects such as logging in, launching programs, creating launchers, and we'll also explore applications bundled with Linux Mint.

3

Getting Acquainted with Cinnamon

By now, you should have a fully functional installation of Linux Mint ready to do your bidding. Whether you have already installed the distribution or you are running it from live media, Linux Mint is at your command. Right out of the box, you can browse the web, create and manage files, listen to music, watch movies, and even connect to and administer other machines. In the default installation, Mint includes everything you need to be productive. In this chapter, we'll explore the most popular Mint desktop environment (**Cinnamon**) and how to use and customize it.

In this chapter, we will discuss the following topics:

- What is Cinnamon?
- Logging in to Cinnamon
- Launching programs
- Task management
- Workspaces
- Notifications
- Creating launchers
- Bundled applications
- File management with Nemo
- Configuring Cinnamon settings
- Changing the default search engine in Firefox
- Changing the themes of the desktop

Getting familiar with Cinnamon

Cinnamon is a **desktop environment**. This is the term that the Linux community uses to describe a user interface thrown on top of the Linux kernel. With Linux, you don't actually need a desktop environment. In the case of Linux servers, it's not uncommon to see them with no user interface at all; instead, the administrator would rely on shell commands to configure and interact with a system. In fact, it's even possible to perform all the basic desktop functions (such as modifying files, listening to music, and browsing the web) using shell commands. These commands call programs that can run without a user interface. However, when using Linux on your desktop or laptop, installing a desktop environment makes things much simpler. Most distributions (such as Mint) include a desktop environment in the default installation. Nowadays, Linux desktop environments have become so efficient that terminal commands are no longer a necessity; you can operate your computer with the comfort of your traditional mouse just like you would with Mac OSX or Windows.

Cinnamon is not the only desktop environment available for Linux. As mentioned earlier, there are others such as GNOME, KDE, MATE, and Xfce. Each desktop environment offers a different style of interacting with your computer graphically. Some may enjoy the eye candy that KDE provides; others may prefer the simplicity of Xfce, while those that use virtual workspaces heavily may enjoy GNOME. If you don't like one user interface, you can always try another one. Workspaces will be discussed later in this chapter.

Cinnamon is a desktop environment that tries to cater to all types of users. There is plenty of eye candy (such as KDE); it offers a great support for workspaces (such as GNOME), runs fast (like Xfce), and has a few tricks of its own. Due to its popularity, it's unofficially assumed to be the default desktop environment of Mint. Many of the same developers of Mint work on it even though Cinnamon is actually not exclusive to Mint.

In fact, Cinnamon is actually a fork of GNOME 3.x. When the 3.x series of the GNOME desktop was released for Linux, many users were displeased due to its radical departure from how the environment functioned in the 2.x series. Cinnamon was built on top of GNOME 3.x, but changed dramatically to become its own environment. As of Cinnamon 2.0, it's now completely separate from GNOME, though its origin remains.

The following screenshot shows off the Cinnamon desktop, which you'll see right after logging in. We will explore its various functions in the following sections of this chapter.

Logging in to Cinnamon

When your Linux Mint computer has completed the start-up procedure, the first thing you'll see is the **MDM (Mint Display Manager)**, which will allow you to log in to the system by providing the username and password that you created during the installation.

If you choose the option for automatic login during installation or if you are running Mint from live media (such as a USB stick or DVD), the MDM screen will be bypassed and you'll immediately be logged in to Cinnamon. If this is the case, feel free to move on to the next section and come back to this one if you need a run through of how the MDM functions.

At first, the only user account you'll be able to log in with is the one that you created during installation. In *Chapter 8, Managing Users and Permissions*, the process of creating additional users will be explained.

When the MDM first appears, you will be shown a list of users on the left-hand side, and you will have an opportunity to type in your user name and then press *Enter* to begin the login process. If your hand is already on your mouse, it may be quicker just to click on the desired username on the left-hand side rather than typing in the username manually. Next, you will need to provide your password when the system will ask for it, and then you can either click on **OK** or press *Enter* to begin logging in to the system.

While this is all you really have to know in order to access your system, the MDM has a few additional features as well. As we've discussed, there are more desktop environments available other than just Cinnamon. However, one thing that is not yet mentioned is that you can actually install more than one environment at a time by simply installing the required packages to install another desktop environment. Installing additional programs is covered in *Chapter 6, Installing and Removing Software*.

If you have any additional desktop environments installed, you can choose the one that you'd like to use on the MDM screen prior to logging in. To do so, click on the middle icon on the lower-left side of the desktop in between the power icon and flag. When you do so, you will be given a selection of which desktop environment to use. For example, you could use Cinnamon as your main interface, but also install Xfce to use from time to time.

Launching programs

Once you're logged in to Cinnamon, you're able to launch applications and start working. On the bottom-left side of the Cinnamon desktop, you'll see **Menu**, titled appropriately enough, next to an icon that looks like a gear. Clicking on this will launch Cinnamon's application menu, as shown in the following screenshot:

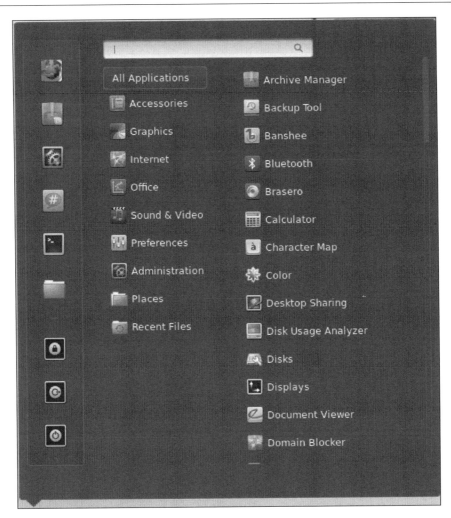

 If you have a Windows logo key on your keyboard, you can press this key to immediately launch the application menu without having to use your mouse.

The application menu in Cinnamon is not a simple menu; it's full of features designed to make it easy to find the items that you want. For example, if you already know the name of the application that you want to launch, you can start typing its name in the search box at the top of the window. This will narrow down a list of applications as you type. In addition, the **Recent Files** section will store the files that you've been working on lately, so you can get right back to work. Similarly, **Places** stores the most recent folders that you've accessed.

The middle section of the application menu is a list of applications broken down by category. The first entry, **All Applications**, shows every graphical application installed on the system, though other entries such as **Graphics** and **Office** show more specific results. For example, if you're looking for **Libre Office Writer** (a word processor) you'll find it either in **All Applications** or **Office**.

For advanced users, if you know the command for the application you'd like to launch, you can save some time by pressing *Alt + F2* on your keyboard. This will open a box in which you can type a command. Type the name of the application (for example, firefox), and it will open straight away. In most cases, the command for an application is its name in lowercase characters.

On the left-hand side of the menu, you'll see a list of icons. These are applications that have been saved as favorites, thus allowing you quick access to the programs that you use the most. By default, Firefox, Software Manager, System Settings, XChat, Terminal, and Nemo are saved as favorites and are immediately visible on the left-hand side of the menu. If you right-click on an application within the menu, you'll have an **Add to favorites** option to add it on the left pane of the menu along with the others. If you'd like to remove an application that is already listed as a favorite, locate that icon within the menu, right-click on it, and select **Remove from favorites**.

With each application that you add to your favorites, the application menu will grow taller. Keep this in mind as you add favorites, so the menu doesn't grow to an uncomfortable size.

Finally, the last three icons on the bottom-left corner of the desktop screen allow you to lock your session, log out, and shut down, respectively.

Monitoring tasks

Managing running programs in Cinnamon is very similar to other user environments. Just like Mac OSX and Windows, there is a close, maximize, and minimize icon on the edge of the window border. On the bottom of the screen is a panel that shows a list of running applications as well as the date/time and messages from individual applications.

You may notice a few standalone icons on the left-hand side, next to the **Menu** icon. These are pinned applications similar to the quick-launch area of the Microsoft Windows taskbar. Here, you can store launchers for your favorite applications. By default, there is a Show Desktop button and program icons for Firefox, launching a Terminal, and opening Nemo. If you'd like to remove any of these, simply right-click on them and you'll have the option to do so. To add new pinned applications, right-click on the desired application within the application menu and click on **Add to panel**.

The typical use case of the Cinnamon desktop consists of a user launching an application from the application menu (and pinning it if desired). This creates an entry for the running program in the panel. Then, the user can minimize the application to free screen space or close it. The running applications will be listed in the panel in the order in which they were launched.

Another method of cycling through open applications is known as **Scale Mode**. To activate it, press *Alt* + *Ctrl* + the down arrow on your keyboard. When you do so, your desktop will zoom out showing you a bird's-eye view of the applications that are currently open. Next, you can either click on the application you'd like to bring to the front or press *Esc* to exit the menu.

From time to time, you may want to take a look at the applications that are running on your system and their impact on resources such as CPU or RAM usage. For this purpose, Mint includes **System Monitor** that you can use to not only check resources' usage but also to close misbehaving applications and see which programs are being the greediest. An example of the **System Monitor** is pictured in the following screenshot:

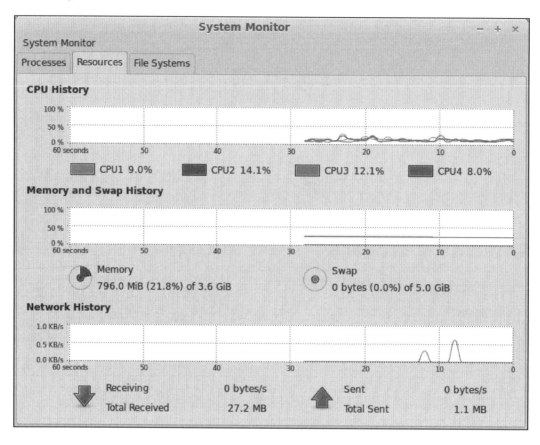

To access the **System Monitor**, open the application menu and you'll find it under **System Tools**. Feel free to pin it to the panel or the application menu for quick access later. One example of the usefulness of the **System Monitor** is the following scenario. Imagine you're not working with any intensive application, but mysteriously, the fan on your computer starts running abnormally high. You could then check the **System Monitor** to easily determine which application is using the most of your CPU. Then, you'll know which application to focus your troubleshooting on.

Utilizing workspaces

So, what do you do when you have too many applications open? One of the most popular elements of most Linux desktops is the concept of **workspaces**. When your screen becomes full of applications, it can become hard to manage. Thankfully, you can separate applications into different workspaces, which are essentially additional Cinnamon screens that you can work with.

By default, Cinnamon has two workspaces available. To see this concept in action, simply move your mouse to the upper-left corner of your screen. This activates **Expo Mode**, which allows you to view and switch between your workspaces. At first, you should see two workspaces. The first is the one that you've been using all along; however, you'll also see a blank Cinnamon interface ready for your use. If you click on the second (blank) interface, you're brought into an entirely different workspace that is a blank slate. You can then launch applications inside this second workspace. These applications are not shown on the same screen as those that were running on the first workspace. You can create additional workspaces by clicking on the **+** icon on the left-hand side of the **Expo** screen. You can close existing workspaces by pointing to them and clicking on the **x** icon that will appear.

 You can also enter Expo mode by pressing *Ctrl* + *Alt* + the up arrow on your keyboard.

By default, the workspaces are displayed horizontally. This is fine if you only have a few workspaces to cycle through. However, once you start adding a bunch, you'll notice that it can be hard to see them all as the Expo screen zooms out with each workspace you create. To remedy this, try the following steps:

1. First, open **System Settings** (available in the application menu) and then switch to advanced mode by clicking on the link at the bottom of the window.

2. Next, click on the Workspaces icon and enable the **Display Expo view as a grid** option. You should notice the difference the next time you activate the Expo screen. If you plan on using a large number of workspaces, you may find this layout easier to follow.

Once an application is running, it's not glued to the workspace that you opened it in. If you'd like to move an application that is already open to another workspace, you can easily do so via one of the following two methods:

- The first method is to right-click on the open application's entry on the panel, and then you can click on **move to left workspace** or **move to right workspace**. This will immediately move the application one workspace to the left or right.

- Alternatively, you can also right-click on the window border (the top edge of the application window), which will have the same options as mentioned in the preceding method.

Notifications

At various times, you'll see several notifications while you use Mint. For example, you may see notifications such as updates are available to be installed, removable media has been inserted, how much battery power is remaining, or a wireless network has become available. Whenever an event occurs, the Cinnamon desktop will immediately display a notification in order to let you know.

Cinnamon will notify you in one of two places when a noteworthy event occurs. For example, you may see a notification bubble on the top-right corner of the screen when a wireless network becomes available or your machine is disconnected from a connection. If you miss a notification, don't worry. Each time a notification appears, it is stored in the panel for viewing later, underneath an icon that looks like a speech balloon, which is shown as follows:

Removable media notifications are handled a bit differently. If you insert media, such as a flash drive or DVD, a notification will not appear on screen but will be immediately available in the panel. By default, the contents of removable media will immediately open in the file manager (Nemo). Notifications for removable media are stored underneath a separate icon, shown as follows, which looks similar to a hard disk:

There is a series of notifications for audio as well. On the panel, there is an icon for controlling the volume, which you can adjust either by clicking on it and adjusting the slider or hovering your mouse pointer over it and moving the scroll wheel. If you are playing audio (for example, listening to MP3 files in Banshee), the icon will turn into a musical note instead, but you'll still be able to adjust the volume in the same way. However, when you click on the volume icon while the music is playing, you'll see a section used to control music in addition to the controls that are normally available. The following screenshot shows the Cinnamon notification area (with the audio icon clicked on) while the music is playing:

Creating launchers

Some users may desire to have their favorite applications available on the desktop in the form of shortcut icons. The Cinnamon interface features two ways of creating launchers. These allow you to create icons to launch applications or commands.

The easiest way to create a launcher is to find the application in the application menu and right-click on it. One of the options that appears in this menu is **Add to desktop**, which will create the icon for you. Then, you can drag the icons to arrange them as you like.

Additionally, you can also create a launcher manually. This is useful if you cannot find the application in the menu or you'd like to create a custom icon different from the one available in the menu; to do so, right-click on an empty portion of the desktop and click on **Create Launcher**. A window will appear with some fields for you to fill out in order to create a launcher. However, since you'll need to know the command used to launch the application, this may be a method catered more toward intermediate users. However, if you'd like to create a launcher to a file location (such as your Documents folder), this is best accomplished by this method.

The fields to fill out in order to manually create a launcher are as follows:

- **Type**: Choose whether the launcher will be an application, terminal application, or a location.
- **Name**: Provide the name of the application; you can type anything you want here.
- **Command**: Provide the command used to open the application. This is only visible while creating an application launcher.
- **Location**: Provide the location of the folder you want the launcher to point to. This is only visible while creating a location launcher.
- **Comment**: Provide a comment regarding the application or location. This is not required.

The following screenshot is an example of creating an application launcher:

Bundled applications

Although most of the applications bundled with Mint are not specific to Cinnamon, they are discussed here as each compliments the environment by providing a basic functionality. As discussed earlier, Mint includes just about everything you'll need to be productive immediately. Whether you want to browse the Web, check your e-mail, or watch movies, you're covered. In this section, we'll go through some of the noteworthy applications included out of the box. In *Chapter 6, Installing and Removing Software*, we'll run through the process of installing new applications, so you will get a chance to install some additional applications, discussed as follows, that will make your experience even more complete.

- **Firefox**: The default web browser in Mint is Mozilla Firefox, which is a great choice because it is cross platform (it's essentially the same Firefox that you can download for use with Windows and Mac OSX) and recognized in the industry. The main difference in Mint's version is that the process of changing the default search engine has been customized. We will discuss how to change the default search engine in Firefox later in this chapter.

- **Thunderbird**: Thunderbird is a cross-platform e-mail client, which will allow you to consolidate your e-mail accounts into one application. Nowadays, cloud e-mail solutions (such as **Gmail**) have largely replaced standalone applications such as Thunderbird. However, it's still very useful for ISP e-mail services and even Gmail itself can be accessed with it. If you prefer a standalone e-mail solution over a cloud-based solution, Thunderbird is for you.

- **Pidgin**: Chatting with instant messaging services (such as AOL Instant Messenger or Yahoo Chat) is a snap with Pidgin. Pidgin allows you to connect to all of your chat services in one application with a single contact list. Like Firefox and Thunderbird, Pidgin is also a cross-platform application. It's available on Windows as well.

- **Transmission**: Transmission is a client of **Bit Torrent**, one of the best services available for Linux. Bit Torrent itself is a very useful service that facilitates the transfer of large downloads. The Linux community uses Bit Torrent heavily for downloading large distribution ISO files (for example, the Crunchbang distribution can only be obtained this way). However, like most services created for the purposes of good, Bit Torrent is often abused in order to distribute illegal copies of paid applications and media as well. It's important to use responsibility and good judgment while using it.

- **XChat**: XChat is a full-featured client of **IRC** chat. While some may see IRC as an archaic technology, it's still very popular in the Linux community, so using it is recommended. For most (if not all) of the major Linux distributions, an IRC channel is available.

- **Libre Office**: Libre Office is a cross-platform productivity suite featuring a Word processor (**Writer**) as well as a spreadsheet application (**Calc**) and presentation application (**Impress**). Libre Office is a very capable Office suite on all the platforms; it's available on Linux, Mac OSX, and Windows, so learning it is highly recommended. By default, Libre Office saves files in open formats, though you can save files in Microsoft formats should you need to send documents to someone who uses Microsoft's Office suite.

- **GIMP**: GIMP (**GNU Image Manipulation Program**) is a free alternative to Adobe Photoshop. GIMP is very useful for editing, cropping, and manipulating photos and is a welcome addition to any graphic designer's tool set.

- **Simple Scan**: If you own a scanner, Simple Scan will facilitate your document-scanning needs. Simple Scan is easy to use, thus making things such as creating multi-page PDF files a cinch.

- **Banshee**: For those of you who have a collection of MP3 files, Banshee is a very capable music manager. With Banshee, you can not only listen to your MP3 files but also edit metadata, create playlists, listen to podcasts, and so on.

- **Brasero**: Brasero is a multipurpose media creator. If your computer has a rewritable DVD or CD drive, you'll be able to create music and data discs with this program. Brasero also allows you to create bootable CDs and DVDs from downloaded ISO files, so it is an important part of any Linux administrator's tool kit.

- **Software Manager**: A Mint-specific application, Software Manager is your gateway to discovering new applications. Although installing and removing applications is covered in *Chapter 6, Installing and Removing Software*, feel free to have a look around at the various categories of applications available. In addition, although Software Manager was developed by the Linux Mint team, it has found its way to other distributions since its debut.

- **Synaptic**: Synaptic is an application that does essentially the same thing as the Software Manager, but is catered more toward power-users. Synaptic is a tried-and-true package manager, having existed for well over 10 years. Intermediate to advanced users will likely prefer Synaptic over Mint's Software Manager.

- **Update Manager**: During the time in which a version of Mint is within its support cycle, security and feature updates are regularly released. Updates may include new versions of applications such as Firefox or even the Linux kernel itself. Although Linux is inherently secure, keeping it up to date is the best security practice recommended on any platform. Keeping your system up to date is discussed in *Chapter 6, Installing and Removing Software*.

- **Videos**: Videos is a generic video player application with a generic name. By default, all video files (clips, movies, and so on) stored on your hard disk will open with this program.

- **VLC**: VLC is also included for viewing video files. It's very similar to the Videos application, but much more capable and available on just about every platform in existence. There are few types of video files that won't open with VLC. In many ways, VLC is actually superior to the default Videos application.

- **Document Viewer**: Document Viewer allows you to view PDF files, which you would normally view using Adobe Reader on other platforms.

- **gThumb**: gThumb comes to the rescue when you need to view images. Not only does gThumb handle the viewing of images currently in your collection, it allows you to import new photos from a digital camera if you have one.

File management with Nemo

Every operating system has its method of managing saved files and browsing the filesystem; in Windows, it's File Explorer; in Mac OSX, Finder is used for this purpose; and in the case of Linux, there are many file managers. Each desktop environment has its own file management application. For example, the Xfce environment uses Thunar, KDE ships with Dolphin, GNOME features Files, and Cinnamon includes Nemo. There are others; however, we have a choice with Linux. In fact, it's not uncommon to see Linux users mix file managers or even install one that is completely separate, such as **Krusader** or **Midnight Commander**.

Nemo, Cinnamon's preference for file management, is a very capable file manager. With it, you can complete any task you'd normally perform in any other file manager. Copying, moving, renaming, and deleting files and folders is a breeze. In addition, you can browse network locations within Nemo as well. The following screenshot shows the Nemo file manager:

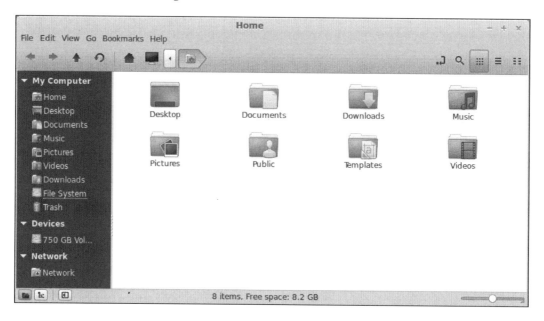

Browsing your filesystem within Nemo is as easy as clicking on objects to open them. In the main section of the window, you're presented with the contents of the current folder. Along the top of the window, you'll see the path you've navigated to, and on the left-hand side is a pane that shows the shortcuts to various locations.

 If you insert a removable media (such as a disc or USB disk), it will automatically mount and show up in the left-hand pane of Nemo. To safely remove the attached media, click on the Eject icon that appears next to its heading on the left pane.

In the preferences menu, you can customize Nemo to your liking; perhaps, the default icon view isn't your favorite layout. You can view the content of folders as a list instead, which is similar to the Detailed List view in Windows Explorer. To access the preferences menu, click on **Edit** in the file menu and then select **Preferences**. The options here are self-explanatory, so feel free to adjust them to your liking and see what effect each setting has.

On the top-right side of each Nemo window are three additional icons you can use to adjust your view. The icons are shown as follows:

The first, which looks like a curved arrow, changes the location bar from an icon view (also known as **breadcrumbs**) to a text path that allows for keyboard input similar to an address bar in a web browser. The magnifying glass opens a menu that allows you to search folders for specific files should you forget where something is. Finally, the remaining three icons allow you to switch views without having to access the preferences menu.

Feel free to navigate around the filesystem and do some exploring; however, don't worry too much about what each of the individual folders is for just yet. We'll explore the filesystem in greater detail in the following chapter.

Configuring the settings of Cinnamon

Cinnamon is highly configurable; it's very easy to make it your own. You can customize everything from the theme all the way to power events such as choosing what happens when you close your lid (if you're using a laptop). Just about everything is customizable, thus making your installation of Mint truly your own. To get started with customizing your installation, open the **System Settings** application. You'll find it in the application menu under **System Tools**. By default, Mint has **System Settings** pinned on the left-hand side of the application menu for easy access. The following screenshot shows the Cinnamon **System Settings** application:

By default, not all categories are shown as **System Settings** will open in normal mode the first time you open it. In order to be able to access the complete array of settings, it's recommended that you switch to an advanced mode right away. To do so, click on the **Switch to Advanced Mode** link on the lower-left side of the **System Settings** window. You will see more categories appear instantly.

Next, we'll go through the most useful modules within **System Settings**, which are described as follows. Feel free to experiment to create your own perfect desktop.

- **Backgrounds**: Here, you can select a wallpaper for your desktop. A nice set of default backgrounds are included. To disable wallpapers altogether, expand **Advanced options** and change the picture aspect to **No picture**.

- **Effects**: By default, some of your video card resources are utilized to provide flashy effects during transitions. For example, with the effects enabled, minimizing a window will show it fading away rather than just simply disappearing from view. If you are on a slower system and need to conserve resources, disable this feature.

- **Themes**: Your entire desktop can be themed, thus changing its appearance completely. There are several items that can be individually themed to create your own look for the desktop. This process is explained later in this chapter.

- **Desktop**: Here, you can configure which icons are visible on the desktop. By default, the Computer and Home icons are visible as well as the icons for any removable media you may have inserted. In addition, you can also choose to show icons of the trash folder and available network servers.

- **Hot corners**: In this menu, you can configure what happens when you move the mouse into any corner of the screen. By default, the upper-left corner is configured to access the Expo mode. If you find yourself accidentally enabling the Expo mode frequently, you can disable it here (or simply use *Ctrl + Alt +* the up arrow instead). You can configure the other corners as well to activate Expo, Scale, or even activate a command if you wish. For example, you could configure Cinnamon to launch Firefox each time you move your mouse to the upper-right corner of the screen.

- **Networking**: In most cases, you won't access this module often. Here, you can configure networking (both wired and wireless) if you need custom settings. To connect to a wireless network, it's much easier to click on the wireless icon in the tray. However, in *Chapter 9, Connecting to Networks*, we will go over the networking functions in more detail, so it's a good idea to at least know where the settings can be found.

- **Power Management**: In this module, you can configure when to suspend the system. This is especially useful if you are using a laptop. For example, you may want the laptop to suspend (sleep) when the lid is closed.

Be very careful with the sleep settings on laptops. While it's a good idea to configure your laptop to sleep while not in use or when the lid is closed, make sure you also exercise good judgment. For example, only stow your laptop in your bag if you are *absolutely sure* that it has entered a suspended state. You can typically tell if a laptop is suspended by the activity of the LEDs, which may be in the form of a sleep indicator or a blinking power LED depending on the model. Placing a non-suspended laptop in your bag can easily cause it to overheat and suffer hardware failure as there is no airflow inside laptop bags. Not all laptops will turn themselves off when the temperature gets too hot.

- **Device Drivers**: Most of the time, Mint finds drivers that it needs for your specific hardware. In some cases, proprietary drivers may be available that may offer improved performance. A typical example of this is video cards. While support for video cards in Linux is great nowadays, sometimes the open source drivers may not be as functional as those available from the manufacturer. As a general rule, don't fix it if it's not broke.

If you are having issues with your system (low frame rates in games, unable to access wireless networks, and so on), then you may try accessing this module to see if you have proprietary drivers available that will provide you with added functionality. Whenever possible, it's recommended to either use the drivers that ship with the distribution, as they have been thoroughly tested, or the open-source drivers, as the developers have access to the source code and so they can fix bugs.

In regards to proprietary drivers, being closed source means that the Linux community has no visibility into the code to fix potential issues.

Regardless of the overall opinion of proprietary drivers, it's important to make the decision that's best for you. If you need such drivers to make full use of your hardware, there's no reason why you shouldn't do so. This is especially true nowadays as resource-intensive gaming applications (such as Steam) have become available on the Linux desktop.

Changing the default search engine in Firefox

In the preceding section, it was mentioned that the version of Firefox included with Mint differs from the others in the way that the search engine settings are configured. In this section, we'll walk you through the process.

 If you are already satisfied with Mint's default search engine (Yahoo), then there is no need for you to complete this activity. Feel free to skip it if you wish.

So, why does Mint use Yahoo as its default search engine? The main reason is revenue. Maintaining and developing a Linux distribution is a very expensive job. A lot of bandwidth is regularly consumed not only by those who are downloading the ISO image itself but also by the many updates that are released and regularly downloaded by its users. Yahoo shares revenue, which its users generate while searching online, with Linux Mint. This is one of the ways that Mint generates funding to keep itself going.

The process of changing the default search engine in Firefox is as follows:

1. First, locate the search box next to the address bar. There is a down arrow located in the search box. If you click on it, you'll see an option to **Manage Search Engines...**.

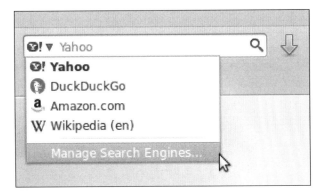

2. In the **Manage Search Engine List** window that appears, click on the **Get more search engines** link at the bottom of the window, as shown in the following screenshot:

3. A new tab will open to a customized Mint URL that explains the rationality behind changing the way in which search engines are managed in Mint. If you scroll down, you'll find icons for other search engines, such as Google, eBay, YouTube. Click on the one you want to add.

4. Another new tab will open. While this page is displayed, click on the down arrow in the search box again like you did in step 1. A new option to add the selected search engine will appear that was not there earlier.

5. The selection to the search provider you added will then be displayed in the search box. From this point forward, you can use this newly added search engine to conduct searches online.

6. If you'd also like to change the default search provider for address bar searches, the process is different. To do this, type about:config into the address bar.

7. Click on the button labeled **I'll be careful, I promise!**

8. In the search box, type `keyword.url`.

9. Double-click on **keyword.url**.

10. Change the search string in the dialog box to the one that matches the one for the provider you'd like to use. If you don't know what the search engine string is, you can find a list online. For example, type the following to make Google handle address bar searches:

```
http://www.google.com/search?&q=
```

Changing themes

One of the greatest aspects of Cinnamon is how customizable it is. Nearly every aspect of the environment can be changed, including (but not limited to) the colors of applications, desktop wallpaper, and even the theme of the Cinnamon interface itself.

To start customizing your environment, use the following steps:

1. Open **System Settings** and locate the **Themes** section in the first row.

2. A new menu will appear with three tabs: **Installed**, **Get More Online**, and **Other Settings**.

3. The **Installed** tab shows which Cinnamon themes are currently installed. If you've never customized themes before, you'll only have the two default themes listed (the following two screenshots). There is a green check mark next to the currently active theme.

4. Feel free to switch to the **Cinnamon** theme to see the changes right away. The colors of the panel as well as the application menu will change. Make note of the fact that the color of application windows (such as Nemo) did not change.

5. In the next tab, **Get more online**, you can download new themes from Mint's `spices` repository. When it finishes refreshing, you'll see a list of new Cinnamon themes for you to download.

6. Feel free to download a few Cinnamon themes that look good to you. When you're done installing the themes, switch back to the **Installed** tab and you'll see your newly downloaded themes listed there.

7. Activate one of your newly downloaded themes by double-clicking on it. Notice that the Cinnamon interface is now using your newly downloaded theme.

The last section, **Other settings**, allows you to theme components other than Cinnamon. Unfortunately, there are no integrated means to download themes for other components like you can for Cinnamon. Although we'll cover installing new software in *Chapter 6, Installing and Removing Software*, you can find new themes in the **Software Manager** by simply searching for `themes`. The type of themes you're looking for are known as **GTK** themes, which set the themes for individual applications, and **Metacity** themes, which allow you to change the window borders of applications.

If you have downloaded additional **GTK** or **Metacity** themes, you can select them in the **Other settings** tab. To illustrate how different these themes can make applications appear, the following screenshots shows the screens before and after applying the theme. The following screenshot shows Nemo with the default Mint-X theme applied to it:

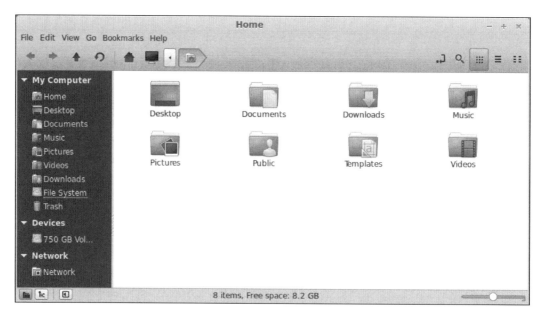

The following screenshot shows Nemo with a custom desktop theme applied to it:

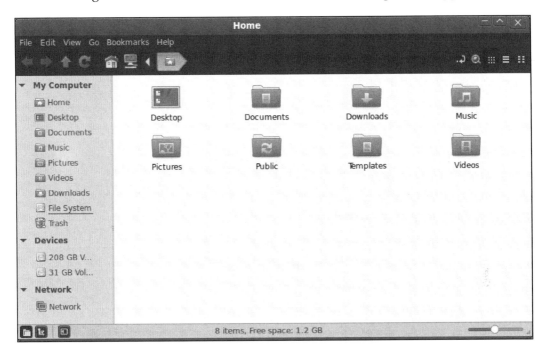

In addition, the theme for the MDM display manager can be changed. As a reminder, the MDM is the login screen that you see when you first start your Mint computer. By default, there are quite a few themes for the MDM that you can choose. You can change the MDM theme by accessing the login screen section of **System Settings**. The following screenshot shows off this configuration menu:

Summary

In this jam-packed chapter, the Cinnamon desktop environment was covered in depth. First, we explored what Cinnamon is and how it fits in with other desktop environments such as GNOME and KDE. Next, we discussed logging in to the environment and how to launch applications. We also covered task management, switching between workspaces, and notifications. In addition, some of the bundled applications were listed, Nemo was featured, and then we configured the Cinnamon settings and themes.

In the following chapter, we'll get started with executing shell commands in the terminal to boost your knowledge even further. We'll cover how to access the Linux shell, manage files without a GUI, navigate the filesystem, and more!

4
An Introduction to the Terminal

So far in our adventure, we are yet to leave the comfort of Mint's graphical desktop environment. Our time with Mint so far has been spent clicking on icons, launching GUI applications, and working from within windows. For most people, there is little need to leave this comfort zone. Mint is an incredibly rich experience, and it may seem that the developers have thought of everything and included a graphical application to configure just about anything you can think of. However, for those who aspire to be an administrator of Linux systems or just want to achieve advanced skills, learning shell commands is definitely recommended. For some tasks, executing commands can actually save time. In this chapter, we'll learn the basics of the Linux shell and commands related to it.

In this chapter, we will discuss the following topics:

- Why should we use the terminal?
- Accessing the shell
- Executing commands
- Navigating the filesystem
- Managing files
- The nano text editor
- Reading manual pages with the `man` command
- Searching for files
- Using the `watch` command
- Introduction to scripting

Why should we use the terminal?

With Mint containing a complete suite of graphical tools, one may wonder why it is useful to learn and use the terminal at all. Depending on the type of user, learning how to execute commands in a terminal may or may not be beneficial. If you are a user who intends to use Linux only for basic purposes such as browsing the Internet, checking e-mails, playing games, editing documents, printing, watching videos, listening to music, and so on, terminal commands may not be a useful skill to learn as all of these activities (as well as others) are best handled by a graphical desktop environment.

However, the real value of the terminal in Linux comes with advanced administration. Some administrative activities are faster using shell commands than using the GUI. For example, if you wanted to edit the /etc/fstab file, it would take fewer steps to type sudo nano /etc/fstab than it would to open a file manager with root permissions, navigate to the /etc directory, find the fstab file, and click on it to open it. This is especially true if all you want to do is make a quick change. Similarly, typing sudo apt-get install geany may be faster if you already know the name of the package you want, compared to opening up Mint Software Manager, waiting for it to load, finding the geany package, and installing it. On older and slower systems, the overhead caused by graphical programs may delay execution time.

Another value in the Linux Shell is scripting. With a script, you can create a text file with a list of commands and instructions and execute all of the commands contained within a single execution. For example, you can create a list of packages that you would prefer to install on your system, type them out in a text file, and add your distribution package's installation command at the beginning of the list. Now, you can install all of your favorite programs with a single command. If you save this script for later, you can execute it any time you reinstall Linux Mint so that you can immediately have access to all your favorite programs. If you are administering a server, you can create a script to check the overall health of the system at various times, check for security intrusions, or even configure servers to send you weekly reports on just about anything you'd like to keep yourself updated on. There are entire books dedicated to scripting, so we won't go in detail about it in this book. However, by the end of the chapter, we will create a script to demonstrate how to do so.

Accessing the shell

When it comes to Linux, there is very rarely (if ever) a single way to do anything. Just like you have your pick between desktop environments, text editors, browsers, and just about anything else, you also have a choice when it comes to accessing a Linux terminal to execute shell commands. As a matter of fact, you even have a choice on which **terminal emulator** to use in order to interpret your commands.

Linux Mint comes bundled with an application called the **GNOME Terminal**. This application is actually developed for a completely different desktop environment (GNOME) but is included in Mint because the Mint developers did not create their own terminal emulator for Cinnamon. The GNOME Terminal did the job very well, so there was no need to reinvent the wheel. Once you open the GNOME Terminal, it is ready to do your bidding right away. The following screenshot shows the GNOME terminal, ready for action:

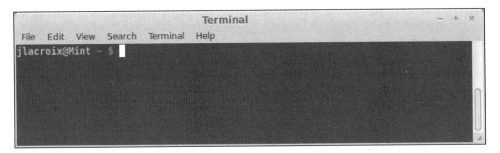

As mentioned earlier, there are other terminal emulators that are available. One of the popular terminal emulators is **Konsole**. It typically comes bundled with Linux distributions, which feature the KDE environment (such as Mint's own KDE edition). In addition, there is also the **xfce4-terminal**, which comes bundled with the Xfce environment. Although each terminal emulator is generally geared toward the desktop environment that features it, there's nothing stopping you from installing them if you find that GNOME Terminal doesn't suit your needs. However, each of the terminal emulators generally function in much the same way, and you may not notice much of a difference, especially when you're starting out.

You may be wondering what exactly a terminal emulator is. A terminal emulator is a windowed application that runs in a graphical environment (such as Cinnamon in Mint) that provides you with a terminal window through which you can execute shell commands to interact with the system. In essence, a terminal emulator is emulating what a full-screen terminal may look like, but in an application window. Each terminal emulator in Linux gives you the ability to interact with that distribution's chosen shell, and as each of the various terminal emulators interact with the same shell, you won't notice anything unique about them regarding how commands are run. The differences between one terminal emulator and another are usually in the form of features in the graphical user interface, which surround the terminal window, such as being able to open new terminal windows in tabs instead of separate instances and even open transparent windows so that you can see what is behind your terminal window as you type.

While learning about Linux, you'll often hear the term **Bash** when referring to the shell. Bash is a type of command interpreter that Linux uses; however, there are several others, including (but not limited to) the **C shell**, the **Dash shell**, and the **Korn shell**. When you interact with your Linux distribution through a terminal emulator, you are actually interacting with its shell. Bash itself is a successor to **Bourne shell** (originally created by Stephen Bourne) and is an acronym for "**Bourne Again Shell**." All distributions virtually include Bash as their default shell; it's the closest shell to a standard one in terms of shells that Linux has. As you start out on your Linux journey, Bash is the only shell you should concern yourself with and the only shell that will be covered in this book.

 Scripts are generally written against the shell environment in which they are intended to run. This is why when you read about writing scripts in Linux, you'll see them referred to as **Bash Scripts** as Bash is the target shell and pretty much the standard Linux shell.

In addition, terminal emulators aren't the only way to access the Linux shell for entering commands. In fact, you don't even need to install a terminal emulator. You can use **TTY** (**Teletype**) terminals, which are full-screen terminals available for your use, by simply pressing a combination of keys on your keyboard. When you switch to a TTY terminal, you are switching away from your desktop environment to a dedicated text-mode console. You can access a TTY terminal by pressing *Alt + Ctrl* and one of the function keys (*F1* through *F6*) at the same time. To switch back to Cinnamon, press *Alt + Ctrl + F8*.

Not all distributions handle TTY terminals in the same way. For example, some start the desktop environment on TTY 7 (*Alt + Ctrl + F7*), and others may have a different number of TTYs available. If you are using a different flavor of Mint and *Alt + Ctrl + F8* doesn't bring you back to your desktop environment, try *Alt + Ctrl + F7* instead.

You should notice that the terminal number changes each time you switch between TTY terminals. For example, if you press *Alt + Ctrl + F1*, you should see a heading that looks similar to **Linux Mint XX ReleaseName HostName tty1** (notice the `tty` number at the end). If you press *Alt + Ctrl + F2*, you'll see a heading similar to **Linux Mint XX ReleaseName HostName tty2**.

You should notice right away that the TTY number corresponds to the function key you used to access it. The benefit of a TTY is that it is an environment separate from your desktop environment, where you can run commands and large jobs. You can have a separate command running in each TTY, each independent of the others, without occupying space in your desktop environment. However, not everyone will find TTYs useful. It all depends on your use case and personal preferences.

Regardless of how you access a terminal in Linux to practice entering your commands, all the examples in this book will work fine. In fact, it doesn't even matter if you use the bundled GNOME Terminal or another terminal emulator. Feel free to play around as each of them handles commands in the same way and will work fine for the purposes of this book.

Executing commands

While utilizing the shell and entering commands, you will find yourself in a completely different world compared to your desktop environment. While using the shell, you'll enter a command, wait for a confirmation that the command was successful (if applicable), and then you will be brought back to the prompt so that you can execute another command. In many cases, the shell simply returns to the prompt with no output. This constitutes a success. Be warned though; the Linux shell makes no assumptions. If you type something incorrectly, you will either see an error message or produce unexpected output. If you tell the shell to delete a file and you direct it to the wrong one, it typically won't prompt for confirmation and will bypass the trash folder. The Linux Shell does exactly what you tell it to, not necessarily what you want it to. Don't let that scare you though. The Linux Shell is very logical and easy to learn. However, with great power comes great responsibility.

To get started, open your terminal emulator. You can either open the GNOME Terminal (you will find it in the application menu under **Accessories** or pinned to the left pane of the application menu by default) or switch to a TTY by pressing *Ctrl + Alt +F1*.

You'll see a prompt that will look similar to the following:

`username@hostname ~$`

Let's take a moment to examine the prompt. The first part of the prompt displays the username that the commands will be executed as. When you first open a terminal, it is opened under the user account that opened it. The second part of the prompt is the host name of the computer, which will be whatever you named it during the installation. Next, the path is displayed. In the preceding example, it's simply a tilde (~). The ~ character in Linux represents the currently logged-in user's home directory. Thus, in the preceding prompt, we can see that the current directory that the prompt is attached to is the user's home directory. Finally, a dollar sign symbol ($) is displayed. This represents that the commands are to be run as a normal user and not as a root user.

For example, a user named C. Norris is using a machine named Neptune. This user opens a terminal and then switches to the /media directory. The prompt would then be similar to the following:

`cnorris@neptune /media $`

Now that we have an understanding of the prompt, let's walk through some examples of entering some very basic commands, which are discussed in the following steps. Later in the chapter, we'll go over more complete examples; however, for now, let's take the terminal out for a spin.

1. Open a prompt, type `pwd`, and press *Enter*. The `pwd` command stands for **print working directory**. In the output, it should display the complete path that the terminal is attached to. If you ever lose your way, the `pwd` command will save the day. Notice that the command prints the working directly and completes it. This means that it returns you right back to the prompt, ready to accept another command.

2. Next, try the `ls` command. (That's "L" and "S", both lowercase). This stands for **list storage**. When you execute the `ls` command, you should see a list of the files saved in your current working directory. If there are no files in your working directory, you'll see no output.

3. For a little bit of fun, try the following command:

   `cowsay Linux Mint is Awesome`

This command shows that the Mint developers have a sense of humor and included the cowsay program in the default Mint installation. You can make the cow say anything you'd like, but be nice. The following screenshot shows the output of the preceding cowsay command, included in Mint for laughs:

```
 Terminal                                         − + x
 File  Edit  View  Search  Terminal  Help
jlacroix@Mint ~ $ cowsay Linux Mint is Awesome

< Linux Mint is Awesome >
 ------------------------
          \   ^__^
           \  (oo)_____
              (__)\       )\/\
                  ||----w |
                  ||     ||
jlacroix@Mint ~ $ █
```

Navigating the filesystem

Before we continue with more advanced terminal usage, it's important to understand how the filesystem is laid out in Linux as well as how to navigate it. First, we must clarify what exactly is meant by the term "filesystem" as it can refer to different things depending on the context. If you recall, when you installed Linux Mint, you formatted one or more partitions with a filesystem, most likely ext4. In this context, we're referring to the type of formatting applied to a hard-disk partition. There are many different filesystems available for formatting hard disk partitions, and this is true for all operating systems.

However, there is another meaning to "filesystem" with regards to Linux. In the context of this chapter, filesystem refers to the default system of directories (also known as **folders**) in a Linux installation and how to navigate from one folder to another. The filesystem in an installed Linux system includes many different folders, each with its own purpose. In order to understand how to navigate between directories in a Linux filesystem, you should first have a basic understanding of what the folders are for.

You can view the default directory structure in the Linux filesystem in one of the following two ways:

- One way is to open the Nemo file manager and click on **File System** on the left-hand side of the window. This will open a view of the default folders in Linux, as shown in the following screenshot:

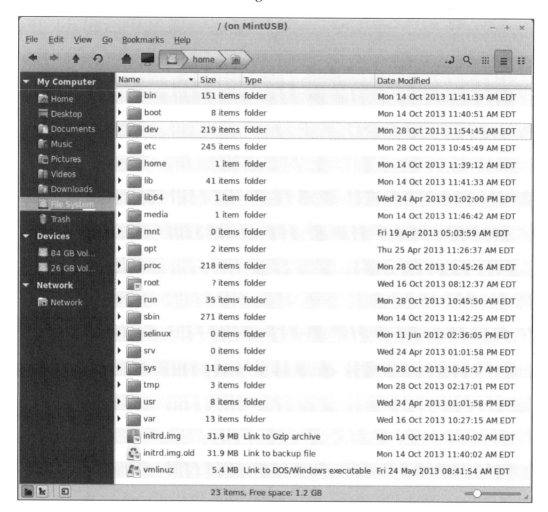

- Additionally, you can execute the following command from your terminal emulator:

```
ls -l /
```

The following screenshot shows the output of the preceding command from the root of the filesystem:

```
Terminal                                        − + ×
File  Edit  View  Search  Terminal  Help
drwxr-xr-x   2 root root  4096 Oct 14 11:41 bin
drwxr-xr-x   3 root root  4096 Oct 14 11:40 boot
drwxr-xr-x  16 root root  4500 Oct 28 11:54 dev
drwxr-xr-x 147 root root 12288 Oct 28 10:45 etc
drwxr-xr-x   3 root root  4096 Oct 14 11:39 home
lrwxrwxrwx   1 root root    32 Oct 14 11:40 initrd.img -> boot/initrd.img-3.8.0-
19-generic
lrwxrwxrwx   1 root root    33 Oct 14 11:21 initrd.img.old -> /boot/initrd.img-3
.8.0-19-generic
drwxr-xr-x  22 root root  4096 Oct 14 11:41 lib
drwxr-xr-x   2 root root  4096 Apr 24  2013 lib64
drwx------   2 root root 16384 Oct 14 11:21 lost+found
drwxr-xr-x   3 root root  4096 Oct 14 11:46 media
drwxr-xr-x   2 root root  4096 Apr 19  2013 mnt
drwxr-xr-x   4 root root  4096 Apr 25  2013 opt
dr-xr-xr-x 173 root root     0 Oct 28 10:45 proc
drwx------   7 root root  4096 Oct 16 08:12 root
drwxr-xr-x  23 root root   740 Oct 28 16:02 run
drwxr-xr-x   2 root root 12288 Oct 14 11:42 sbin
drwxr-xr-x   2 root root  4096 Jun 11  2012 selinux
drwxr-xr-x   2 root root  4096 Apr 24  2013 srv
dr-xr-xr-x  13 root root     0 Oct 28 10:45 sys
drwxrwxrwt   7 root root  4096 Oct 29 13:56 tmp
drwxr-xr-x  10 root root  4096 Apr 24  2013 usr
drwxr-xr-x  13 root root  4096 Oct 16 10:27 var
lrwxrwxrwx   1 root root    29 Oct 14 11:40 vmlinuz -> boot/vmlinuz-3.8.0-19-gen
eric
```

The first point to understand, especially if you're coming from Windows, is that there is no drive lettering in Linux. This means that there is no C drive for your operating system or D drive for your optical drive. The closest thing that the Linux filesystem has for a C: drive is a single forward slash, which represents the beginning of the filesystem. In Linux, everything is a subdirectory of /. When we executed the preceding command (ls -l /), we were telling the terminal emulator that we'd like a listing of / or the beginning of the drive. The -l flag tells the terminal emulator that we would like a long alphabetical listing rather than a horizontal one.

Paths are written as shown in the following command line example. In this example, the path references the `Music` directory under Joe's `home` directory:

`/home/joe/Music`

The first slash (`/home`) references the beginning of the filesystem. If a path in Linux is typed starting with a single forward slash, this means that the path starts with the beginning of the drive. In the preceding example, if we start at the beginning of the filesystem, we'll see a directory there named `home`. Inside the `home` folder, we'll see another directory named `joe`. Inside the `joe` directory, we'll find another directory named `Music`.

The `cd` command is used to change the directory from the current working directory, to the one that we want to work with. Let's demonstrate this with an example. First, let's say that the prompt Joe sees in his terminal is the following:

`joe@Mint ~ $`

From this, we can deduce that the current working directory is Joe's home directory. We know this because the ~ character is shorthand for the user's home directory. Let's assume that Joe types the following:

pwd

Then, his output will be as follows:

`/home/joe`

In his case, ~ is the same as `/home/joe`.

Since Joe is currently in his home directory, he can see the contents of that directory by simply typing the following command:

ls

The `Music` directory that Joe wants to access would be shown in the output as its path is `/home/joe/Music`.

To change the working directory of the terminal to `/home/joe/Music`, Joe can type the following:

cd /home/joe/Music

His prompt will change to the following:

`joe@Mint ~/Music $`

However, the `cd` command does not make you type the full path. With the `cd` command, you can type an absolute or relative path. In the preceding command line using `cd` command, we referenced an absolute path. The absolute path is a path from the beginning of the disk (the single forward slash), and each directory from the beginning is completely typed out. In this example, it's unnecessary to type the full path because Joe is already in his home directory. As `Music` is a subdirectory of the directory he's already in, all he has to do is type the following command in order to get access to his `Music` directory:

`cd Music`

That's it. Without first typing a forward slash, the command interpreter understands that we are referencing a directory in the current working directory. If Joe was to use `/Music` as a path instead, this wouldn't work because there is no `Music` directory at the top level of his hard drive.

If Joe wants to go back one level, he can enter the following command:

`cd..`

Typing the `cd` command along with two periods tells the command interpreter that we would like to move backwards to the level above the one where we currently are. In this case, the command would return Joe back to his home directory.

Finally, as if the difference between a filesystem in the context of hard drive formatting and filesystem in the context of directory structure wasn't confusing enough, there is another key term you should know for use with Linux. This term also has multiple meanings that change depending on the context in which you use it. The word is **root**.

The user account named `root` is present on all Linux systems. The root account is the Alpha and Omega of the Linux system. The root user has the most permissions of any user on the system; `root` could even delete the entire filesystem and everything contained within it if necessary. Therefore, it's generally discouraged to use the root account for fear of a typo destroying your entire system. However, in regards to this chapter, when we talk about root, we're not talking about the root user account. We'll get to that in *Chapter 8, Managing Users and Permissions*; however, for now, there are actually two other meanings to the word root in Linux in regards to the filesystem.

First, you'll often hear of someone referring to the root of the filesystem. They are referring to the single forward slash that represents the beginning of the filesystem. Second, there is a directory in the root of the filesystem named `root`. Its path is as follows:

`/root`

Linux administrators will refer to that directory as "slash root", indicating that it is a directory called `root`, and it is stored in the root (beginning) of the filesystem. So, what is the `/root` directory? The `/root` directory is the home directory for the root account. In this chapter, we have referred to the `/home` directory several times. In a Linux system, each user gets their own directory underneath `/home`. David's home directory would be `/home/david` and Cindy's home directory is likely to be `/home/cindy`. (Using lowercase for all user names is a common practice for Linux administrators). Notice, however, that there is no `/home/root`. The root account is special, and it does not have a home directory in `/home` as normal users would have. `/root` is basically the equivalent of a home directory for root. The `/root` directory is not accessible to ordinary users. For example, try the following command:

```
ls /root
```

The `ls` command by itself displays the contents of the current working directory. However, if we pass a path to `ls`, we're telling `ls` that we want to list the storage of a different directory. In the preceding command, we're requesting to list the storage of the `/root` directory. Unfortunately, we can't. The root account does not want its directories visible to mortal users. If you execute the command, it will give you an error message indicating that permission was denied.

> Like many Ubuntu-based distributions, the root account in Mint is actually disabled. Even though it's disabled, the `/root` directory still exists and the root account can be used but not directly logged in to. In *Chapter 8, Managing Users and Permissions*, we'll clear this mystery a little more. For now, the takeaway is that you cannot actually log in as root, though in *Chapter 8, Managing Users and Permissions*, we'll demonstrate a way to run commands with root permissions.

So far, we've covered the `/home` and `/root` subdirectories of `/`, but what about the rest? This section of the chapter will be closed with a brief description of what each directory is used for. Don't worry; you don't have to memorize them all. Just use this section as reference.

- `/bin`: This stores essential commands accessible to all users. The executables for commands such as `ls` are stored here.

- `/boot`: This stores the configuration information for the boot loader as well as the initial ramdisk for the boot sequence.

- `/dev`: This holds the location for devices to represent pieces of hardware, such as hard drives and sound cards.

- `/etc`: This stores the configuration files used in the system. Examples include the configuration for Samba, which handles cross-platform networking, as well as the `fstab` file, which stores mount points for hard disks.

- /home: As discussed earlier in the chapter, each user account gets its own directory underneath this directory for storing personal files.

- /lib: This stores the libraries needed for other binaries.

- /media: This directory serves as a place for removable media to be mounted. If you insert media (such as a flash drive), you'll find it underneath this directory.

- /mnt: This directory is used for manual mount points; /media is generally used instead, and this directory still exists as a holdover from the past.

- /opt: Additional programs can be installed here.

- /proc: Within /proc, you'll find virtual files that represent processes and kernel data.

- /root: This is the home directory for the root account.

- /sbin: This consists of super user program binaries.

- /tmp: This is a place for temporary files.

- /usr: This is a directory where utilities and applications can be stored for use by all users, but it is not modified directly by users other than the root user.

- /var: This is a directory where continually changing files, such as printer spools and logs, are stored.

Managing files

Now that you have an understanding of how to navigate the filesystem, it's time to take a look at some basic file management. After all, what good is accessing a terminal if you don't know how to create, delete, move, and rename files and directories? Once you learn the basics of navigating the filesystem, the rest will be easy. File management in the Linux Shell is very logical but also very important to learn. Take some time to go through the following examples to manage some files on your system.

First, let's take a look at creating a file. There is more than one way to do this, but the following command line accomplishes the goal very easily:

```
touch myfile
```

With the touch command, we created a new file named myfile. The touch command will create a file in your working directory. Thus, if your working directory was your home directory, you'll now have a file called myfile in that directory.

However, the file that it created isn't very useful, is it? In fact, the file is completely empty. In the next section, we'll go over how to modify this file and add content to it. Being able to create files in Linux is an important first step, and you have successfully done so with the touch command.

 If you execute the touch command against a file or directory that already exists, the modified time of the file or directory will be updated, though its contents would not have changed. This is useful if you are using a backup program that looks for files with a certain modification time. Thus, you can execute the touch command against a file or directory that already exists to update the modification time and trigger a backup of that item.

So, what if you wanted to remove the file you created in the previous step? This is also very easy. The following rm command will allow you to easily remove the file:

```
rm myfile
```

So, what about directories? It's just as easy to create a directory instead of a file using the following command:

```
mkdir myfolder
```

If we want to remove the directory later, we can do so with the rm command but with the -r flag added to it. Keep in mind though; if you delete a directory, you delete everything inside it as well. The command line to remove the directory is as follows:

```
rm -r myfolder
```

Now you know how to create files and directories as well as how to remove them. What about renaming files or moving a file or directory from one place to another? To set up a walkthrough of further manipulating files and directories, let's create some files and directories to work with. They are as follows:

```
touch myfile
touch myfile2
mkdir myfolder
mkdir myfolder2
```

Now, we have some files and directories to play around with. First, let's rename myfile to myfile1 to make it look better. The mv command will allow you to move from its old name to a new one. This can be done using the following command line:

```
mv myfile myfile1
```

If you execute ls to list the storage in your working directory, you'll see that there is no file named myfile anymore; the preceding command moved it to myfile1. We can also rename directories in the exact same way using the following command line:

```
mv myfolder myfolder1
```

Renaming files and directories isn't the only thing that can be done with the mv command. In addition, you can move a file from one place to another. Let's move myfile1 into myfolder1:

```
mv myfile1 myfolder1
```

Now, myfile1 is no longer in the working directory. It now resides inside myfolder1. You can confirm this by typing the following command:

```
ls myfolder1
```

You can also move a folder into another directory using the following command:

```
mv myfolder1 myfolder2
```

As you can see, the mv command takes care of the logic for you. You don't have to clarify whether the file you are moving or the destination is a file or directory. It's able to figure it out by itself. Type the following command in the terminal:

```
mv myfolder2 myfile2
```

You would get an error. As myfile2 is a file and not a directory, you cannot move a directory into it.

In the preceding examples, we used the rm and mv commands with files and directories that existed in our working directory. It's important to note that you are not required to be within the directory where the files are located in order for you to be able to modify them. Both the mv and rm commands accept path arguments as well. For example, if you wish to delete a file called mydocument contained under /home/users/Documents, but your working directory was some other path, you could type the following command line:

```
rm /home/user/Documents/mydocument
```

As ~ is shorthand for /home/user, you can simplify the command line even further, as follows:

```
rm ~/Documents/mydocument
```

Many commands accept path arguments in much the same way. Once you master relative paths, absolute paths, and how to navigate around, you're well on your way to becoming a shell guru!

The nano text editor

Until now, we have used single purpose commands to achieve very basic goals such as creating empty files and directories. In the Linux Shell, there is more to life than simple commands. There are actually complete programs, which are able to run completely within your shell window. One example is **nano**, which is a text editor. There are many text editors available (such as `vi` and `emacs`), but `nano` is quite possibly the easiest to learn when starting out. There are two ways to open the `nano` text editor. The first way is by simply entering the `nano` command in the terminal.

The `nano` text editor immediately opens and you are able to start typing. However, when you enter the `nano` command by itself, you aren't actually editing a file until you save it. To save the file, press *Ctrl + O* (the letter O) and you are prompted to save the file. If you simply type the name, such as `myfile.txt`, the file will be saved to wherever your current working directory is. For example, if your working directory was `/home/user/mydocs` when you entered the command and you saved the file as `myfile.txt`, it would create the `myfile.txt` file underneath `/home/user/mydocs`.

If you already know the name of the file you want to create and where you'd like to save it, you can type all of it into a single command, as shown in the following command:

```
nano /home/user/mydocs/anotherfile.txt
```

With this command, `nano` will open as normal. However, when you press *Ctrl + O* in order to save the file, it will default to the path and filename you specified. If the file already existed when you entered that command, the contents of the file would be displayed on your screen, and you'd be able to modify it.

Feel free to play around with the `nano` text editor as it is very easy (and useful) to learn. Files are edited in `nano` in much the same way as graphical text editors by pressing the *Enter* key to move to a new line, the arrow keys to move your insertion point around the document, the Backspace key to delete characters, and the *Tab* key does exactly what you'd expect. As mentioned earlier, *Ctrl + O* brings up the save dialog. After you press *Ctrl + O*, confirm the name you'd like to use and press *Enter* to finalize the save process. To cut some text in order to paste later, press *Ctrl + K* to cut the line and then press *Ctrl + U* to move the line to where the insertion point currently is. To exit `nano`, press *Ctrl + X*.

Not all Linux distributions ship `nano`, especially older distributions or server-based platforms. If your goal is to become a Linux administrator, you should learn another terminal-based text editor as well. A good recommendation is the `vi` text editor, which is more advanced but very common in the field. You may run into a situation where `vi` is the only option on the server you are working on.

Reading manual pages with the man command

So far, you've learned several very useful commands to form the basis of your terminal skills. However, we haven't yet gone over the most important command of all—the `man` command.

The most important skill that any Linux administrator will ever learn is how to find useful information when in a jam. Being resourceful in the face of disaster is what separates hobbyists from professionals. In today's age, there's a wealth of information available at your fingertips. When faced with a nasty error message, often a quick Google search will find an online posting where someone has already been through the same problem and may have typed a response indicating what the solution is. In the worst case scenario, you may stumble across a bug report instead and discover that your problem is a known issue, and the developers of the software are already working on resolving it.

When you don't have the comfort of an Internet browser by your side or you'd like to quickly look up some details on a specific command, *ask the man*. The `man` command (short for **manual**) is one of your biggest allies in the Linux world. Knowing how to use it will help make you resourceful. You'd be surprised how much information the `man` command can provide. To use it, all you have to do is execute the `man` command and use another shell command as an argument. After you are done, simply press *q* on your keyboard to exit.

For example, try executing the `man` command against the `ls` command, as follows:

```
man ls
```

The following screenshot shows the output of the man command:

```
Terminal                                    – + ×
File  Edit  View  Search  Terminal  Help
LS(1)                          User Commands                          LS(1)

NAME
       ls - list directory contents

SYNOPSIS
       ls [OPTION]... [FILE]...

DESCRIPTION
       List  information  about  the FILEs (the current directory by default).
       Sort entries alphabetically if none of -cftuvSUX nor --sort is speci-
       fied.

       Mandatory  arguments  to  long  options are mandatory for short options
       too.

       -a, --all
              do not ignore entries starting with .

       -A, --almost-all
              do not list implied . and ..

       --author
              with -l, print the author of each file

       -b, --escape
Manual page ls(1) line 1 (press h for help or q to quit)
```

As you can see, there is much more to the ls command than what has been discussed in this chapter. There are many arguments that you can pass along to the ls command to change the way the results are displayed. For example, from the man entry for ls, you will discover that you can pass the -a argument to ls (so the command becomes ls -a) to view hidden files along with the rest of the output.

Files or directories that begin with periods, also known as **dot files**, are hidden. These files will neither show up in the normal ls output in the shell nor will they appear in the Nemo file manager unless you explicitly configure it to show hidden files. As mentioned in the man page for ls, you can use the -a flag to show hidden files, or you can view hidden files in Nemo by enabling **Show Hidden Files** in the **View** menu. Try this in your home directory, and you will see that there are many more files there than you might have thought.

Feel free to try the `man` command against other commands and view the output. In fact, you can even discover more about the `man` command itself by executing it:

```
man man
```

However, not all commands have manual entries. For example, you can try the following command:

```
man cd
```

However, it won't work. The manual entry for the `cd` command is not included in Linux Mint. Feel free to give the `man` command a try and see what manual entries you're able to come up with.

Searching for files

Now that you've had a crash course on how to create and manage files, you probably have quite a few files all over the hard disk that you've created. However, what do you do when you want to update a file, but you've forgotten where it is? The `find` command comes to your rescue.

The `find` command will allow you to search your filesystem for files based on the search criteria. To use it, you type `find`, a path to start the search from, the search criteria, and then the name of the file. For example, consider the following command line:

```
find / -name myfile
```

In the preceding example, we chose to start our search in / (the beginning of the filesystem). We are searching for a specific name (`-name`), and the name we're looking for is `myfile`. After executing the command, a search will be conducted for the file, and the output returned is the full path of the file once (and if) it's found.

However, you are more likely to see one or more errors when executing the preceding command. As we started our search in /, the search would have been conducted in directories that a normal user may not have access to. Therefore, we can narrow down the search by starting it further up the filesystem tree using the following command:

```
find /home/user -name myfile
```

This is better. The search should be faster as we're not searching the entire hard disk for the file that we're only looking for in our home directory.

 The find command is also very useful from a system administrator's standpoint. For example, if you wanted to edit a configuration file in /etc, but you weren't sure of where exactly it was located, you can search for the file. If you were looking for the smb.conf file, the find command would find it under /etc/samba/smb.conf. You would then know where the file that you'd like to edit is.

Sometimes, you may not know the actual filename you're trying to find. Perhaps you were working on a file during the last week, but you don't remember what you named it or where you saved it. The find command can still save the day. Instead of passing the -name option, you can pass -mtime (stands for **modified time**) instead. Let's take a look at the following example:

```
find /home/user -mtime -7
```

In the preceding example, we're looking for all files contained in /home/user that were modified seven or less days ago. Unfortunately, if you use a web browser or similar software which saves its local configuration in your home directory, this command will likely display a large list of junk files. If you also know the file extension you used, you can narrow the results down even further.

```
find /home/user -mtime -7 -name *.txt
```

In this example, we used the same find command with –mtime, as used in the preceding command, but we also appended -name, as done in our first example. The *.txt portion returns all files that end with the .txt file extension. After you put it all together, you're essentially searching for all files in your home directory that were modified seven or less than seven days ago and have a filename ending in .txt.

There are other variations of the find command. Check out the main page for the find command and experiment with finding other files in your filesystem.

Using the watch command

Another command that is very useful for system administration is the watch command. Even better is the fact that the watch command is extremely easy to learn as what it does is simple. It repeats the command typed immediately after it every two seconds by default. For example, you can view the output of the ls command every two seconds by typing the following command:

```
watch ls /home/user
```

This is not very exciting, is it? To illustrate what `ls` does, open another terminal window. In that window, create a new file in your home directory. You should see the new file appear in the output of the first window. If you delete the file, you'll see the file disappear from the `watch` output.

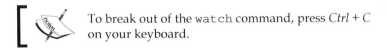

To break out of the `watch` command, press *Ctrl* + *C* on your keyboard.

While this may be useful for monitoring a single directory, it may not be a very exciting example. For an even better example, try the following command:

`sensors`

As long as your motherboard supports it, the `sensors` command will output the current temperature of your CPU. Some (but not all) computers will display the fan rotation speed as well. You've just printed the temperature of your CPU to your terminal. However, it would be more useful to have the output automatically updated without having to execute the `sensors` command again. As you would have guessed, the `watch` command can automatically update the output of `sensors` every two seconds. This can be achieved using the following command line:

`watch sensors`

In the following screenshot, the `watch` and `sensors` commands are used to monitor the system temperature:

```
Terminal                                                        − + ×
 File  Edit  View  Search  Terminal  Help
Every 2.0s: sensors                            Tue Oct 29 14:08:54 2013

acpitz-virtual-0
Adapter: Virtual device
temp1:        +40.0°C  (crit = +103.0°C)

thinkpad-isa-0000
Adapter: ISA adapter
fan1:         3154 RPM

coretemp-isa-0000
Adapter: ISA adapter
Physical id 0:  +43.0°C  (high = +87.0°C, crit = +105.0°C)
Core 0:         +43.0°C  (high = +87.0°C, crit = +105.0°C)
Core 1:         +39.0°C  (high = +87.0°C, crit = +105.0°C)
```

Now, this is more useful. If you were running a very CPU-intensive program and wanted to keep an eye on the temperature of your processor, this is one way to do so. However, of course, it gets better. Two seconds is still a bit of a delay. Let's update the output more frequently using the following command line:

```
watch -n 1 sensors
```

By adding the -n option, we can change the number of seconds in which the output of watch updates. In the preceding example, we tell the watch command that we'd like it to update every second rather than the default two seconds. Now, the output of the sensors command is much more useful.

You can use the watch command against virtually any shell command with varying results. In fact, there may be a time where even updating every second is too slow. Take the following command for example:

```
date
```

The date command simply prints the current date and time. If you were to do so with the watch command with updates every second, which is shown in the following command line, the results may not be very reliable:

```
watch -n 1 date
```

Every second is pretty close, but not exact to the clock. You aren't limited to seconds with the watch command. You can update in fractions of seconds as well, using the following command:

```
watch -n 0.1 date
```

With the preceding command, our output is closer to real time. It may not be 100 percent perfect, but it's good enough to suit any purpose that would require monitoring the time.

Introduction to scripting

Now that you are beginning to grasp how to enter shell commands, it's a good time to introduce scripting. Although this book will not go into scripting in great detail, covering the very basics of it here will help you study scripting should you decide to do so.

 If you do decide to further your scripting skills (it's a very useful skill for you to learn), there are many books available that are dedicated to this very subject. One such book is *Linux Shell Scripting Cookbook, Second Edition, Shantanu Tushar* and *Sarath Lakshman, Packt Publishing*

Bash scripts are actually just text files. So, to get started, you'll need to fire up a text editor. You can use whichever text editor you'd like, such as `nano` (discussed earlier in this chapter) or even `gedit`, which is a graphical text editor that ships with Mint. Scripts are executed from the terminal, so you may want to use `nano` to edit your scripts as you will end up in the terminal at some point during this process anyway.

To get started, type the following command into your text editor:

```
#!/bin/bash
```

What you just typed is known as a **hashbang**. This is the first line that should be typed into any script you create. In the hashbang, we declare which interpreter we'd like to use to execute the commands that will follow. In most Linux distributions, Bash is primarily the only option, so you're unlikely to diverge from this instruction.

Next, we can type any command we would like in the lines following. You can have a single command per line or as many commands as you wish.

For example, you can add the `ls` command to the next line. Now, your script will look as follows:

```
#!/bin/bash


ls
```

To execute the script, save it and then mark it as executable. To do so, exit the text editor, and execute the following command:

```
chmod +x myscript
```

Be sure to change `myscript` to whatever you named your script. Now, to execute it, simply type the following command:

```
./myscript
```

In the preceding command, we executed the script that we created. However, rather than just simply typing the name of the script, we prefixed it with a period and forward slash. The reason we did this is because by default, when you type a command (a script is treated as a command), the interpreter will look for the command to be located in folders such as `/bin`, `/usr/bin`, `/usr/local/bin`, and so on. By prefixing the name of the script with a period and forward slash, we're telling the terminal emulator that we want to execute a command (script) that is stored in our current working directory. If you missed the period and forward slash, you would have received the following error:

```
bash: myscript: command not found
```

Once you execute the script, you should see the contents of your current directory. This is because the script simply executes the `ls` command. Unfortunately, this isn't very useful, is it? It's much easier to type `ls` than it is to type `./myscript`. This script saves us no time at all. We can make a more useful script by removing `ls` from within the script and replacing it with the output of the `sensors` command. For example, try the following script instead:

```
#!/bin/bash


watch -n 0.1 sensors
```

Save the script with a simple name (such as `cputemp`) and mark it executable, as described earlier. Now, each time you execute `./cputemp`, you'll see an almost real-time representation of your CPU temperature. Now, this is useful.

From here, Bash scripting becomes more and more complex. In fact, there's little that separates Bash from actual programming languages as you have access to utilize variables, branching statements, and many other advanced techniques to create programs that can automate complex tasks.

Summary

In this chapter, we went over quite a bit of information regarding the Linux Shell and how to execute commands. We started with some reasons on why you'd want to use the terminal in the first place and then we discussed the Linux filesystem and how to navigate it. The `nano` text editor was also shown, which is a great text editor to use from within your terminal to create and edit text files. We also discussed basic file management, how to search for files, the `watch` command, and how to create a simple script. This knowledge will serve you well through the remainder of the book, where each chapter will feature one or more new commands for you to learn to administer your Linux Mint system.

In the following chapter, we'll take a look at all things storage. We'll look at how to access removable media (such as flash drives) and mount volumes, analyze what is using up space, how to burn CDs and DVDs and use the USB Image writer, and much more.

5
Utilizing Storage and Media

So far in our adventure, we have learned the basics of how to install and configure a Linux Mint system. We have looked at the best practices for installation, how to use the Cinnamon user interface, as well as how to execute commands in a Linux shell. However, we are yet to cover how Mint handles storage. With cloud-based storage becoming more and more accessible to all users (even beginners), removable media such as flash drives and external hard drives are not used as often as they used to be. However, removable media is still an important subject today, and it is important to know about managing internal storage as well.

Linux Mint offers custom tools for managing removable storage. For example, there is a tool for analyzing exactly where your used disk space is being heavily utilized, burning optical media, formatting USB flash drives, and even a tool for writing Linux ISO images to flash drives so that you can boot from them.

In this chapter, we will discuss the following topics:

- Accessing removable media
- Formating flash drives
- Mounting and unmounting volumes
- Automatically mounting volumes at boot time
- Analyzing disk usage
- Gibibytes versus gigabytes, and mebibytes versus megabytes
- Burning CDs and DVDs
- USB Image Writer
- Universally Unique Identifiers

Accessing removable media

As mentioned earlier in the book, the lack of drive lettering is one of the most difficult thought habits for Windows users to leave behind in the Linux world. In Windows, drive letters are ingrained into the culture. A typical Windows user may associate the A drive with floppy disks, the C drive with local OS storage, and the D drive with optical media. Flash drives are typically given the first available drive letter when inserted. A user would open My Computer (or more recently, simply Computer), and the flash drive or optical media will be listed there for access.

In Linux, removable media is handled very differently from the Windows platform. The insertion and access of removable media in Linux is mostly the same as Windows. Once a flash drive or optical media is inserted, the user is either shown the contents straight away or given a prompt to allow the individual to choose what he or she would like to do as a result of inserting the media. In most cases, once the removable media is inserted, an icon for it will appear right on the desktop as My Computer is not a typical inclusion in Linux.

Although each desktop environment (Cinnamon, GNOME, KDE, Xfce, and others) contains a largely different user experience, removable media is typically handled very similarly on each one. If you insert a flash drive into your computer, most environments will either create an icon for it on your desktop, in the notification area, in the file browser, or in all the three locations.

If all that you would like to do is access the contents of removable media (such as a flash drive) to save or read files, there's nothing more you would need to know. In the case of Cinnamon, an icon for your flash drive would appear on the desktop, so all you would have to do is double-click on the icon, and the contents of the drive would appear in Nemo for you to peruse. When you're finished and wish to remove the flash drive, you would click the Eject icon in Nemo next to the drive to safely disconnect it from the filesystem. Although accessing flash drives is fairly straightforward, more advanced concepts come into play when you wish to perform tasks such as reformatting or repartitioning a drive.

Right out of the box, flash drives work fine in most Linux distributions. Flash drives are typically preformatted from the factory with the FAT filesystem (in some cases, exFAT for larger flash drives), and most Linux distributions are able to utilize them as they are without any trickery or hackery. However, it's important to understand that the FAT filesystems are a proprietary of Microsoft, and no Linux distro is required to recognize proprietary formats. While most do recognize them, you may run into a situation where you're using a distribution that doesn't. In the case of Mint, there's nothing you need to do to add support for these devices. You're good to go, as all the tools you need are included right from the beginning.

As not all Linux distributions are able to access FAT-formatted devices, formatting flash drives in a format that Linux inherently understands (such as EXT2 and EXT3) may be beneficial. This may become an issue if you're using a flash drive in more than one environment as not all platforms recognize Linux formats either. So, which filesystems should you use on your flash drives? The basic rule of thumb is if you have a mixed environment (Windows, Mac, Linux, and so on), you can leave the flash drives formatted as FAT. If you use only Linux, you may consider changing the filesystem to EXT3 for greater compatibility.

Formatting flash drives

In the earlier versions of Mint, there was no official method of formatting flash drives. Users typically would download and install a third-party utility (such as gparted) to format flash drives. Thankfully, a new graphical application (USB Stick Formatter) is included, beginning with Linux Mint 16.

Accessing this application couldn't be simpler. To format a USB stick using this graphical tool, simply right-click on the icon shown for your flash drive and click on **Format**. Then, choose a label, click on **Format**, and that's it. Once the format is done, you're all set. The following screenshot shows the Linux Mint USB formatter window:

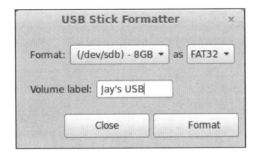

It goes without saying, but make sure you format the correct device. If you use more than one flash drive, you could format the wrong one. Additionally, if you use command-line tools to format a USB stick, it's very easy to format your main device accidently, thus resulting in data loss. Take your time, and also ensure that you have current backups before formatting any file system, just in case.

As with most activities in Linux, if there's a way to do it in the GUI, there's also a way to do it via shell commands (and vice versa). If a desktop environment isn't available to you or you prefer command-line tools, read on for another method to format your flash drive.

First, ensure that your flash drive is not mounted (in use). If you are using a desktop environment, look for an Eject icon next to the flash drive in Nemo. If it's there, click on it to safely remove the device. If you're not using the GUI, you can try the following commands instead.

To determine the device name of your flash drive, execute the following command before and after inserting your flash drive:

```
sudo fdisk -l
```

Compare the output. The device that shows up after inserting your flash drive but does not show up in the output before inserting it is probably the drive you're looking for. It should be fairly easy to determine which entry is the flash drive you wish to format using the process of elimination. In most cases, you'll definitely want to leave `/dev/sda` alone. Others that show up on the list may be removable devices. Try comparing the size of the devices against your flash drive, and the one that is your target should immediately become apparent. For example, if `/dev/sdc` is a 4 GiB partition in the fdisk output and your flash drive is 4 GB, chances are that it's the one you're looking for. Unless you have more than one 4 GB flash drive inserted, in this case, `/dev/sdc` would be the device you would want to format. The following screenshot shows the terminal output from the fdisk command:

```
                              Terminal                          _ + x
/dev/sda1    *         2048    50333695     25165824   83   Linux
/dev/sda2        50333696    85985279     17825792   82   Linux swap / Solaris
/dev/sda3        85985280   250066943     82040832   83   Linux

Disk /dev/sdb: 7743 MB, 7743995904 bytes
239 heads, 62 sectors/track, 1020 cylinders, total 15124992 sectors
Units = sectors of 1 * 512 = 512 bytes
Sector size (logical/physical): 512 bytes / 512 bytes
I/O size (minimum/optimal): 512 bytes / 512 bytes
Disk identifier: 0x00032638

   Device Boot      Start         End      Blocks   Id  System
/dev/sdb1    *         2048    10929782     5463867+  83   Linux
/dev/sdb2        10932222    15124479     2096129    5   Extended
/dev/sdb5        10932224    15124479     2096128   82   Linux swap / Solaris

Disk /dev/sdc: 4004 MB, 4004511744 bytes
116 heads, 51 sectors/track, 1322 cylinders, total 7821312 sectors
Units = sectors of 1 * 512 = 512 bytes
Sector size (logical/physical): 512 bytes / 512 bytes
I/O size (minimum/optimal): 512 bytes / 512 bytes
Disk identifier: 0x00000000

   Device Boot      Start         End      Blocks   Id  System
/dev/sdc1    *           32     7821311     3910640    c   W95 FAT32 (LBA)
jlacroix@Euphoria ~ $ █
```

To unmount the device, look at the partition number. A flash drive typically only has a single partition; in this case, /dev/sdc1. (Additional partitions might be /dev/sdc2, /dev/sdc3, and so on, but this is not common with flash drives.) The following command would unmount the flash drive:

```
umount /dev/sdc1
```

(replace sdc1 with the partition number in the fdisk output).

Now, you're ready to format your device. Use the mkfs command in the following format to do so:

```
mkfs.ext2 /dev/sdc1
```

In the preceding command, replace ext2 with the filesystem type you would like to use. However, ext2 is more than sufficient for most uses. The ext2 filesystem doesn't include the added overhead of the ext3 filesystem. It is also more stable than newer filesystems such as ext4. With a maximum size of 32 TB, it will be quite some time until typical removable media sizes outgrow ext2.

Next, give your flash drive a label (if desired). This can be done using the following command line:

```
sudo e2label /dev/sdc1 "My Label"
```

Again, replace sdc1 with the device name of your flash drive. Finally, give your user account access to the entire drive using the following command line:

```
sudo chown username -R /media/username/nameofdevice
```

If you're using Cinnamon, it's preferable to use the graphical USB Stick Formatter in order to format your flash drive as it is simpler to use; however, for those who wish to become Linux administrators, learning the command-line methods is recommended.

Mounting and unmounting volumes

As mentioned earlier, removable media is typically handled automatically in Linux Mint. When you insert a device, it is detected and mounted. In most cases, the content of the removable media will appear on your screen, and an icon will be created for it on your desktop. When you finish using the device, it is important to unmount it before removing it. When using a desktop environment such as Cinnamon, this is easy. Simply click on the Eject icon next to the device you would like to remove. The following screenshot shows the Unmount icon next to a flash drive named **MULTIBOOT** in Nemo:

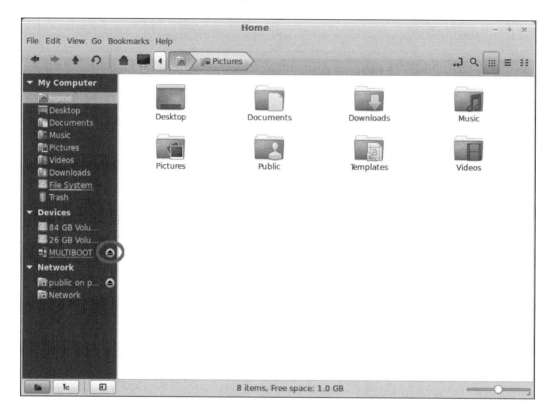

However, you may not always have a GUI available. If you plan to work with shell commands, it's important to understand how to mount and unmount filesystems as well.

If, for some reason, your desktop environment isn't functioning or you would like to operate in the Linux shell, you would need to mount a flash drive manually to use it. In order to mount a flash drive manually, we first need a folder to which the flash drive needs to be attached. This folder should be in our filesystem. In the `/media` folder, you should notice a folder under your name. For example, try the following command:

```
ls /media
```

Inside the folder, you should see another folder named after your username. Generally speaking, this is the place that is recommended to mount removable media. You aren't required to mount your removable media under this folder, but it is a good practice. In order to mount your flash drive manually, first create a folder for it. You can name the folder as you wish in the following manner:

```
mkdir /media/myusername/myflashdrive
```

Next, let's mount the flash drive using the following command line:

```
sudo mount /dev/sdc1 /media/username/myflashdrive
```

From this point onwards, the contents of your flash drive will appear underneath the folder you created. When you finish using your flash drive and wish to remove it, execute the following command:

```
sudo umount /dev/sdc1
```

As you can see, there are several steps involved in mounting removable media in Linux. For casual use on a system with a desktop environment installed on it, using the automatic method is preferable due to its ease of use. However, if you find yourself using a Linux system without a GUI or you are unable to start your desktop environment due to a software issue, mounting file systems manually is a good skill to learn.

There are additional options, such as specifying the file system and setting permissions, for the mount command. For the most part, the mount command will automatically detect the filesystem type. If you wish to take a look at the advanced parameters of the mount command, check its man page.

Automatically mounting volumes at boot time

Another scenario we've not gone over so far is automatically mounting filesystems when your system is booted. A great example of this is adding a secondary hard disk. As your needs grow, adding more fixed storage may make sense. Your author, for example, recently added a new hard disk to his PC due to the fact that so many virtual machines were installed, and there was no room for them on the primary hard drive. In this example, a secondary hard disk offers the benefit of segregating virtual hard disks onto their own dedicated storage. Another example may include setting up a secondary hard drive for a backup program to use. While another hard drive inside the same physical PC is not technically considered a backup (one good power surge or a fire could render all hard drives inside the same case useless), it's still better than nothing.

It's important to note that it's not required to ensure that secondary storage is mounted at boot as you can always double-click on a secondary hard disk in Nemo when you're ready to use it. The benefit of having a disk automatically mounted at boot time is that it would then be available right after the booting, so you don't have to remember to do it. In the preceding example of a virtual machine program storing its files on a secondary disk, the software would show an error message if you tried to use it, and its storage wasn't available. If you set up the disk to mount during boot, you wouldn't have to remember to mount the drive before starting the virtual machine software. Another example is backup software that automatically backs up your PC. If your backup disk isn't mounted, then the backup software wouldn't be able to access it and complete your backup.

It would become somewhat annoying to manually mount your secondary storage each time you start your PC. If you forgot to do so, the files stored on that hard drive would not be available. A tried-and-true (and very old) method of solving this issue is the /etc/fstab file. The fstab file is a simple text file containing information for local storage. The file is automatically generated when you install a typical Linux distribution, and it is located where the mountpoints for your root filesystem and any other partitions you created during installation are designated. As an example, execute the following command to see the current contents of the fstab file:

```
cat /etc/fstab
```

The following screenshot shows the sample `fstab` file output:

```
                            jlacroix@Pandora:~                          - + x
jlacroix@Daphne ~ $ cat /etc/fstab
# /etc/fstab: static file system information.
#
# Use 'blkid' to print the universally unique identifier for a
# device; this may be used with UUID= as a more robust way to name devices
# that works even if disks are added and removed. See fstab(5).
#
# <file system> <mount point>   <type>  <options>       <dump>  <pass>
# / was on /dev/sda1 during installation
UUID=5c499020-4d7d-47c2-a22f-a25e343c90c4 /             ext4    errors=remount-ro 0       1
# /home was on /dev/sda3 during installation
UUID=994be3ee-e391-4c5a-a1b9-0b276f36f8fb /home         ext4    defaults        0       2
# swap was on /dev/sda2 during installation
UUID=07f371e5-672c-452b-8333-808e01dfc015 none          swap    sw              0       0
jlacroix@Daphne ~ $
```

The output will show storage devices that are currently configured to be mounted automatically. At first, this will consist only of your local storage devices, the one you set up during installation. In the second column, you'll see the mountpoints for each of your devices places in the filesystem. In the `fstab` output, the installation uses a separate home and root partition designated by / and `/home`, respectively. The long series of characters you see on the screen after the term **UUID** is the **Universally Unique Identifier** of the drive. We'll discuss what this means near the end of this chapter. However, for now, just think of it as a generated serial number of the partition that allows the system to differentiate it from others. Finally, you'll see some additional options such as the filesystem type and the order in which the partition or drive is checked for errors.

The beauty of this file is that it can be edited, allowing you to create entries for additional media earlier and beyond what was created during the installation. Not only does it allow you to automatically mount secondary hard disks, you can also use it to automatically mount network shares and treat them as if they were local devices. Again, the `/etc/fstab` file is not the only method that you can use in order to mount secondary hard drives. If you have a secondary hard drive installed in your computer, you can simply access it from the GUI without editing any configuration files. However, adding the drive to the `/etc/fstab` file gives you a bit more control, such as which folder it is mounted in, so you can expect the contents to be not only mounted automatically but always available in the same place.

In order to best describe how to edit the `fstab` file, let's use an example. Suppose you purchased an additional hard disk and have already installed it on your computer and formatted it with the ext3 filesystem. After starting your computer, you can execute the following command in order to determine the virtual device file for the hard drive's partition(s):

```
sudo fdisk -l
```

Like we discussed earlier, with flash drives, the output will allow you to determine the virtual device file for your disk. Based on this knowledge, you can then add a mountpoint for the drive by copying an existing entry and placing it at the end of the file. The following command line will suit this example:

```
/dev/sdb1   /mnt/mydisk   rw,relatime,data=ordered 0 0
```

In the preceding example, we're going to mount `/dev/sdb1` (the first or only partition of the secondary disk) to the `/mnt/mydisk` directory. If `/mnt/mydisk` doesn't exist, you will need to create it. Note that you can use just about any directory you wish for the mountpoint, thought it has to actually exist. Next, after the mountpoint, we have some options. The `rw` option is likely self-explanatory; it means that we would like the disk to be mounted, read, and written, so changes can be made to the data it will contain. The latter options control when data is written to the disk. You can learn more about the various `fstab` options by perusing the output of the `man` command against `fstab` (`man fstab`).

When you make changes to the `/etc/fstab` file, the changes are not immediately active. When you restart your computer, the `fstab` file will be parsed on startup and all entries will be made active. However, the easiest way to test your `fstab` file is to execute the following command in your terminal:

```
sudo mount -a
```

When you execute that command, you may not get any output at all. If not, that's good — this means that the command didn't have a problem with your `fstab` file. If, on the other hand, you do get an output, it will be the errors that will give you a clue as to which line of the `fstab` file the command has an issue with. This way, you can test your `fstab` file without having to reboot your computer. This will definitely save your time.

Analyzing disk usage

We've spent a great deal of time in this chapter going over how to access media and mount storage devices. However, it's also important to understand how to manage that data and know how to determine how the space is being used. Finding the amount of free space on a volume couldn't be simpler. In Cinnamon, if you open the storage device in Nemo, you'll see the amount of free space on that volume shown at the bottom of the window. If you're working from a terminal window, the following command does the trick:

```
df -h
```

The `df` command will show you a list of volumes and the amount of free space available on each one. (The `df` command stands for **disk free** and the `-h` flag tells `df` that we want human readable output or rather shows the size of the disk in megabytes/gigabytes.) This certainly is useful information but not exactly what we want if we need to find out what is taking up all the space on a drive. For example, if a production server is running out of space, you would certainly want to drill down and determine the items that are the most responsible for the usage.

The **Disk Usage Analyzer** comes to the rescue. The Disk Usage Analyzer comes preinstalled with Linux Mint and allows you to generate a graphical overview of the items that take up the most space on a volume. To use it, locate the tool in your application menu and then click on the volume you'd like to interrogate. Immediately, the program will begin scanning the volume. Once finished, you will see a list of folders ordered from the largest to the smallest as well as a graphical depiction on the right-hand side of the window. Using your mouse, you can point to a section in the graphical display to reveal the name of the folder that it represents. The larger the data inside the folder, the larger is the block inside the display.

The following screenshot shows the **Disk Usage Analyzer** in action:

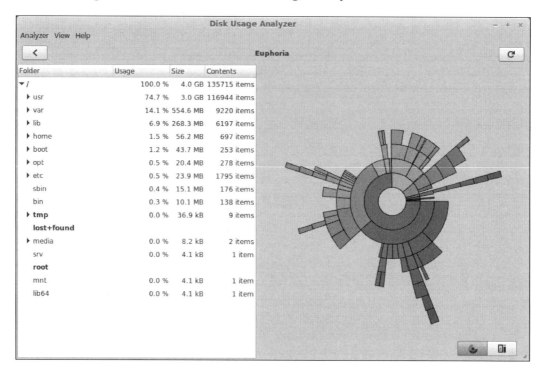

Go ahead and try it for yourself. Take a look at each of your volumes and find out which takes up the most space. If you already have established a Linux system with a good amount of data, you may even discover things you don't need, which can be removed.

The Disk Usage Analyzer is not limited to Mint or Cinnamon. Quite a few Linux distributions include it by default. However, if they don't include it, you can easily install it. Although the title of the application is **Disk Usage Analyzer**, the actual package is named baobab and most Linux distributions make it available in their repositories if it is not installed by default.

Understanding gibibytes versus gigabytes and mebibytes versus megabytes

While learning more about Linux, you may become confused about some terminology you're likely to find relating to storage devices. In the field, most people refer to data sizes as megabytes, gigabytes, and so on. While this is also true of Linux, you may see other terms, such as **mebibytes** and **gibibytes**, used to describe data sizes as well,. So, what's the deal?

First, it's important to understand that the storage measurement terms you're probably accustomed to, such as megabyte (MB) and gigabyte (GB), are part of the **International System of Units** (**SI**). This is a standard form of measurement for scientific data that has been used for quite some time. Typical words in the SI system include kilo, mega, giga, and others. Therefore, when the SI system is applied to computer storage (bytes), we get kilobyte, megabyte, gigabyte, and so on.

However, there was a bit of error when applying the SI system to measuring computer storage. The SI recognizes kilo as 10^3, mega as 10^6, and giga as 10^9. (The caret (^) symbol in the context of this section refers to powers. For example, 10^6 should be read as 10 to the sixth power.) However, computers represent the same levels of storage as 2^10, 2^20, and 2^30, respectively. This has caused quite a bit of confusion in the industry. In fact, there was a time period where consumers were quite angry that the advertised space for the hard drives they were purchasing didn't give them as much storage as advertised, so some new measurement terms were created.

The solution was to create a new measurement system with some new words. Instead of measuring data in kilobytes, we now have **kibibytes** (2^10), **mebibytes** (2^20), and **gibibytes** (2^30), which is what you'll see quite often in Linux distributions nowadays. These are abbreviated as **KiB**, **MiB**, and **GiB**, respectively. Although this new unit of measurement is largely considered to be politically correct, it hasn't caught on everywhere in Linux land just yet. As you may have noticed in the Disk Usage Analyzer screenshot in the previous section, not all applications are adopting this new system. Therefore, you'll that see both units are used throughout Linux for now.

> The KiB, MiB, and GiB storage terms are not Linux specific, but are mentioned in this book because Linux distributions were some of the first software releases to implement and accept this new method. Microsoft Windows, for example, still uses the older KB, MB, and GB terms at the time of writing this book.

Burning CDs and DVDs

Although it can be argued that optical media is slowly dying out (quite a few computers are sold without optical drives nowadays), burning media is still an important task for a lot of people. Burning CDs and DVDs is useful for creating Linux distribution media, bootable rescue discs, and short term backups.

 If you are considering burning DVDs or CDs to back up your important files and documents, *don't*. Burnable CDs and DVDs are *not* a reliable method of backing up important data. Unlike factory-pressed media (such as movie DVDs and computer software discs), burnable media is unreliable, and the data actually starts to fade in a short period of time. There isn't an exact estimate of how long burnable media lasts, but some argue that they can start to fade in as little as 17 months. However, your author has had some cease functioning sooner than that and some much later. Burnable media should be used only for short term projects.

The **Brasero** disc burning utility is included with Linux Mint. Brasero can be compared to well-known media burning programs such as Nero Burning Rom or Cyberlink Power2Go, which are available on competing platforms. With Brasero, you can create audio CDs, data discs, video discs, and you can also copy existing discs or create media from ISO images. The following screenshot shows **Brasero**, a powerful disc-burning application:

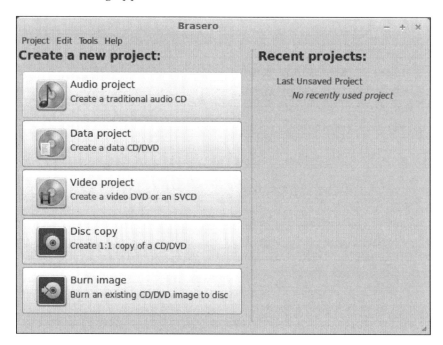

Brasero is a very straightforward application, especially if you've used other disc-burning applications on Linux or other platforms. To create a data disc for example, simply click on **Data project** and a new project window will open up. Then, you can drag files into the project window to start building your media. At the bottom, a space indicator displays the remaining space on the media. Once you've added all your files, click on the button labeled **Burn...** in the bottom-right corner of the application window, as shown in the following screenshot:

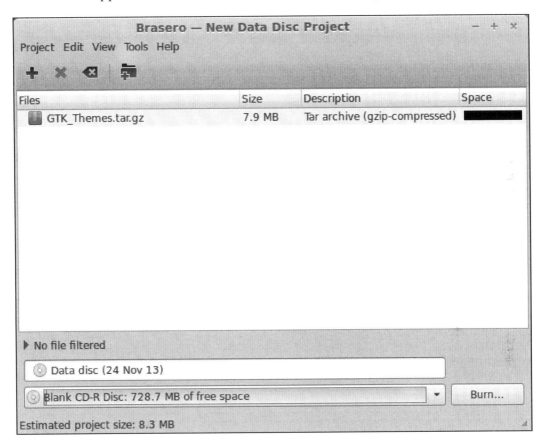

Similarly, creating an audio CD is just as easy. After clicking on **Audio project** from the main **Brasero** menu, you can drag MP3 files into the window, which is shown in the following screenshot, in the same way as you would drag data files. The difference is that the files will be arranged by tracks and you can reorder them.

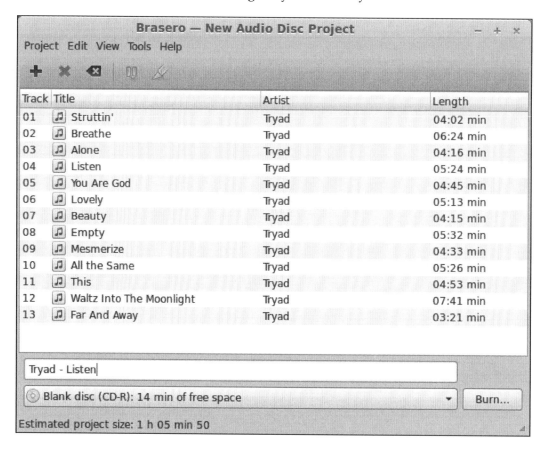

Brasero is not the only disc-burning application available in Linux. If for some reason it doesn't work well for you or you'd like to try something else, applications such as **K3b**, **xfburn**, and others are available for installation as well. Package installation is covered in *Chapter 6, Installing and Removing Software*.

Using the USB Image Writer

As mentioned, optical media is in the beginning stages of fading away. Some proponents of optical media may argue against this as many people still use optical media. However, with more and more computers shipping without optical drives, the fate of optical media has been written. The Linux Mint developers must understand this because a custom application is included to facilitate the creation of bootable USB flash drives for installing Linux or running utilities. The **USB Image Writer** makes the creation of bootable flash drives a cinch and is included in the default Mint installation. You'll find it in your **Applications** menu. The following screenshot shows the Mint's USB Image Writer application in action:

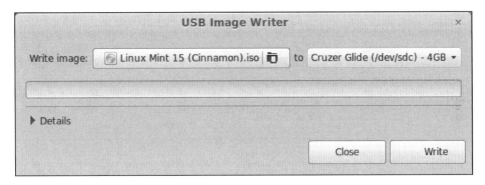

To use this tool, select a previously downloaded .iso file (such as a distribution of Linux) and then select the flash drive you'd like to use. When you're comfortable with the selections, click on the **Write** button and the process will begin, typically taking a few minutes to complete. It goes without saying that this will erase your flash drive. Make sure you're comfortable with the flash drive you've chosen before you begin the process.

You can simplify the process a bit by right-clicking on the .iso file you've downloaded, and then clicking on **Make a Bootable USB Stick**. This will fill in the ISO selection field for you and then all that you'd have to do is select the flash drive you'd like to use.

The USB Image Writer may not work with all ISO files. If you create bootable media with an ISO file and it fails to function properly, consult the information pages for the ISO file you've downloaded and see if they have a preferred method. Some Linux distributions prefer that you use the dd command to create bootable flash drives from their ISO files and include instructions on their pages for doing so.

Understanding how Universally Unique Identifiers work

The last section of this chapter deals with another aspect of storage in Linux that some may find confusing. This is **Universally Unique Identifiers** (**UUIDs**). You've no doubt seen Linux names storage devices using virtual device files such as /dev/sda, /dev/sdb, and so on. In the preceding sections, you had seen this everywhere, even in the /etc/fstab file when listing the partitions that are mounted each time you start your system, created during installation. However, there was a bit of a problem with this type of system that UUID tried to solve.

In today's day and age, we remove and insert media constantly. A typical desk drawer may contain a plethora of flash drivers, and in the typical desktop PC, we may have multiple hard disks and may add additional storage devices later. Each time we add media to the computer, it is assigned a virtual device file by the kernel. Typically, the first partition on the first hard drive used by Linux will be /dev/sda1, the second on the same drive will be /dev/sda2, and the first partition of the second hard drive will be /dev/sdb1, and so on.

This can be a major problem when swapping storage devices. If the storage device /dev/sda (which will likely contain your boot loader) is seen by Linux to be a different disk or if you add storage devices and the virtual devices change order, your system may not boot or the disks may not be located in the filesystem where you expect them to be. To solve this dilemma, UUIDs are used by virtually all Linux distributions today to ensure that disks and their partitions are assigned in the proper order and to the appropriate places in the filesystem.

You may have noticed several UUIDs displayed in the fstab screenshot earlier in this chapter. The lines began with UUID=. The UUID values are generated based on several factors of the disk and are expected to be unique to that disk. Having two disks or partitions that generate the same UUID is immensely unlikely. Thus, when the system looks for specific UUIDs when mounting disks and partitions, it's extremely unlikely that the system will ever be confused about which partition should be mounted where. Therefore, you can reorder your disks and not expect to suffer issues while booting, at least as far as the Linux kernel is concerned. Think of UUIDs as generating a unique serial number for each of your storage devices.

However, the UUID system is not without its own set of flaws. If a partition is resized, the UUID would change and would need to be adjusted manually. The same would occur if you wanted to upgrade your hard drive to a larger one. If you cloned your current disk to a new larger disk, the UUID of the target disk would be different, and Linux would be confused during the boot process. If you manually cloned a disk, you would need to manually update GRUB (the bootloader) as well as the /etc/fstab to reflect the new UUID values. To see the current UUIDs for your disk and partitions, execute the following command:

```
ls -l /dev/disk/by-uuid
```

You may recall that when modifying the fstab file , we used the following line:

```
/dev/sdb1   /mnt/mydisk   rw,relatime,data=ordered 0 0
```

Instead, we could have (and possibly should have) used a UUID to direct the fstab file to the partition we wished to mount. The preceding line could be changed to the following after generating a UUID:

```
UUID=b679d5bc-736a-46be-8e6b-b3d40e6e4caa    /mnt/mydisk
rw,relatime,data=ordered 0 0
```

Now that we have converted our fstab entry to use a UUID, we can be certain that the disk will always be mounted where we designated it. If we ever resize or replace this volume, all we'd need to do is determine the new UUID and replace it in our fstab file, and we would be good to go.

Summary

Storage devices in Linux are handled very differently compared to other platforms. In this chapter, we have gone over the ins and outs of media, including how to format, mount, and add extra storage. We also took a look at the Disk Usage Analyzer, which is useful to determine where your storage is being consumed, so you can best make a decision on how to clean up unused files and reclaim valuable space.

In the next chapter, we'll finally take a look at package management and learn how to install new applications to extend Mint even further. The topics discussed in the next stage of our adventure will include installing new software packages, removing software packages, installing updates, as well as what makes software management different in Mint compared to other platforms.

6
Installing and Removing Software

Linux Mint ships with just about everything the average person needs in order to be productive right away. By default, Mint includes a complete office suite, applications to listen to music files and watch movies, a web browser, the ability to burn CD/DVD media, and much more. But even though Mint is one of the most complete distributions around, the software it includes is by no means all there is available. Mint benefits from the Ubuntu package repositories, which feature tens of thousands of packages to install. Managing software on your local machine is the next step in mastering Linux Mint. In this chapter, we'll explore the multitude of ways to obtain new software in Mint, as well as how to manage currently installed applications.

In this chapter, we will discuss the following topics:

- Managing packages in Linux Mint
- Using the Mint **Software Manager**
- Installing new applications
- Removing applications
- Using the Synaptic Package Manager
- Configuring software sources
- Advanced package management
- Keeping your system up to date

Managing packages in Linux Mint

A concept known as package management separates the method by which software is distributed in Linux versus other platforms. If you've used other environments such as Windows or Mac OS X, you may have become very familiar with their methods of installing new programs. With Windows, you typically download an executable installer (for example, .exe or .msi) and navigate through an installation routine known as a **wizard**. On Mac OS X, you can download installation images (.dmg or .iso files) and install them into your Applications folder. Linux, on the other hand, uses **packages** that are downloaded from **repositories**.

What may be confusing to new users is the fact that not only is the method of obtaining new software very different in the Linux world, but also, each distribution has its own way of handling packages. In fact, a distribution's method of package management is one of the biggest differences that sets each of the distributions apart from one another. For example, Debian-based distributions (Debian, Ubuntu, and so on) use DEB (.deb) packages to distribute software. When it comes to Red-Hat-based systems (Red Hat, Fedora, CentOS, and so on), software are released in RPM (.rpm) formats. Each package type has specific commands used to manage them. In Debian-based distributions, you'll use the dpkg or apt commands, and with Fedora, you'll use the rpm or yum commands.

Linux Mint is based on Ubuntu, so naturally, we'll explore how to utilize DEB packages in this book. However, don't let the intricacies of Linux package management scare you off. There are several GUI tools available to help you manage installed applications, without forcing you to memorize the commands straight away. The best thing about graphical tools is that they take care of the command logic for you, as they are frontends to the underlying commands that the distribution uses in order to install packages. In this chapter, we'll start off by using the GUI tools, and then proceed into the specifics. That way, you'll learn the best of both worlds.

Using the Mint Software Manager

As mentioned earlier, there are GUI package management tools available in various distributions. Not all distributions ship with GUI tools to manage installed software, but all of the distributions aimed toward entry-level to intermediate users do. In Debian-based distributions, **Synaptic** is a very popular GUI tool (and is also available for use in Mint) and there are also other distribution-specific tools, such as the **Ubuntu Software Center**. Mint takes it one step further and includes its own GUI application for package management that is very easy to use; the Mint **Software Manager** is that tool, and it makes package management a breeze. The Mint **Software Manager** is available in your **Applications** menu. Go ahead and launch it. The following screenshot shows the main window of Mint's **Software Manager**:

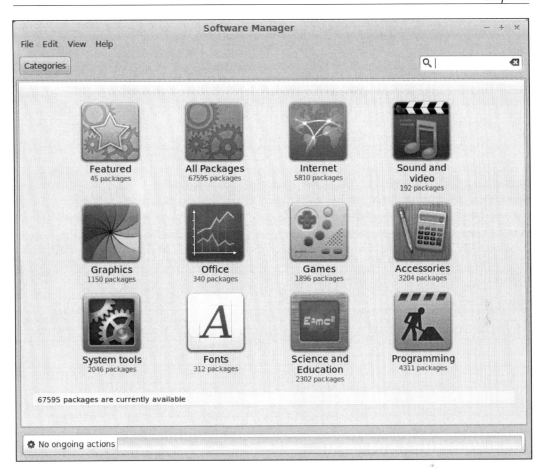

Before you dive into the **Software Manager**, first you will be prompted for your password. The password that you'll enter is the same as the one you used when you logged in. If you recall, you were asked to create a login password when you first installed Mint. But the password you set is more than just something to facilitate logging into your computer; it also doubles as your sudo password. This means that the user account you create during installation is able to use the sudo command, which essentially means that this user account is similar in concept to the administrator on Windows machines. Don't worry if this confuses you, as we'll discuss this in more detail later in *Chapter 8, Managing Users and Permissions*. For now, the thing to take away is that users with sudo rights are able to modify things on a machine that normal users cannot, such as using the **Software Manager** to install packages.

Once opened, the **Software Manager** will display a list of categories, which include available applications sorted into **Graphics**, **Internet**, **Sound and Video**, and others. If you're looking for a specific type of application, you can usually find it under the category you'd expect to find it. For example, if you were looking for a new web browser, you should be able to find what you're looking for under **Internet**, exactly as you may expect. The following screenshot is an example of one of the categories available:

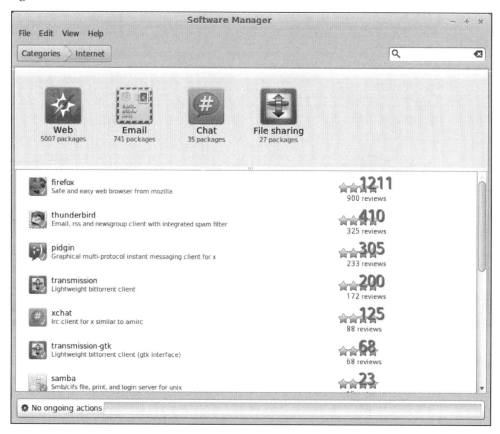

Installing new applications

Using Mint's **Software Manager**, installing new software couldn't be easier. Of course, you can learn all of the terminal commands to manage your installed software by hand, but you don't have to; the **Software Manager** should meet all your basic package management needs.

There is a great deal of applications available such as games, web browsers, music/video players, instant message clients, and more. There's most likely a program available to fit any need you can think of. To get some practice, let's grab a few new programs.

To install a new software package, first find it within the **Software Manager** application. You can click on a category and browse the available applications if you would like. Once you find an application you'd like to install, double-click on it, and then in the next screen, click on the **Install** button. Your new application will start downloading from Mint's repositories and then will be installed right away. Once the installation is complete, your new application will appear in your **Applications** menu in its respective section.

If you know the name of the program you would like to install, you can save some time by searching for it in the **Software Manager** window using the search bar in the upper-right corner. To get you started, here are a few applications you may enjoy. If you want to install one of them, simply search for the title, and follow the same directions.

Frozen Bubble

Frozen Bubble is a fun game where you must break the bubbles by matching their colors before they reach the bottom of the screen. The game is controlled solely by the arrow keys on your keyboard. You move the pointer with the left and right arrows and fire with the up arrow. There are many levels, and you can even create your own. The package for this game is titled "frozen-bubble"; so, if it doesn't show up by title, including the hyphen may help. The following screenshot shows Frozen Bubble—a fun game starring cute characters:

FileZilla

For those of you who develop web pages or have a need to upload files to an FTP server, it doesn't get much better than **FileZilla**. FileZilla is a cross-platform FTP application (available for Linux, Mac, and Windows) that has grown in popularity to the point where it's become an industry standard. The following screenshot shows FileZilla—a full-featured, cross-platform FTP application:

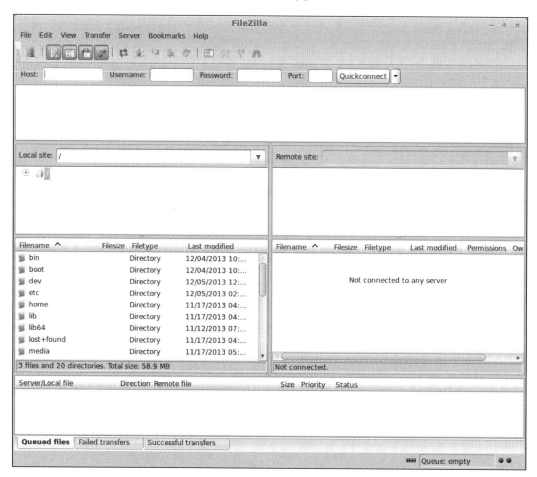

Minitube

Minitube is an application that is more or less a frontend to YouTube. Although, in Mint, YouTube works out of the box in Firefox, if there is ever a problem with the compatibility of YouTube in Linux (Flash plugin failures and so on), Minitube is an excellent application, and some even prefer it to watching videos in the browser, since Adobe's Flash plugin has been known to cause browser crashes when installed. The following screenshot shows Minitube, a YouTube client:

Steam

If you enjoy games, **Steam** is something that you should definitely consider installing. At one point in time, the lack of commercial games was long considered a weakness of Linux. Now, Steam brings with it the capability to play some very exciting commercial-quality games. The number of available games on Linux is growing quite fast, and Steam is a large part of this growth. Once you install Steam, you'll be able to purchase games designed for Linux. Note that not all games on Steam are available for Linux, but the number grows larger every day. The following screenshot is of Steam, a popular cross-platform game-distribution platform:

In order to fully practice how to install applications in Linux, it's highly recommended to search the Internet for the best Linux apps, and you should very easily find several articles that contain Linux users' picks of their favorite apps. Check out some reviews online, and even some articles from individuals switching to Linux from other operating systems. Not only will you get some inspiration as far as what applications to install, you'll also gain some practice with installing new applications on your system.

Removing applications

So, at this point, you've likely installed quite a few applications. Some of them may be great, but perhaps other applications might have failed to impress you. Using the **Software Manager**, you can easily remove unneeded applications.

To do so, open the **Software Manager** and search for the application that you would like to remove by typing your query into the search field at the top-right corner of the window. Once the search results are loaded, click on **View** in the file menu and uncheck **Available packages** so that only **Installed packages** remains checked. Then, double-click on the application you would like to remove and click on the **Remove** button on the next screen.

> If you'd like, you can even remove applications that came bundled with Mint if you don't think you'll ever use them. But be careful, if any of the applications you attempt to remove are a dependency of another application, you'll lose both. Pay careful attention to the output of the removal process, especially if it pops up a message saying that removing one package will cause others to be removed as well. When you're first starting out, it may be a good idea to not remove any applications unless you've installed them yourself.

The **Software Manager** application does the job for basic package management, but it does not include all the features for managing your software. In the following sections, we'll cover more advanced tools.

Using the Synaptic Package Manager

The **Synaptic Package Manager** has been around for over a decade. Synaptic is essentially a frontend to package management just as the **Software Manager** is, but with more advanced options available. The average person may not need to use it, though power users and administrators may appreciate having more control. Synaptic is also installed by default in Linux Mint, and is available in the **Applications** menu underneath **Administration**.

The first thing you will likely notice is that Synaptic is not as polished as the **Software Manager**. On the left-hand side, you will see a list of sections by default, which are the same idea as the categories in the **Software Manager**. You may also notice that there are many more sections in Synaptic with more advanced sections such as kernels, modules, and libraries. The following screenshot shows the main window of the **Synaptic Package Manager**:

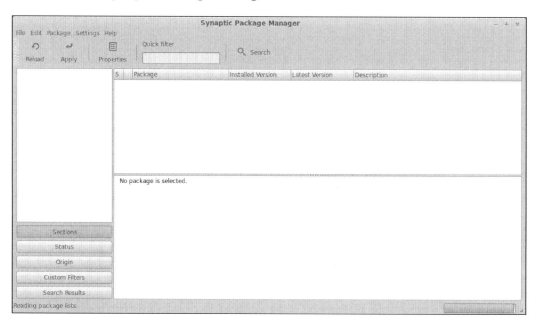

To illustrate the main differences, the best way is to use Synaptic for both adding and removing software. If you know the name of a package you would like to install, you can click on the **Search** button at the top of the window and type in the name of the application in the box that appears. (The **Quick filter** box that's also on the top of the window just filters the current list instead of doing a full search.) If you don't have an idea of a package you would like to install, some of my favorites include chromium, neverball, filezilla, geany, terminator, supertux, and wesnoth.

The `chromium` package installs a game called **Chromium BSU**, which is a spaceship-shooting game controlled by your mouse. Another package is very similarly named (chromium-browser) and installs a web browser that is very similar to Google Chrome and even compatible with the same plugins. Don't be confused if both show up in your search.

Once you find an application that you want to install, click on the checkbox to the left of its entry in the list. You will have only one option that's not grayed out and unavailable, and that is to mark the package for installation. Once you do, you will be notified of any dependencies (additional packages that a program may need in order to run) that might also be installed along with the application. Then, click on the **Mark** button if the dependency window appears. Finally, click on the **Apply** button in the top-left corner. A summary window will appear to allow you to take another look at what you're about to do before you confirm your changes. The following screenshot shows the final summary window that appears before package installation:

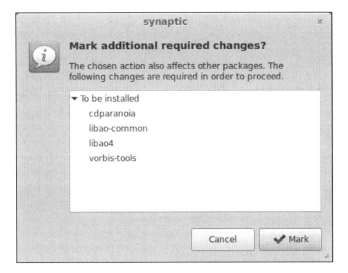

From here, Synaptic will download the requested packages (and any possible prerequisites) and install them for you. When it's done, the application you requested will be found in the **Applications** menu.

 You don't have to install applications one at a time. If you have several applications that you would like to install, you can search for another application without losing your selections and check them for installation as well. When you click on the **Apply** button, it will install all your requested packages. You won't lose your selections unless you close the program.

So far, you may be wondering what the benefit of the **Synaptic Package Manager** is over the **Software Manager**, since there were more steps involved to complete tasks that we have done previously. One of the many features that the **Synaptic Package Manager** has over the **Software Manager** is the number of options you get when removing software. To illustrate the difference, try removing the application that you just installed. All you have to do is search for the package again (if it's not still on your screen) and click on the same checkbox as before. If you've changed screens, simply search for the package you would like to remove before clicking on the checkbox. You'll have more options that are open to you now. The following screenshot shows the selections available for an installed package:

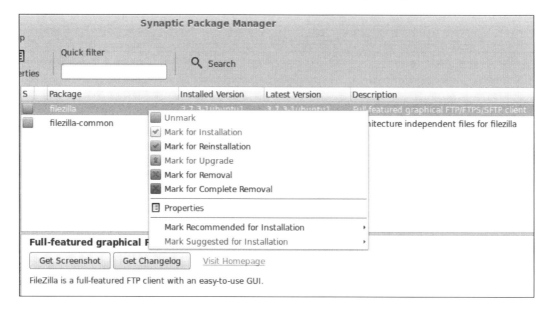

Following is a list of the options available from the right-click menu after searching for an application:

- **Unmark**: If you've selected an application for installation or removal (but you didn't mean to), this option will allow you to deselect the changes.
- **Mark for Installation**: If a package is not yet installed, this option is available. This option will download the application from your software sources, as well as any dependencies required to make it work, if any.
- **Mark for Reinstallation**: In cases where you have a misbehaving program, it may sometimes help to reinstall it. That's exactly what this option does; it gives you a chance to reinstall an application already installed on your machine.
- **Mark for Upgrade**: If a package upgrade is available for the selected item, you'll have a chance to install it. This option is rarely used, since updates are primarily handled through the **Update Manager**.

- **Mark for Removal**: As mentioned before, this option removes an application from your machine. However, it doesn't remove any configuration files that the application may have created on your filesystem.
- **Mark for Complete Removal**: The final option removes the application from your system, as well as any configuration files it may have created.

Another worthwhile feature of Synaptic is generating a list of installed applications. You can also do that in the **Software Manager**, but you would have to view the list on a category-by-category basis. In Synaptic, you can view a single list of everything installed on the machine—all on a single screen. This is a very useful technique when auditing the installed software on a machine, allowing you to prune your applications as you see fit. To generate this list, ensure **All** is selected on the left column of the Synaptic window. Then, click on **Status** and then select **Installed**. The following screenshot shows the installed software list in Synaptic:

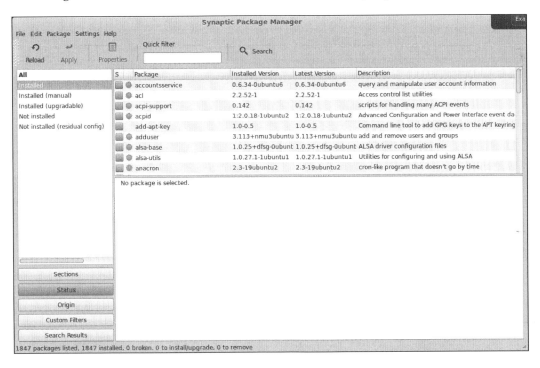

The **Synaptic Package Manager** certainly has many more options than Mint's **Software Manager**. However, in Linux, there is almost never a single correct solution. You may find that the **Software Manager** fits your needs best, or perhaps you may be a power user who enjoys the greater options of the **Synaptic Package Manager**. Whichever your case, choose the one that works best for you.

Configuring software sources

In most Linux distributions, Mint included, software is distributed by repositories. As mentioned earlier, one of the most distinctive differences between one distribution and another is the format of the available software packages and the way they are installed. Typically, packages are changed and then placed into a repository. By default, a distribution would ship with the default set of repositories allowing you to install new packages right away. For most users, the default repositories are all that's needed. However, over time, you may find that you want to use a software package but you're unable to find it while searching for the package in the **Synaptic Package Manager** or **Software Manager**. This could simply mean that you mistyped the name of the package while searching, but most commonly it means that the package may not be available in the repository.

One example of this is Google's web browser, **Chrome**. If Chrome is a web browser you like to use and you searched for the package, you would get several results but not the actual Chrome web browser itself. The Chromium web browser would likely show up in the search, but it's not quite the same thing (though it is very similar). If a user didn't know better, they may assume that Chrome isn't available for Linux. However, that's not the case. It's just not included in Mint's repositories as an available package. There may also be other software packages you might want to run which aren't included in the default repository. When this occurs, usually a quick Google search will point you in the right direction.

In the case of Google Chrome, Google makes a number of packages available for Linux. In order to install it, go to the page that comes up in the search, and you should stumble across a page that contains packages for Debian-based Linux distributions. Choose your package, and when it's done downloading, Mint should recognize the file and allow you to install it by double-clicking on it. Just make sure that you choose the right package. For example, recall whether or not you installed the 32-bit or 64-bit version of Linux Mint.

Downloading a package manually from the Internet and installing through the downloaded package is not a typical way of installing new software in Linux, but some softwares are made available via this method from time to time. In the case of Chrome, it will install its own repository to your system, so that way when a new version is released, Mint's **Update Manager** will catch it and offer it to you. Over time, software repositories may add up, and at some point or another you may wish to remove an add-on repository that you no longer need. In other cases, when you search the Internet for a package that's not available in Mint's own repository, you may find that an article calls for you to enter a repository manually.

In the past, this meant that you would need to open up a terminal, then open the `/etc/apt/sources.list` file in a text editor, and then add the required entry to add the extra repository that contains the software you need. While this is perfectly fine for intermediate and advanced users, it would be so much better if there was a graphical application that you could use in order to manage software repositories. Actually, Mint does include such a tool, which is simply called **Software Sources**. If you search for it in your **Applications** menu, you should be able to find it in the search results. The following screenshot shows Mint's **Software Sources** application:

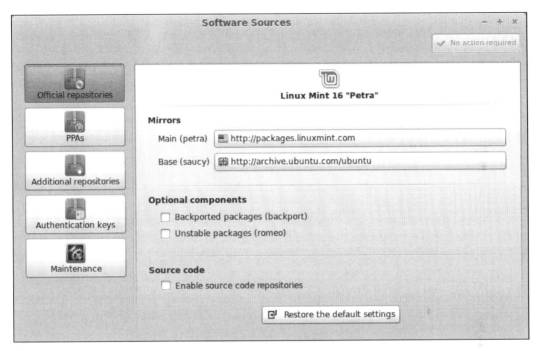

On the first screen, the one that opens up when you first launch the application, you're given various regional options. In a nutshell, Mint's software sources default to a software repository near you. As you can see from the American flag in the screenshot from my machine, it's defaulting to a software repository in the USA. If I were to visit another country and take my machine with me, I could select a different repository (otherwise, reaching the same repository from somewhere else may take a long time). If these values are correct and are already set to your local country, you probably won't need to make any changes here, but it's nice to know that you can make changes if you ever needed to.

Where the **Software Sources** app really shines is with the other options it gives you. The second button down on the left, **PPAs**, allows you to set up a **PPA (Personal Package Archive)**, which are smaller repositories set up to fill small gaps in the available software. One example of this is the **Handbrake** program, which allows you to copy DVDs to your hard drive (those that you are legally entitled to copy, of course). Handbrake isn't available in Mint's software selection at the time of writing this book. So, if you searched Google for the keywords "Linux Mint" and "Handbrake", you would most likely find yourself reading an article regarding an available PPA that allows you to download and install the software.

Personal package archives are not specific to Mint. PPAs are an Ubuntu technology that allow developers to set up repositories to host software that they have compiled for Ubuntu to easily make their software available for others. There are PPAs available for all kinds of different packages. Since Mint uses Ubuntu as its base, it automatically inherits the ability to use PPAs. Mint went a step further though, and facilitated the installation of PPAs in its **Software Sources** application. This is a great thing, because in the past, the only way to add a PPA was to use a terminal command. A complete beginner would likely feel intimidated by having to manually install a PPA. Thanks to Mint, you can use the **Software Sources** application to add a PPA to your system. To add a PPA, all you have to do is click on the **Add a new PPA...** button and enter the URL you are given from the PPA site and then follow the prompts to add it to your system. After adding it to your system, the software included in the PPA would then be displayed in search results in both Synaptic and the **Software Manager**. The following screenshot shows the PPA insertion dialog:

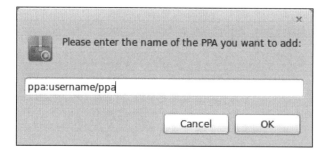

Generally, PPAs are created by volunteer developers who want to make a package available for Mint/Ubuntu that normally isn't part of the default repositories. While PPAs are useful to fill any gaps in the software available for your distribution, the continued usefulness of the PPA solely depends on the individual who created and/or maintains it. If for some reason the volunteer abandons the PPA, new versions of the application would no longer be made available. It's recommended that you use PPAs only if you really need to. PPAs are not tested by Ubuntu developers, and if a package stops being updated, that means you aren't getting security updates for it either. Use PPAs at your own risk.

The third option, **Additional repositories**, is very similar to the idea of PPAs, though repositories are usually larger and maintained by developers closer to the project; however, this isn't always the case. If you find that a software package you would like to install requires its own repository, you can set it up in this section of the **Software Sources** application. You may find some additional repositories listed in this dialog, especially if you've installed software packages from the web, such as Google Chrome. Google Chrome, for example, creates its own repository, so you would see it listed here. If later on you would like to remove a repository, you can do so through this section. The following screenshot shows the software repository section with an add-on repository installed:

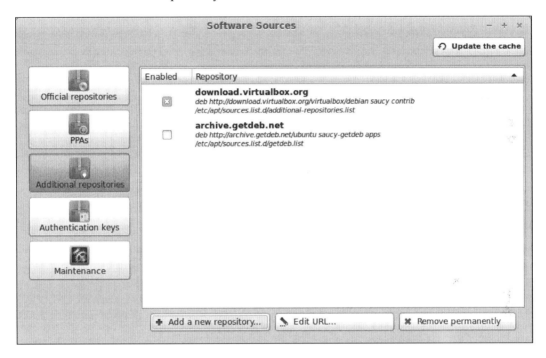

In the **Authentication keys** section of **Software Sources**, you are shown a list of currently installed authentication keys and you can also add a new one. These keys are used to sign packages to make sure that they are trusted, and each repository has its own key. This is not a section that you will make use of very often, typically only when instructed to do so when adding a new repository or when you would like to remove keys for a repository that you no longer use.

Finally, the **Maintenance** section gives you two options: **Fix MergeList problems** and **Purge residual configuration**. These options are useful to solve error messages that you may run into down the road, and are shown here in case you need them. However, in normal usage, you should not run into these issues, and detailed information about these options and why they are needed is beyond the scope of this book. However, if you do end up getting an error message regarding a mergelist issue, you may make use of this tool. In regards to residual configuration, this refers to the ability to remove dependency packages that were installed when you installed an application that may not be installed anymore. Unless you really want to clean up your application list or you are running low on disk space, it's best to avoid this option. An application that's considered a dependency application may be something that you use, so using this option is not advised on a normal basis.

Advanced package management

As mentioned earlier in this chapter, the graphical tools available for package management in various distributions are merely frontends to the underlying package commands specific to that distribution. These graphical tools take care of the logic for you. In fact, you could completely skip learning the underlying commands and work entirely within the easy-to-use graphical tools to manage your installed software. However, it's very useful to understand how the internals of package management work in case you find yourself in a situation where the GUI tools fail to function.

Here's an example that can help clear up the relationship between package management commands and graphical tools such as the **Software Manager**. Take the following command, for example:

```
sudo apt-get install filezilla
```

When the preceding command is run in the terminal, it will instruct your system to fetch the FileZilla application from Mint's repositories and install it. Your system will also install any and all dependencies required to make FileZilla function. Sounds familiar? It should. That's exactly the same thing that occurs if you were to instruct the **Software Manager** or Synaptic to install the FileZilla application. The graphical tools are simply using the underlying command to install the application. In the case of Mint, the **Software Manager** (when instructed by you to install a new application) is simply calling the apt-get command in the background and using it to install the package you asked for.

Similarly, the `apt-get` command, shown as follows, can be used to remove packages as well:

```
sudo apt-get remove filezilla
```

If you don't think you'll need to use an application again and don't feel you need to retain its configuration, you can remove the application as well as its configuration at the same time:

```
sudo apt-get remove --purge filezilla
```

In addition, you can also search via a terminal command to see if an application is available for installation. For example, we can run the following command to determine if Eclipse (an application for development) is available:

```
apt-cache search eclipse
```

 Package names in Linux are usually lowercase, though this is not always the case. When in doubt, search for package names in lowercase first.

With the preceding command, we're searching for any package that includes `eclipse` in the name. You may have noticed that we didn't use "sudo" in the preceding command. That's because unlike installing or removing packages, elevated permissions are not required to merely search the package database in order to see what's available.

There are many different `apt` commands available for other purposes. Feel free to check the man page for `apt-get` to learn even more.

Keeping your system up to date

Software updates in the Linux world are typically released for one of the three purposes. New versions of packages are released to fix bugs, patch security vulnerabilities, or add new features. By now, you've most likely come across Mint's **Update Manager** if you were at any point prompted to update your system (which typically first happens right after installation finishes). Keeping your system up to date is strongly recommended. However, it's not out of the realm of possibility that a theoretical bad update could crash your system. This rarely happens, but it's always a good idea to keep current backups just in case, especially when administering your system.

In Linux Mint, there are two ways to update your system. You can use a subcommand of `apt-get` (which we'll get into shortly), but Mint also provides a graphical utility simply known as **Update Manager** that will also accomplish your needs. Whichever method you use is up to you, but Mint's **Update Manager** is actually recommended, as it categorizes the updates based on how likely they are to break your system. (Again, this is extremely rare, but it's better to be safe than sorry.) The following screenshot shows Mint's **Update Manager** application:

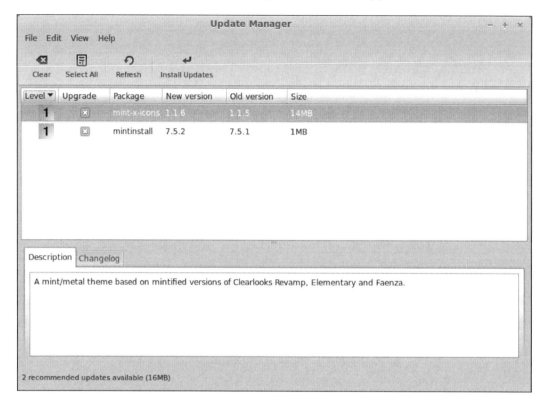

In the **Update Manager**, there are 5 levels of security updates. The lower the security level, the safer the update is perceived to be. The higher the level, the more unsafe a package is believed to be; by default, levels 4 and 5 are disabled. Levels 1 and 2 are tested by the Linux Mint community for stability, but levels 3 and 4 typically aren't. When you view a list of updates, you will see a number associated with each one.

By default, installing the default levels 1 to 3 of updates should suffice for more users. However, depending on current events, you may sometimes consider higher level updates. For example, there may come a time someday where you hear about a really bad Linux virus making its way around the Net. Upon reading the update, you may find that a specific Linux kernel update closes the security hole that the virus uses to spread. In this case, you may enable levels 4 and 5 to make sure that you get the update. To do so, click on **Edit** and then **Preferences** and enable the latter two levels. The following screenshot shows Mint's **Update Manager** application with security level descriptions displayed:

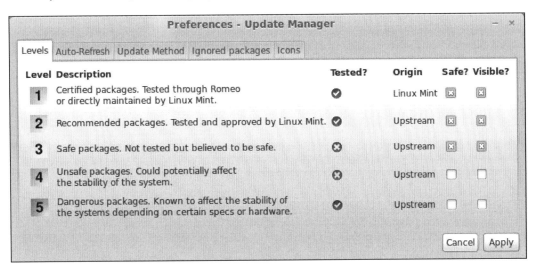

Also, on the **Preferences** configuration screen, you can select your update frequency. At times, Linux distributions may release updates quite frequently, sometimes several times a week or more. This is great in the sense that new features and security updates are constantly coming. But it may get frustrating to have your work interrupted several times with offers to update your system. In the next tab of the **Preferences** configuration window, you can select the **Auto-Refresh** frequency. **Auto-Refresh** refers to how often your computer communicates to your repositories to see what has changed. When the refresh occurs, you are then notified if there are updated packages. One possible solution is changing your update frequency to 7 days, so that way you can choose a specific day that is less busy for you to install your updates. It's definitely recommended that you keep all the applications up to date, but do so at a time that's convenient for you.

As mentioned, you don't necessarily need to use the **Update Manager** in order to update your system, though it is recommended. You can also update your system using terminal commands. This may come in handy if your system doesn't open a graphical user interface for some reason, and it's believed that installing the latest updates may help. To do so, first you need to manually refresh your available updates. You can do this with the following command:

```
sudo apt-get update
```

After entering your password, your system will download the latest list of available packages from your repositories. This doesn't actually install anything, it just ensures that your system has an up-to-date list of what's available in the repositories. Once that's done, you can download and install updates by running the following command:

```
sudo apt-get dist-upgrade
```

 When using terminal commands to update your system, the updates will not be broken down by security level. All updates are applied using this command, even level 4 and 5 updates. Use them at your own caution.

Summary

In this chapter, we went over how to install new software packages as well as updates. We started out with an overview of the basics of how software management differs in Linux than in other platforms. The **Software Manager** was demonstrated, and hopefully you used it to browse available packages and found some great applications. We also covered removing programs, the **Synaptic Package Manager** and how it differs from the **Software Manager**, as well as how to install and remove packages using terminal commands. We finished the chapter with an overview of installing package updates.

In the next chapter, we'll have even more fun by enjoying some multimedia files in Mint. You will be shown how to perform activities such as listening to MP3s, playing DVDs, importing photos from a digital camera, and more!

Enjoying Multimedia on Mint

Now that we've learned how to get our work done in a Linux Mint system as well as how to maintain it, it's time to show you how to have some fun and relax. Out of the box, Linux Mint comes preconfigured to allow you to enjoy multimedia files such as videos and music. In addition, more applications are available in the repositories to enhance your media even further. In this chapter, we'll take a look at listening to music, playing video files, photo management, and desktop recording.

In this chapter, we will discuss the following topics:

- Understanding issues concerning codecs
- Playing music files
- Ripping an audio CD
- Editing MP3 tags
- Playing video files
- Playing a DVD
- Viewing photos
- Editing photos with GIMP
- Accessing your webcam
- Recording your desktop

Understanding issues concerning codecs

Codecs (**C**oder **Dec**oder) are software plugins that allow multimedia files, such as MP3 and AVI, to be recognized on a system. For example, if your system lacks the necessary codec to support MP3 files, you won't be able to play these files on your system. At first, you might be thinking, "What's the big deal?" These types of files work immediately on Windows and Mac OS X. In these platforms, you typically double-click on a multimedia file or insert a DVD, and the content plays without any extraordinary effort on your part. It's very easy to take this ability for granted, as most people expect these types of things to work. In Linux, however, it is the norm for these types of things to need a bit of configuration on the user's side to function properly. As a result, media files such as MP3s, some video formats, and DVDs won't play unless you manually install the software that makes them work.

So, why don't all distributions just give their users a break and include these codecs by default? For the most part, the reason has to do with licensing as well as ethics. Various codecs (such as those required to play MP3 audio and DVD video) are not free, and many Linux developers prefer not to include any technology that has a proprietary license attached to it. As a result, users of some distributions are forced to do a bit of search on Google to figure out how to get various multimedia formats working on their systems.

Some distributions make this easier than others. Ubuntu, for example, will display a pop-up box to give you an option to install the missing software as you run into files that need them. Other distributions such as Debian and Arch barely facilitate this and need you to perform some magic in order to find out how to manually add the missing software. Thankfully, Mint chooses to include these built-in codecs so that all of your multimedia files will work right away, without forcing you to investigate what you need to install to get things working. In short, everything will just work.

In regards to ethics, some developers in the Linux world will refuse to include drivers or codecs that are not free in their distributions due to their beliefs that all software should truly be free. In the Linux community, there are often two types of developers and users: those that will use proprietary technologies where required as a means to an end and those who will refuse to use proprietary technologies even if it means less functionality or slower performance. The Mint developers fall into the first category. They prefer not to use proprietary technologies, though they will use proprietary components wherever it's absolutely required in order to facilitate common usage. In the Mint community, it's believed that it's better to include proprietary technologies where required rather than hearing comments such as, "Mint sucks, because it can't play MP3 files" from those who don't understand or care about the politics.

Depending on where you live, using proprietary codecs that you don't hold a license for may fall into somewhat of a legal gray area. Whether or not it is illegal for you to use these codecs depends on your local laws as well as whether or not you hold a license for such codecs. With regards to personal use, such as enjoying multimedia files on your computer, you're safe; however, if you work in a company that produces multimedia files for profit, it's best to ensure that you hold a license for the technologies that you plan to use in your projects. Especially in corporate environments, it's important that you do your research. Neither the author nor Packt Publishing is accountable if you choose to not respect licensing rules.

> Linux Mint also releases a "No Codecs" version of its releases. If you reside in a country where it is illegal to use codecs you haven't paid for, you can either purchase licenses for the required codecs or download the No Codecs release instead. To do so, head over to the following site, find a mirror near you, and then browse the mirror for the No Codec version:
>
> `http://www.linuxmint.com/mirrors.php`

You may be wondering how Linux Mint is able to offer preinstalled multimedia codecs if there are legal/ethical issues surrounding their use. The Linux Mint developers make no assumptions based on whether or not you are legally allowed to utilize the codecs that are not free in your country, and leave the research up to you. The developers wanted Mint to support all the typical formats out of the box, and they included the codecs for this purpose.

A detailed discussion regarding licensing and patents is beyond the scope of this book (and the subject of many debates in the Linux community). If you would like to learn more, conduct an Internet search on the topic. If you search for the phrase, "Why should we pay for codecs when working on a Linux Operating System", you will find a PDF document by Fluendo that explains this further, though be advised that it is a sales document.

Playing music files

Music files, including MP3 and OGG/Vorbis files, work pretty much as you'd expect. If you have downloaded a music file, all you have to do is double-click on the file and it will start playing. **Banshee** is included as the default music player in Linux Mint. The following screenshot shows Banshee, a music player and manager:

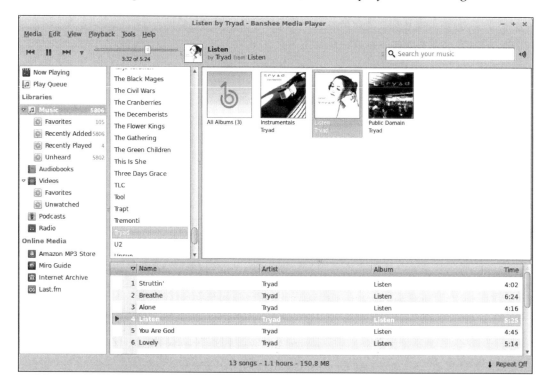

While Banshee is a very capable music player, it's able to do much more than simply play music files. If you take a look at the side bar, you'll notice some additional options such as **Podcasts** and **Amazon MP3 Store**. If you choose to store your music files in the **Music** folder located in your home directory, Banshee can import the files into your collection. To do so, click on **Tools** at the top of its window and then select **Rescan Music Library**. Banshee will then audit any audio files you may have in your **Music** folder and sort them into its database. After the audit is complete, you'll be able to find your music files in Banshee's database and sort your songs by artist, album, or song title. You can also create playlists of your favorite songs. You can add new music to your **Music** folder at any time; all you have to do is click on **Rescan Music Library** again and Banshee will import any new audio files that it finds.

The **Podcasts** feature of Banshee is also worth pointing out. The first time you click on the **Podcasts** section on the left-hand side of the window, you're given an option to use **Miro Guide** to download new podcasts. If you click on **Open Miro Guide** in the bottom-right corner of the window, you can search for podcasts you may be interested in. The following screenshot shows **Miro Guide** opened within Banshee after searching for linux action show:

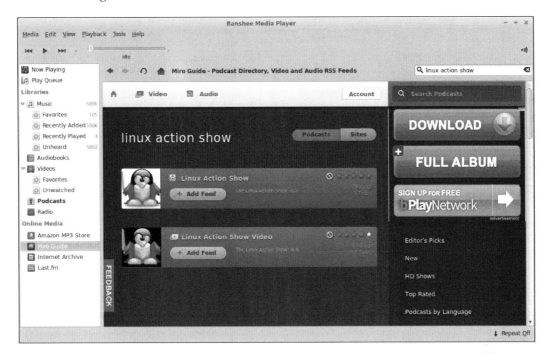

After adding a podcast, Banshee will periodically download new episodes and save them in the Podcasts directory in your home folder.

Be sure to keep an eye on your free space. If your home folder is on a smaller partition, the downloaded podcasts can start to eat up your free space. To combat this, feel free to delete any podcasts you've already listened to. You can download them again later if you feel the need.

Ripping an audio CD

Perhaps, you have an audio CD that you would like to import into Banshee. By default, Mint does not contain a program to convert (rip) an audio CD into MP3 files. Despite this, we are going to discuss ripping CDs in this chapter, because it's a very common task that many music fans will find themselves wanting to do.

> Although the recording industry may not be fond of the practice, it's very common for music fans to rip CDs into MP3 files with an MP3 player or car stereo. Of course, you should only rip CDs that you own, and it's illegal to share them with those who haven't paid for the content. However, for your own purposes, ripping CDs falls into fair use.

To facilitate ripping an audio CD, you'll need to install an extra package from Mint's repositories. There are several programs available that facilitate this type of task. To make your search easier, one program that's recommended for this purpose is **Asunder**. To install Asunder, two packages are needed. Both packages can be installed in a single `apt-get` command as shown in the following command line:

```
sudo apt-get install asunder lame
```

You can search for them in Synaptic or **Software Manager**. In the preceding command, we installed two packages with a single `apt-get install` command. The `asunder` package contains the actual Asunder program itself, and the `lame` package provides Asunder with the ability to encode MP3 files. Once Asunder is installed, you'll find it in the **Applications** menu. To get started with ripping an audio CD, insert an audio CD into your computer and launch Asunder.

> Although it is preferable to rip CDs into OGG files rather than MP3s (since OGG files use an open source codec that is completely legal), ripping CDs into MP3s is explained instead, because many devices that play music do not support OGG files today. Although MP3s use a codec that is not free, they are the assumed file type in virtually all physical music players and car stereos. If you do not need to listen to MP3s on a proprietary device, you may consider the OGG format instead.

Once **Asunder** opens, you'll see the main window. However, before ripping your CD, it's best to set up the program for the best quality audio. You only need to do this once, as the next time you open **Asunder**, it will remember your settings. The following screenshot shows the main window of **Asunder**:

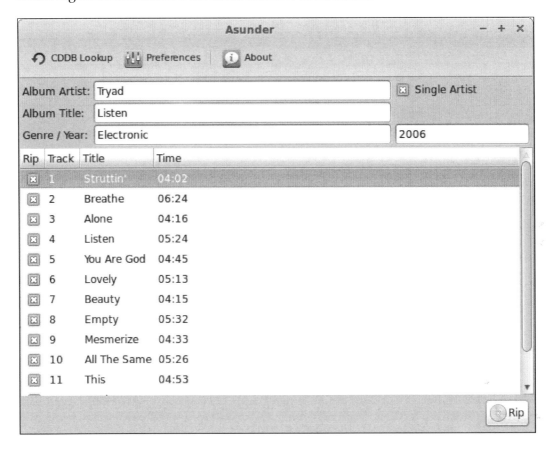

To set up the best quality for creating MP3 files, click on the **Preferences** tab at the top of the **Asunder** window. Once the **Preferences** menu opens, click on the **Encode** tab. The following screenshot shows the **Preferences** menu of **Asunder**, where the **Encode** settings are located:

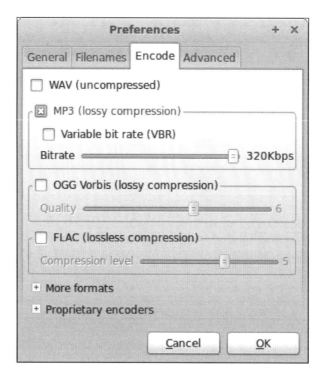

The following settings are ideal for the highest quality MP3 files that **Asunder** is able to provide:

- **WAV (uncompressed)**: Disabled
- **MP3 (lossy compression)**: Enabled
- **Variable bit rate (VBR)**: Disabled

- **Bitrate**: Slide all the way to the right (**320Kbps**)
- **OGG Vorbis (lossy compression)**: Disabled
- **FLAC (lossless compression)**: Disabled

Once you have configured your settings, you're ready to go. Click on **OK** and then on **Rip**. The process will take around 5 to 10 minutes, depending on your computer and the length of the CD. By default, music files are stored in the root of your /home directory, so when done, be sure to move the files into your **Music** directory so that music players such as Banshee can find them.

 Most of the time, Asunder will find the album information and automatically fill in the track names and album information. However, with rarer albums, you may have to input this data yourself.

Editing MP3 tags

MP3 files contain metadata that music managers such as Banshee read from when sorting the files into their databases. These are known as **ID3 Tags** and are embedded into the MP3 files themselves. If this metadata ever becomes inconsistent, you may end up with invalid data in your music player. Examples of this might be a song being listed with an incorrect track number or a typo in the album title that causes the files to be read under two different albums. Editing MP3 tags is especially useful after ripping a CD. Most of the time, even despite entering the proper information into a program such as Asunder, you'll end up with some missing information.

Banshee has some capability of correcting metadata issues. If you click on **Tools** at the top of the **Banshee Media Player** window, there is a selection named **Fix Music Metadata**. If you click on it, you'll see a new screen where you'll be shown any inconsistent data that leads to duplicate artist names, album names, or genres. Here, you'll be able to fix these issues so that the files are organized into playlists properly. However, the capability of this menu is limited.

To view and display all the metadata for a song, locate a particular song in Banshee's playlist and right-click on it. At the bottom of the right-click menu, you'll see a selection, **Edit Track Information**. Using this option, you'll be able to edit more than just the artist, album title, and genre. The following screenshot shows Banshee's **Track Editor**:

In addition to the track editor, there is also a more powerful solution available for download in Banshee. **Easytag**, available in the default repositories, allows you to edit music metadata in bulk, with features such as pattern-matching. This program is beyond the scope of this book, though. However, if you need to edit a large collection of MP3 files in bulk, Easytag is a good solution that's worth checking out. Feel free to open Synaptic or the **Software Manager** and search for easytag if you'd like to take a look at it.

Playing video files

Much like music files, video files (MPG, AVI, and so on) work out of the box in Mint and will typically play as soon as you double-click them. Interestingly, Mint features two video player programs. The default player is simply called **Videos**, but **VLC** is installed as well. It's not certain why Mint features two video players, but if your file won't open in Videos, it's likely that VLC will be able to play it. VLC is a powerful cross-platform video player (it's available in Windows and Mac OS X as well) and is able to play just about anything. If VLC is unable to play a video file, it's likely that nothing will.

If you end up preferring to use VLC, it's easy to switch the default. In order to do so, right-click on a video file, click on **Properties**, and on the very first tab, you'll see a drop-down menu that will allow you to select the default player. Please keep in mind that you'd have to repeat this for all video file types. For example, setting the default player for MPG files does not set it for AVI files and so on.

Playing a DVD

As mentioned earlier, Mint supports commercial DVD movies out of the box. The recommended application to use for DVD video is VLC. To play a DVD, insert it into your DVD drive and give it a little bit of time to spin up. Then, in VLC, click on the **Media** menu on the top–left side and then click on **Open Disc**. Finally, click on **Play** to begin playing the movie.

Once the movie starts playing, VLC is able to handle all the basic DVD controls you would expect it to. If you peruse the file menu, you'll see options to skip to the menu, skip to the next chapter, choose a specific chapter, and so on.

Most DVDs can be played in Linux. However, every now and then, you may run into a DVD that won't play at all in Linux but may work fine in a regular DVD player such as those that hook up to a television. If you run into such a disc, it doesn't mean that there's anything wrong with the disc or your computer. The multimedia industries go to great lengths to make sure that their movies won't work in anything other than the devices they've approved. So sometimes, this copy protection may prevent the movie from working in Linux, despite Mint building DVD capability into their distro. This doesn't happen too often, but it can and sometimes does.

Viewing photos

In Mint, viewing photos works pretty much as you would expect. If you double-click on an image, it will open up in Mint's default image viewer program. This program is simply called **Image Viewer** in the **Applications** menu. The following photo is opened in the **Image Viewer**:

Once you've opened a photo, you're able to cycle through any additional photos that may exist in the same directory. At the top of the window, you'll see icons to move left and right through any additional pictures that may exist in the same location, and you'll also see icons for zooming in and out as well as rotating the picture.

 Although the title of Mint's default image viewer is **Image Viewer** in the menu, you may see it listed as **Eye of GNOME** depending on where you look, as this was its original name. In fact, if you want to launch the **Image Viewer** from the command line, the command is eog and not imageviewer as you may first expect.

For performing any advanced editing such as cropping, you'll need to explore applications outside of Mint's basic image viewer. Thankfully, such an application also comes bundled in Mint and is discussed in the next session.

Editing photos with GIMP

The **GNU Image Manipulation Program** (**GIMP**) is another graphics application included in Mint and is able to handle the advanced needs of image editing. GIMP is very much comparable to **Adobe Photoshop** and is primarily geared toward intermediate to advanced graphic designers or photographers. However, even its most basic features are useful for very common photography tasks. The following screenshot shows how a photo is edited in GIMP:

One example of editing a photo is cropping it. This is something even a photography novice will need to do from time to time. After you've opened a photo in GIMP by clicking on **File** and then on **Open**, you'll find the cropping tool under the **Tools** menu, under **Transform Tools**. After you crop your photo, you can save your changes. However, what you may think of as saving a file in any other program is known as **exporting** a file in GIMP. If you want to overwrite the same file, you'll find an **Overwrite** option in the file menu. However, if you'd like to save the file under a new name, you'll need to click on **Export** instead and then choose a file type.

There is also another feature that even beginners may wish to play around with. The **Filters** section allows you to apply some special effects to your photos. It ranges from useful all the way to just plain wacky. Advanced usage of GIMP is beyond the scope of this book; however, thankfully, the Internet is not short on GIMP tutorials available through a simple Google search.

Accessing your webcam

By default, Mint does not come with an application in order to view and record your webcam. However, there are several webcam applications available for installation, and one of them is known as **Cheese**. Cheese is available for installation in the same way that you would install any other packages. Simply search for it in Synaptic or **Software Manager**, or execute `sudo apt-get install cheese` in a terminal window. Cheese will then be available in the **Applications** menu once it finishes installing.

Cheese is a very basic webcam program, but it gets the job done. With Cheese, you can take simple pictures through your webcam, record video, or even take multiple pictures in a short iteration. In addition, you can also apply special effects to your photos.

Another application available for viewing your webcam is a program called **GTK+UVC Viewer**, which is installable by searching for the `guvcview` package. If, for some reason, Cheese doesn't work well for you, **GUVCViewer** may be an alternative worth checking out. However, **GUVVCViewer** has many advanced features that may be overwhelming for those who only need a very basic usage of their webcam.

Recording your desktop

Some may find the need to record their desktop in order to make an instructional video. The VLC application, which comes bundled with Mint, is capable of recording the screen, but it doesn't do the best job. In fact, these days, screen recording is one of the weaknesses in terms of software availability in Linux, since there is no application available that is equivalent in quality to popular software packages such as **Snag-It** and **CamStudio**.

One application that does come somewhat close to these popular software packages is known as **recordMyDesktop**. It is an application that can be used in a terminal window via shell commands, but it does have a graphical frontend known as **GTK recordMyDesktop**, which is a bit easier to use. Although **recordMyDesktop** seems to work fine, it lacks certain features that are very common. For example, you simply can't save your recorded files anywhere other than the root of your home folder. There's no way to change it. The following screenshot shows the **recordMyDesktop** application used for screen recording:

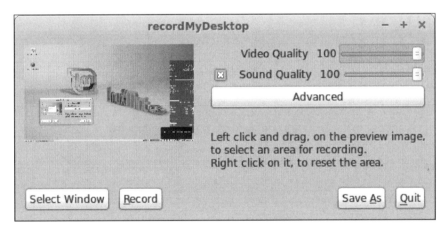

Other screen recording programs in Linux are of varying quality. Some very usable applications to record your screen have come around from time to time, only to disappear into obscurity after a short period of time, and most are largely unmaintained. GTK recordMyDesktop is one application that has stuck around for quite some time.

Using **recordMyDesktop** is anything but simple. Video recording itself seems to work fine enough on most systems. To record your desktop, you click on the **Record** button, and when done, click on the Stop icon, which will show up in the notification tray on your panel. By default, **recordMyDesktop** will record your entire screen. This may not be what you want, depending on your configuration. For example, if you only want to record a specific window, click on **Select Window** first before starting your recording. This is especially important if you have multiple monitors, as the default settings will grab your entire screen, no matter how many monitors it's stretched across.

The main difficulty with **recordMyDesktop** seems to be recording the sound along with your video. In the settings, there is no listing of devices you can choose to record from. The **recordMyDesktop** application chooses what it thinks is your default microphone on your default sound card depending on your configuration, but it may (be and often is) wrong. If you open the settings for the application, you'll notice a default device named **DEFAULT** in the sound tab. This is the device from which **recordMyDesktop** will try to record sound. If you have a USB headset or more than one microphone installed, this may not be what you want.

To list the devices available to record on your system, execute the following command:

```
arecord -l
```

Determining the recording device that you want from the output of the `arecord` command may take some interpretation. When in doubt, experiment. On my system, my USB microphone shows up on **Card 0 Subdevice 0**, so I enter `hw:0,0` into the device field of **recordMyDesktop** in order to access it. The following screenshot shows the example settings used in an instance of **recordMyDesktop**:

Other software packages exist for screen recording, but some of the available ones have been unmaintained for a very long time and may or may not work. Some of them are stable, but others crash constantly and cause you to lose work. When starting out with screen recording, **recordMyDesktop** is most likely your best bet.

Summary

In this chapter, we focused on consuming multimedia in Linux Mint. We started off with an explanation as to why codecs are a controversial matter in the Linux community, and then we explored the applications Mint provides to facilitate playing music, listening to podcasts, and watching videos. Then, we explored how to modify music metadata to keep your collection consistent. We also went over how to watch DVD movies and copy audio CDs into files that can be played on an MP3 player.

The software repositories are full of fun applications to allow you to enjoy your media, so feel free to enjoy yourself and have a look around. You may find some multimedia applications that you enjoy more than those that Mint provides you with. Some highlights to look out for include both the **Rhythmbox** and **Amarok** music players, the **Mplayer** and **Xine** video players, and also **digiKam** to manage your photo collection. In addition, there are several great games in the default repositories, including **Chromium BSU**, **Battle for Wesnoth**, **Nexuiz**, **Supertux**, **Neverball**, and **Planet Penguin Racer**, to name a few.

In the next chapter, we are going to take a look at managing user access, including creating/deleting user accounts, managing user groups, configuring `sudo` access for administrators, and file and directory permissions.

8

Managing Users and Permissions

We've explored quite a bit of Linux Mint, but our journey so far has only been with a single user account. You may or may not want other users to access your computer, but either way, it's highly recommended to learn more about how users and permissions are handled in the Linux world to ensure that your bird's-eye view of Linux functionality is complete. In this chapter, we'll work through examples of user management (creating, disabling, and removing user accounts) as well as file and folder permissions. These concepts will be explored via GUI applications as well as shell command examples.

In this chapter, we will discuss the following topics:

- Creating new users
- Changing passwords
- Temporarily revoking access
- Removing user accounts
- Adding and removing groups
- Running commands or programs as other users
- Administrative access via `sudo` and `visudo`
- Understanding file and directory permissions
- Modifying permissions

Creating new users

As with most things in Linux, there is more than one way to create user accounts in Linux Mint. Mint features a GUI tool to facilitate user management as well as shell commands that will help you get the job done. Although it's much easier to use the graphical tools, which are very simplistic, it's also important to learn how to manage users via shell commands, since your GUI may not always function and most Linux servers do not feature GUI applications. First, we'll explore how to create users with Mint's **Users and Groups** graphical tool, and then we'll explore how to create users via shell commands. The following screenshot shows the **Users and Groups** tool, with the addition of some extra user accounts:

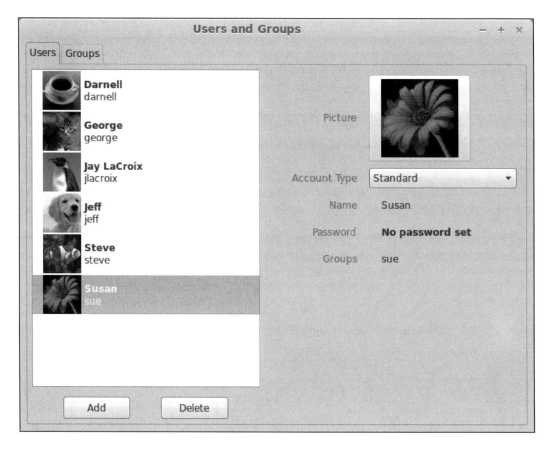

The **Users and Groups** tool is available in the **Applications** menu listed under the **Administration** section. Once you launch it, you'll be able to create a new user account right away. To do so, simply click on **Add** and then a new window will appear, giving you a chance to fill out the necessary information to create the user account.

The **Users and Groups** tool is available in the Cinnamon edition but may not be available in all Mint editions. For example, this tool is not featured in the Xfce edition. In regards to this edition, no GUI tool is included to manage users, so shell commands are the only way to go.

When creating the account, you'll fill in fields such as **Account Type**, **Full Name**, and **Username**. The **Username** is what the user will actually type while logging in, while the **Full Name** is shown as the user's name anywhere a name may be displayed, instead of a username. The following screenshot shows how to create a new user account in the **Users and Groups** tool:

While creating a new user, the **Account Type** field is important. If a user is created with the **Administrator** option, then that user will be able to execute administrative commands on the system.

Only give administrator access to those whom you trust. User accounts with administrative permissions are able to do more than just install software; they can remove packages, as well as delete files, regardless of the ownership. Specifically, this gives the user a sudo access, which is something we'll cover later in this chapter.

Once you create a user account, note that no password is initially set. In order to assign a password to the account, click on the text next to **Password** (which initially reads **No password set**) and you'll be prompted to create the password for the user. The following screenshot shows the dialog box in **Users and Groups**. This dialog appears when changing a user's password.

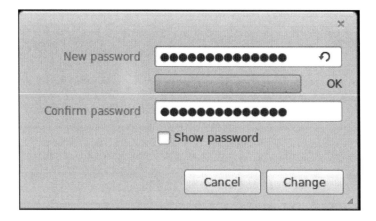

In addition to setting the password, another concept of interest is **Group**s. Directly below the **Password** dropdown, there is a dropdown to add a user to one or more groups. If you click on it, a list of all the groups on the system will appear. You can add a user to any of the listed groups by checking the box next to it. If you set the user as **Administrator**, then the **sudo** group will already be selected for you. You can also create a new group. This will be discussed later in this chapter. The following screenshot shows how to choose groups in the **Users and Groups** tool:

So, what are groups? If you're unfamiliar with the concept of groups, the idea is that you can simplify permissions greatly by adding users to a common group that has the permission to perform a particular task or access particular files. While we'll discuss permissions in greater detail toward the end of this chapter, the basic summary is that files and folders can only be accessed by users who have permission to do so. If you want to give a user access to a directory or individual file, you can either modify the permissions of the file itself or add the user account to a group that has authority over it. The latter is much easier, as you can change who can access various resources by changing just one group membership rather than modifying the access on a file-by-file basis. To use the administrator access as an example, everyone who is a member of the **sudo** group has access to perform administrative tasks. If you no longer wish for a user to have administrative control, simply remove them from the group. Groups are very common in corporate IT environments, which rely on this concept quite heavily. This allows for things such as restricting access to a folder to only those groups whose job duties require it.

This is basically all there is in regard to user administration via Mint's **Users and Groups** tool. The tool is very simplistic; it does not contain any advanced options. For example, if you would like to temporarily disable a user's access to your machine, you won't be able to do so via this tool. There's no option included to suit this purpose, other than possibly changing a user's password to something they don't know. For advanced user management, you'll need to utilize shell commands to do the job. As mentioned earlier, you may not always have access to a GUI, so shell commands are definitely useful.

In order to create a user in Mint via the terminal, the command you'll use is the `adduser` command. In order to add a user, all you have to do is type `sudo adduser` followed by the username, as shown in the following statement:

```
sudo adduser jdoe
```

After you execute the `adduser` command, you'll be walked through the setting of the default parameters for the user, such as their name as well as the password. However, you don't have to answer every question. For example, you can skip adding the person's first and last names as well as their phone number. To skip a field, simply press *Enter* without typing anything. However, the `adduser` command will not let you bypass without creating a password for the user; it will ask you over and over until you provide it. During the process, you may notice that the `adduser` command doesn't prompt for the groups you would like the user to be a member of. For this, we'll use a different command, which we'll get to later.

For now, the takeaway is that the `adduser` command allows us to create a new user, and when you have finished entering in the values for the prompts, your new user account is ready to go. In the next section, we'll discuss passwords.

Changing passwords

With the **Users and Groups** tool, changing passwords is easy. In the preceding section, we discussed how to set a password for a user while creating a new account. To change the password for a user, simply go through the process again by clicking on the text next to **Password**, and then you type in the new password; that's it!

On the shell, the `passwd` command allows a user to change their own password. In fact, a user can even change their own password via the GUI by accessing **System Settings** and then **Account Details**, so using a terminal command such as `passwd` isn't required. However, the `passwd` command can also allow administrators to change the passwords of other users as well.

Although we'll discuss `sudo` in more detail later in this chapter, the `sudo` command allows you to run a command as an administrator, provided you are a member of the **sudo** group. If you execute the `sudo passwd` command, followed by a username, you can change the password for any user you like (even if you don't know their password). This is very useful for IT administrators to assist those who may have forgotten their password.

Be careful when entering the `passwd` command with `sudo` but with no username specified. Doing so will enable the root user account, which may or may not be something you want to do. If you've done so and want to disable the root user account once again, execute the following command:

```
sudo passwd -l root
```

In addition, you may wish to make passwords expire after a period of time, requiring the user to change it after that time. For this, the `chage` command is used. With the `chage` command, you can set a minimum and a maximum age for user passwords. The minimum age is how long until the password can be changed again, and the maximum age is how long until changing the password becomes mandatory. You may be wondering, "Why set a minimum age for a password?" One purpose is due to user behavior. Many users will get accustomed to a particular password. If such a user finds a loophole, they can choose to retain the same password forever; they can and will use it. These types of users may change their password to satisfy the change requirement and then change their password right back to what it was earlier. A minimum password age won't allow the user to change his or her password right away, thereby forcing them to use a new password for a while. Such a policy won't completely stop users from reusing passwords, but it makes it less convenient to do so.

In order to set a maximum password age for a user, execute the `chage` command similar to the following example:

```
sudo chage -M 90 username
```

In this example, the `-M` portion of the preceding command refers to the maximum number of days the password can exist. In the example, 90 days was specified. Therefore, the user will need to change their password in 90 days.

In order to give the user a minimum password age, a command similar to the following example can be used:

```
sudo chage -m 5 username
```

Notice that the -M portion of the command discussed earlier changed to a lowercase -m instead. The -m flag specifies the minimum password age. In the preceding example, we set a minimum password age of 5 days. This means that once the user changes his or her password, they'll be unable to change their password again for the next 5 days.

Keep in mind that a clever user with administrative rights can easily bypass a minimum password age requirement by simply entering the `sudo passwd username` command line and adding their name as the `username` value.

If you would like to see what a user's current password attributes are, execute the following command without making any changes:

```
sudo chage joeuser -l
```

After executing the `chage -l` command, you'll see all the current values for when a user's account will expire as well as the minimum password age. In corporate environments, a large majority of users being unable to access their systems is often caused by users ignoring the repeated prompts on their system that informed them that their password was going to expire, and they likely won't mention this when they ask you for assistance. The `chage` command should reveal the root of the issue right away.

Revoking access temporarily

There may come a time where you would like to temporarily revoke a user's account instead of outright deleting it. Examples of this may be a person who is going on leave, or perhaps you may have a user to whom you no longer wish to grant access, though you still need their files left intact. In Linux Mint, the easiest way to temporarily revoke access to the system is using the **Users and Groups** tool to change a user's password to one that they don't know. Then, they won't be able to log in until you give them the new password.

Of course, this is not the only way you can temporarily revoke access; you can also do so with the terminal. Also, there are several other ways to do so. One of the easier methods is similar to the preceding example: using the `passwd` command to change their password. Another way is to execute the following command to lock an account:

```
sudo passwd -l username
```

In the preceding example, the -l flag will lock an account. If you would like to unlock an account, use the -u flag instead as shown in the following command line:

```
sudo passwd -u username
```

If we are using Linux Mint at home, there may not be many situations where you would need to lock or unlock a user account, but when using Mint in a company, knowing how to quickly modify account access is critical.

Removing user accounts

Of course, removing a user account in Linux Mint is just as easy as creating one. In the **Users and Groups** tool, simply click on the **Delete** button, as shown in the following screenshot:

However, note that doing so will also remove all the files of that user as well as their settings. Using shell commands, you can actually decide to keep the user's files even after removing their account. The `deluser` command will allow you to remove a user account via the Linux shell. For example, to delete user `jdoe`, use the following command line:

```
sudo deluser jdoe
```

Although the preceding command would delete the `jdoe` user, note that it does not delete the user's home directory. If you execute the following command after deleting the user, you will notice that the home directory for `jdoe` will still be listed:

```
ls /home
```

This is a great thing when used in a corporate environment, since you may be tasked with removing a user account but may have retention policies in place that mandate how long you must keep the files around. If you would like to remove the home directory for the user later, you should execute the following command line:

```
sudo rm -r /home/jdoe
```

Although it may go without saying, be very cautious with the `rm -r` command, especially when deleting files in the `/home` folder or in the root of your filesystem. For example, if you were to execute `sudo rm -r /home` without specifying a user folder, you would make every user on the system or server extremely unhappy with you. Similarly, if you execute `sudo rm -r /`, there's a possibility that your system would need to be redone.

Running commands or programs as other users

There may come a time where you need to impersonate another user on your system. In some of our examples so far, we've used the `sudo` command, which essentially runs commands as the root user. On a Linux system, the root account is the account that has access to basically everything. If Linux was a game of chess, think of the root account as the queen—it can go wherever it wants and delete whatever it wants.

In Linux Mint (as well as most Ubuntu derivatives), the root account is disabled by default. Although the root account is disabled, you can still run commands as the root. Technically, the `sudo` command impersonates the root and works even if the root account is disabled. You can enable the root account with the `sudo passwd` command and disable it once again with the `sudo passwd -l root` command.

While we'll go over the technical details of the `sudo` command in the next section, it's important to understand how to run commands as a different user. While the `sudo` command allows you to run commands as if you were the root account, you can actually run commands as any user you want provided you have either root access or the user's password. The `su - username -c "command"` command will allow you to run a command as a different user. For example, to execute `mycommand` as the user `jeff`, you would enter the following command line:

```
su - jeff -c "mycommand"
```

The `su` command stands for **switch user**, and the `-c` flag followed by a command in quotes executes this command as if it were executed by the user you specified. You will then be prompted for that user's password, and only then is the command executed. You can even switch to another user outright by executing the following command line:

```
sudo su - jeff
```

Why might it be necessary to run commands as other users? If you're using Mint on your own personal computer, there's probably not much purpose to do so beyond the `sudo` command. However, in a corporate environment, you may have user accounts that run individual services automatically, and you may need to use such usernames in scripts to run automated tasks. Additionally, you can also assist a family member or friend to perform a task, all without logging out of your own account.

Administrative access via sudo and visudo

The `sudo` command has been mentioned several times throughout this book, so you may already understand its basics and what it does. As mentioned earlier, the basic purpose of the `sudo` command is to run tasks as the root user account. This is much safer than simply logging in to the computer as root, as `sudo` asks you for the root password, which is your reminder that the task you're about to perform is technically reserved for root. While logged into the system as root itself, there are no password prompts, even if you are about to accidentally do something catastrophic to the system. We may be technical people, but even the smartest person is prone to making a mistake from time to time. This is why `sudo` is generally preferred over logging in to the root account itself. As mentioned earlier, many distributions, such as Ubuntu (as well as Mint), leave the root account disabled by default. It's generally safer this way.

Although we've gone through the basic functionality of sudo, we have yet to take a look at how it actually works. The sudo command stands for **super user do** and executes whatever command you type in after sudo as if root was the account performing the task. However, not everyone can use sudo. In Mint, a user can be given rights to use sudo by setting the user as an **Administrator** using the **Users and Groups** tool. However, this is not the only way.

The sudo package in Mint works the same way as in other distributions. The file that controls access to use sudo is /etc/sudoers. There are various declarations of users and groups that are allowed to use sudo inside this file. However, unlike most configuration files in Linux, it's not a good idea to edit this file directly as doing so may cause corruption. Any system that has sudo installed has the visudo command available as well. The "vi" portion of the visudo command refers to the **vi text editor**, which comes standard in many distributions. However, don't let the name fool you; you can use other text editors to edit the sudoers file. However, for good measure, you must edit it through the visudo command.

If you enter the sudo visudo command, your default text editor will open, displaying the contents of the /etc/sudoers file. In the case of Mint, the default text editor in the terminal is nano, so the /etc/sudoers file will open in the nano text editor when you run this command. If for some reason it opens in a different text editor, you can explicitly indicate which text editor you would like to use by using the following command:

```
sudo EDITOR=nano visudo
```

For the preceding example, a little explanation is in order. The first part is easy; we're using sudo, which means that we would like to run the rest of the command as root. The word EDITOR in uppercase is a variable declaration, which we've not talked about much yet. In a nutshell, we're setting the EDITOR variable to equal nano. (We'll discuss Bash shell variables in further detail in *Chapter 11, Advanced Administration Techniques*.) In this case, we're explicitly indicating that we would like to utilize the nano text editor. Then, we execute the visudo command, which tells the system that we would like to edit the /etc/sudoers file. As we declared our editor as *nano*, the system will open the file in nano. That's quite a bit of instruction for just one small line in our Linux shell.

The discussion regarding sudo in this section is not specific to Mint. In most Linux distributions, the same concepts apply. The main difference is that some distributions may not ship sudo by default. However, if they don't, all you should need to do is install it via that distributions package manager. For example, both Mint and Ubuntu ship sudo by default, but some versions of Debian don't and neither does Arch Linux.

So, now that you have the file open and in your terminal, what do you do with it? Feel free to use your arrow keys to scroll through and peruse the file. There will be a few lines of interest, such as the following one:

```
root    ALL=(ALL:ALL) ALL
```

With the preceding line, you can see that the root account has access to sudo in its entirety. If you wanted to, you could add the following line just below it (or anywhere in the file, really) to give complete access to sudo on any other user account:

```
jdoe    ALL=(ALL:ALL) ALL
```

However, before you do that, go down a few more lines, where you'll likely see the following line:

```
%sudo   ALL=(ALL:ALL) ALL
```

Here, we see the declaration that any member of the sudo group has the same access as root does. Therefore, if you want to give a user access to sudo, all you have to do is add that user to the sudo group, and you won't need to touch this file at all. However, there's certainly more to visudo than this. If you would like, you can limit a user to a specific command. Also, you can suppress the password prompt for a command if you like.

For example, let's give our user jdoe the access to update the system and install applications. This can be done using the following command line:

```
jdoe ALL=/usr/local/bin/apt
```

In the previous example, we're allowing the user jdoe to specifically use the apt command (which is used to install packages). If we wanted to, we could also remove the password requirement for apt using the following command line:

```
jdoe ALL= NOPASSWD: /usr/local/bin/apt
```

Now, the user jdoe has access to the apt command, and it won't even prompt him or her for the password. Of course, you should only do this if you believe that the user will not only install and remove packages wisely, but they will also not allow someone else to sneak up to their desk and cause havoc while they are away.

You may be wondering what each field in the sudoers line represents. For example, consider the following command line:

```
jdoe    ALL=(ALL:ALL) ALL
```

The first item is self-explanatory; it is the username that you're editing permissions for. The first ALL represents the host name, tying the command to a specific machine. The second ALL and the third ALL correspond to which user and group, respectively, you're able to run the command from (in this case, all users). The fourth ALL clarifies which commands the user can run as sudo (in this case, all commands).

> Be very careful when modifying user access via visudo. If you're not careful, you may open up your entire machine to those whom you'd rather not grant complete access. If you were an administrator in a company, you would probably want to give users access to specific commands that are required to do their job, and nothing more.

Another trick with sudo allows you to temporarily switch to the root account for an entire session. In all examples so far, we've used the sudo command in front of every command that needed root privileges. However, what if we want to run a bunch of commands as root and don't want to use sudo every time? To do this, we use the following command:

```
sudo -s
```

The sudo -s command will prompt you for your password as usual, but after it does so, it will actually switch your logged-in user to that of root. Therefore, each command you perform will be performed as root until you type exit at the end of the sudo session. Of course, be very careful when utilizing this mode.

Understanding file and directory permissions

The last section of this chapter deals with a very important concept that we haven't touched on so far. Permissions in Linux are handled very differently than those on the Windows platform, but Mac users may already understand these concepts as they are very similar.

While using the Linux shell, you may have noticed funny characters next to file names. For example, when entering ls -l into the shell while in a directory that contains files, you may see the following output:

```
drwxr-xr-x    2 jdoe      users    4096 Dec 24 14:10 Documents
drwxr-xr-x    4 bsmith    users    4096 Dec 31 13:54 Movies
drwxr-xr-x   11 root      root     4096 Dec 24 14:11 Private
```

Before diving into permissions, let's explore the output of the `ls -l` command so that you understand each section. The first section contains the permission string for each file or folder. We'll get into this shortly. Next to the permission string, you'll see a number. This number contains the **link count** for the file or folder. The link count refers to something different depending on whether it is a directory or a file. If it's a directory, the link count refers to how many directory objects are inside it. With the first line, we see that there is a link count of 2. However, in reality, there are no directories stored in this folder despite the link count of 2. Actually, the link count for a folder starts at 2, and if we had another directory nested inside the `Documents` folder, the link count would become 3. This is because there are two hidden directories inside each directory. The first is just a single period ".", and the second is an object named with two periods "..". The single period refers to the directory itself, and the object containing two periods is an object used to represent the parent folder. So, in short, to determine how many actual objects are inside the folder, just subtract 2. So, in our example, the `Documents` folder has no directories in it, the `Movies` folder has two, and the `Private` folder has nine.

The third column lists the user that owns that particular file or directory. In our example, we see that `Documents` is owned by the user `jdoe`, the `Movies` folder is owned by `bsmith`, and the `Private` directory is owned by `root`. The fourth column is the group that owns the file. In our example, the first two directories are owned by the `users` group, and the `Private` folder is owned by the `root` group. The fifth column is the size of the object in bytes. The last sections should be self-explanatory; we see the date and time stamp of the object and then the name of the object.

So, now that we know how to read the output of `ls -l`, we can finally divulge the details of Linux permissions. There are 10 characters in each permission string. For example, the first permission string is `drwxr-xr-x`. What each character means is described as follows:

- `d`: If there is a `d` for the first bit, that means the object is a directory. If the object is a file, the first bit will be a single dash "-".
- `r`: The character `r` stands for **read**.
- `w`: The character `w` stands for **write**.
- `x`: The character `x` stands for **execute**.
- `-`: A single dash means that there is no permission for that bit.

However, in the example permission strings provided, you'll see several of the bits listed several times. Why is that? The reason is because the permissions are broken down into user, group, and other. Each of these gets three permission bits. The very first permission bit is reserved to clarify whether the object is a file or a directory. The permission string drwxr-xr-x breaks down as follows:

Directory or file?	User	Group	Other
d	rwx	r-x	r-x

With the permission string broken down into a table, we see that the user (the user account that owns the object) has all three bits: read, write, and execute. This means that the user that owns the object has full jurisdiction over it. The user can read the file to see what it contains, write changes to it, and even execute it as if it were a program. The Group section of the permission string is missing the w bit in the middle. This means that this group can read and execute the object but cannot change it as w is missing. The same is for Other, which means "everyone else." So, based on this, we can see that everyone (regardless of who they are) can read the object, but only the user who owns it can change it. A more restrictive permission string would be -rwx------. It basically means that the object is a file (the d at the beginning is missing), and the file can only be read, written, and executed by the owner. No other user can even touch it.

It's important to note that the root account bypasses file permissions. If a user created a file with permissions of -rwx------, which in effect means that only the owner can view and modify the file, the root account would effectively have the full rw permissions regardless.

In *Chapter 4, An Introduction to the Terminal*, we briefly used the chmod command and gave executable permissions to a file. This is exactly what the x bit does. If a file has the execute bit set, that means that the file can be executed as a program. If you're writing a script, such as a **Bash script**, this bit needs to be set, or else you'll get the **permission denied** message when trying to run the script. In the next section, we'll cover the chmod command a bit further.

Now that you're building an understanding of the basics, it's time for another curve ball. The permission bits (read, write, and execute) have a different definition depending on whether the bits are referring to a file or a directory. Refer to the following table for a more detailed definition of each bit:

	Read	Write	Execute
File	The file can be read, which means the contents can be displayed.	The file can be modified.	The file can be executed as if it were a program (such as a script)
Directory	The contents of the directory can be listed (the `ls` command).	New files can be added within the directory.	Allows you to change directory (cd) into the directory.

In the preceding table, we can see that the permission string has a slightly different description if the object is a directory than if it is a file. For example, the x bit with a file refers to whether or not it can be executed as a program, while the x bit for a directory determines whether or not you can enter into the directory. This effectively means that it is possible to set a folder to allow all users to enter into the directory but only allow some users to execute the `ls` command to see what's inside it. With a folder, the w bit allows that category to add new files to the directory. This may be confusing at first, but practice reading the permission strings on files and directories on your system, and it will soon make sense.

Another important concept to go over in this section in order to make sure you completely understand permissions in Linux is the numerical permission system. Each permission bit is worth a specific value. The read bit (r) is worth 4. The write bit (w) is worth 2. Finally, the execute bit (x) is worth 1. In each section (User, Group, Other), the permission bits are added up to form a total. For example, let's take a look at the `drwxr-xr-x` permission string.

To determine the numerical value of the permissions, again break up the permission string into three groups. Here, we take off the first bit. We see that it's a directory, so let's omit the d bit for the rest of the discussion. The three permission bits for the user are r, w, and x, and Group and Other both have r-x for their permission bits. Now, let's add the totals of each bit for the user section. As r is worth 4, w is worth 2, and x is worth 1 (and the user has all three), the user section has a numerical value of 7. For Group and Other, the r as well as the x bits are set, so we have a value of 5 for both of these sections. This means that the final permission string translates to 755 with the numerical system. This point is further illustrated in the following table:

Permission string	Numerical value
-rwxrwx---	770
-rw-------	600
-rwxrwxrwx	777
-rw-r--r--	644

Before moving on to the next section, it's a good idea to practice to make sure you understand how to read permissions. There's never any harm in using the `ls` command. Feel free to browse your filesystem and execute the `ls -l` command from within various folders on your system to see how the permissions are set up. Be sure that you can differentiate directories from files and the permissions for each category (`User`, `Group`, `Other`), as well as practice the numerical system.

One final note for this section: using the shell is not the only way to view permissions in Mint. You can view permissions with the **Nemo** file manager as well, and you can do so by right-clicking on a directory or file and then selecting **Properties**. The following screenshot shows the properties window in **Nemo** showing the **Permissions** tab:

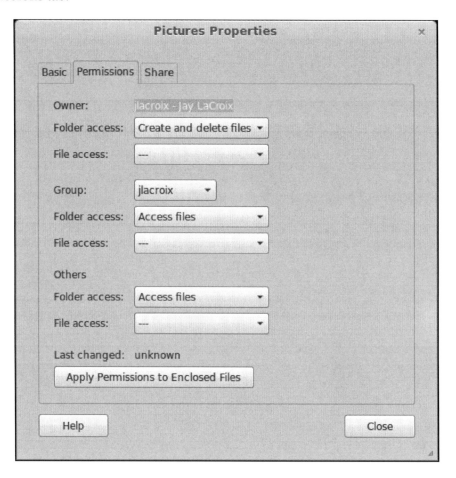

Modifying file and directory permissions

Now that you have a thorough understanding of how to understand the permission system in Linux, we can work on actually changing the permissions of objects. To do so, we have two commands: **chmod** and **chown**. The chmod command is the one we'll use to modify the permission string of an object. The chown command is what we'll use to change the owner or group of an object.

In order to understand these concepts better, create some spare files and directories anywhere on your system so that you aren't modifying any critical component. You can set up a little lab in your home directory, for example, and create several files to modify their permissions. To start with, we'll walk through the basic usage of the chmod command.

For instance, let's assume that we have the following output of the ls -l command in our current working directory:

```
drwxr-xr-x    4 Sally    users   4096 Dec 31 13:54 Budget
drwx------   11 Tom      users   4096 Dec 24 14:11 Music
```

In the preceding example, we see that Sally is allowing *everyone* to see her Budget files. This may not be what she wants. If Sally wants to make her Budget files private (and she should), the following command would do the trick:

```
chmod 700 -R Budget
```

So what exactly did that command do? The chmod command changes permissions, and in this case, Sally is applying the numerical permission of 700 to the Budget folder. Since the r bit is worth 4, the w bit is worth 2, and the x bit is worth 1, the first digit of 7 means full control. The first digit in the numerical value of 700 refers to the user, so Sally is giving herself full access to the folder. As the second and third digits are 0, both the group and other categories are denied any access. If Sally were to list the contents of the working directory, the permission string for the Budget directory would now be changed to the following command:

```
-rwx------
```

Sally also added the -R flag to the command. The -R flag clarifies that Sally not only wants to change the permissions of the Budget folder, but everything inside it as well. If Sally were to omit the -R flag, it would have changed the permissions for the Budget folder itself but not the contents. In this example, Sally could have omitted the -R flag, as neither Group nor Other are given execute permissions (which means that they can't enter the directory anyway). Adding the -R flag makes the permissions of the contents of the Budget folder match those of the parent, so now only Sally and root can access this folder.

Numerically, however, this is not the only way to use the chmod command. Let's take Tom's Music folder as an example. In the previous sample output, the permission string for Tom's Music folder is drwx------. As you can see, only Tom can access it. However, what if Tom wanted to share his music collection with other users on the system? Tom could use the chmod command with a numerical value of 755 (which would give Group and Other access to read and enter into the Music folder, though not change it), or he could use the chmod command with a numerical value of 777 to give everyone complete access. You can actually explicitly state which category of permissions you would like to change by clarifying the bits. For example, consider the following chmod command:

```
chmod g+rx -R Music
```

In the preceding example, g represents group, and the +rx portion of the command means we're adding the read and execute bits. Now, all members of the users group can view the contents of this Music folder. If we changed our mind and wanted to reverse the changes, use the following command line:

```
chmod g-rx -R Music
```

The directory's permission string returns to the way it was. The chmod command can be used with the numerical system or by calling out the bits themselves. You can modify permissions clarifying u for User, g for Group, and o for Other. Then, you can add (+) or remove (-) permission bits: r for Read, w for Write, and x for Execute. As mentioned earlier, the -R flag applies the changes to the contents of a directory as well. If it were a file whose permission you were modifying, you would omit the -R flag.

Permissions in Linux are an important concept to master. Feel free to practice with files on your own system until you learn the concepts. It may be tricky at first, but with a little bit of practice, the concepts will become clear.

Summary

In this chapter, we started off with a walkthrough of creating new users. We explored how to do so using Mint's handy **Users and Groups** tool as well as via the shell. Then, we explored removing a user permanently as well as blocking access on a temporary basis. Next, we went over groups in Linux and how to add and remove them. Our journey then explored how to run commands as other users, and then we had a more in-depth look at the sudo command and how to configure it. This chapter then ended with a detailed look at how permissions in Linux are handled.

In the next chapter, we will explore networking in Mint, including connecting to wired and wireless networks, setting up a static IP, accessing your system via SSH, as well as sharing files.

9
Connecting to Networks

A computer isn't much of a computer if it can't communicate with resources over networks. For the most part, networking in Mint is quite simple, especially if all you want to do is plug in an Ethernet cable and let the automatic configuration do the work for you. However, there are some important aspects specific to Mint and the way that it handles networking that are worth knowing. In addition, features such as SSH paired with the power of the Linux shell add even more power to administration. In this chapter, we'll not only explore how networking is handled in Mint, but we'll also go over some neat tricks that will allow you to control your computer from any other computer.

In this chapter, we will discuss the following topics:

- Connecting to a wired network
- Setting up a static IP
- Connecting to a wireless network
- An introduction to SSH
- Accessing your system via SSH
- Accessing FTP servers
- Sharing files with Samba
- Sharing files with NFS

Connecting to a wired network

With most computers, Mint handles networking pretty much flawlessly. When an Ethernet cable is inserted, it will most likely automatically configure itself using **DHCP (Dynamic Host Configuration Protocol)**, and then you'll immediately see other computers on your network, and you can also access the Internet. However, perhaps, you'd like to set your own address or have a bit more control than just letting Mint do the work for you. In some cases, you may run into an issue where your machine includes a **network interface card (NIC)** that's not immediately recognized, causing you to need to do some configuration before your machine is up and running.

In general, drivers for NICs are built into the Linux kernel. This is both a good thing and a bad thing. The good thing is that quite a few NIC drivers are included by default; there is no need for you to configure anything. However, in other cases, your NIC may not be included. This happens most often when you use a computer that is newer than the date on which your kernel was released. For example, if you have a computer with a Broadwell chipset, but you're using a version of Mint that was published before Broadwell was released, there are chances that your integrated network card will not be supported. We'll talk a bit more about troubleshooting later in this chapter.

As a rule of thumb, you should always download a Linux distribution that was released around the same time or a distribution that is new compared to the manufacturing date of your PC or NIC. For example, if you download a Linux distribution that features the 3.2 kernel (which was released in January, 2012) you're likely to run into problems with hardware support if you use a computer manufactured in 2013 or 2014. In most cases, this may mean issues with your NIC, wireless card, or video card. With this in mind, using a release of Mint closer to or newer than the manufacturing date of your computer is the best approach.

With a recent release of your distribution, in our case, Linux Mint, it's a very rare occurrence that your networking hardware is not recognized. When you plug in an Ethernet cable, you should see the following icon on the panel near the clock that looks like two cables connected together:

If all goes well, the automatic configuration will suffice. Once the Ethernet cable is connected, DHCP will assign the computer an IP address, and away it goes. If you would like to set more advanced settings, such as a static address, you'll need to open your network connections settings to edit them. To do so, click on the icon mentioned earlier on your panel and then click on **Network Settings** to see a list of the connections stored for your system. The following screenshot shows the settings dialog for network connections stored on the system:

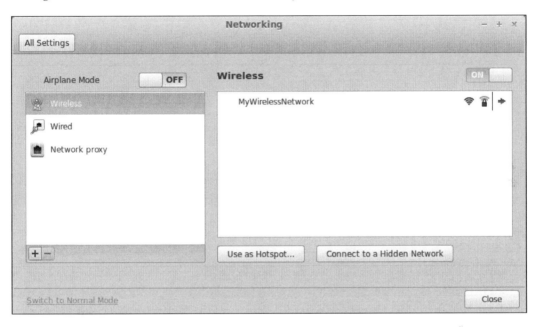

By default, when you first open the tool, you'll most likely see a list of wireless networks or a wired network if your system doesn't contain a wireless card. To edit your wired connection, first click on **Wired** on the left pane, then click on the **Options...** button in the bottom-right corner of the window. A new window will appear that will allow you to fine-tune your wired connection. For example, if you click on the **IPv4 Settings** tab, you'll be able to set a static IP address by selecting **Manual** from the dropdown instead of the default **Automatic (DHCP)** option.

With DHCP, configuration is much easier, as your computer will contact your local DHCP server (which, in most cases, would be a home office router), request an address, and then configure itself. The problem with DHCP addressing is that an IP address can and will expire, and these are subject to change. If you would like to predictably contact your computer on the network via a specific and dedicated IP address, setting a static address is the key.

 A complete set of instructions on networking is beyond the scope of this book. However, a brief look at configuring a static address follows in the next section.

Setting up a static IP

If you prefer your system to be reachable on your network via the same IP address each time, a static IP lease or static IP assignment is recommended. The two terms may sound the same, but the difference comes with who assigns the address. For example, a static lease, also known as a DHCP reservation, is where you configure your router to assign the same IP address to your machine each time. This is by far the easiest way to go, but unfortunately, most small office and home office routers do not feature an option to do this. If your router doesn't have an option to set a static lease (reservation), read on to discover how to change Mint's connection from DHCP to static and set the address manually.

First, you'll need to access your network settings. To do this, click on the network icon located near the clock in your system tray and then click on **Network Settings**. From there, a new window titled **Networking** will appear. On this screen, you'll be able to edit the advanced options for your wired and wireless connections, such as the IP address in this example. To edit an IP address of a wired interface, click on the **Wired** section on the left-hand side pane and then on the **Options...** button in the lower-right corner of the screen. This will bring up yet another window, **Editing Wired connection 1**. If you click on the **IPv4 Settings** tab, as shown in the following screenshot, you'll be able to edit your IP address:

If you're a beginner, you may not want to edit the automatically created connection. Instead, create a new one. This way, if you make a mistake, you can delete the connection you created and go back to the original connection that is known to be working.

Now that you're here, what settings should you provide to create your static connection? While there is no basic rule of thumb, as every network is different, there are a few key rules to keep in mind. As you probably already know, assigning the same IP address to two devices would cause conflict. Therefore, you should ensure that the address you assign is not in use. Most routers start assigning IP addresses beginning with a specific number. For example, perhaps your router exists at 192.168.1.1, and the first IP address it assigns is 192.168.1.100. Considering this IP address, as long as you haven't manually configured any other devices, you should be safe to use anything in between 192.168.1.2 and 192.168.1.99. For the other values, the **DNS servers** and **Gateway** is most likely your router, so you can use your router's IP address for both. **Search domains** is most likely the name of your network; you may or may not have set this.

If you are not sure of what your values are, rather than just assuming that your router is both your gateway and DNS server, the `nm-tool` command will tell you what the IP address is for your DNS server as well as your Gateway address. If you're unsure of which IP addresses are in use within your network, consider logging in to your router's configuration page. Most home and small office routers feature a configuration page that will allow you to see a list of all the connected devices. The following screenshot shows the output of the `nm-tool` command:

```
                              Terminal                          -  +  x
- Device: eth0  [Wired connection 1] -----------------------------------
  Type:                Wired
  Driver:              e1000e
  State:               connected
  Default:             yes
  HW Address:          3C:97:0E:A6:27:8B

  Capabilities:
    Carrier Detect:    yes
    Speed:             1000 Mb/s

  Wired Properties
    Carrier:           on

  IPv4 Settings:
    Address:           172.16.254.235
    Prefix:            24 (255.255.255.0)
    Gateway:           172.16.254.1

    DNS:               172.16.254.1

jlacroix@Athena ~ $
```

Once you have all the variables you need, you're ready to set a static IP address. On the **Editing Wired connection** window, which appeared earlier, choose **Manual** from the **Method** dropdown. Underneath **Addresses**, click on **Add** to add an **IP address**, **Netmask**, and **Gateway** address. After you click on **Save**, the connection will be changed to the values you provided. If you need to switch back to DHCP in the future, navigate back to **Network Settings** and change the dropdown accordingly.

Connecting to a wireless network

Like wired networking, the ability to utilize a wireless card in Mint depends on whether drivers are included in the version of the kernel that ships with your release. Wireless support is fairly good in Linux, but a few vendors are more problematic than the others. Thankfully, Linux Mint has gone to great lengths to support as many wireless cards as possible. There's a good chance that yours will be supported as well.

The icon mentioned earlier for wired connections (located near your clock in the system tray) is also used for wireless connections. If you click on this icon, you should see your local wireless connection listed in the pop-up menu that appears. The following screenshot shows the network connection menu available from the panel, showing an available wireless connection:

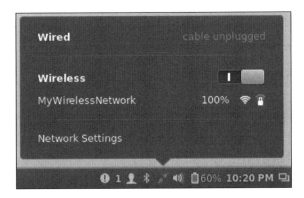

To connect to a network, simply click on it. If a password is required, it will prompt you to enter it. Once you enter the correct password, you should see a message that says you're connected. From this point on, you'll automatically connect to that network whenever you're in range of it.

 You can set up a static IP address for a wireless network as well, should you need to do so. The way to do it is exactly as mentioned in the previous section, though you'll edit your connection underneath the **Wireless** menu, instead of the connection under the **Wired** menu.

If, for some reason, you don't see your wireless network available in the list, the first thing you should check is whether or not your wireless card is enabled. Especially with laptops, it's far too easy to accidentally nudge the hardware switch that enables/disables wireless communication (if you have such a switch). Some laptops have a keyboard key designated to control wireless access; it is very easy to press this key by mistake. Some laptops have the wireless toggle switch on one of their edges. This switch can often catch on the way in and out of a bag.

If you're sure your wireless card is turned on and you still don't see your network listed, your wireless card may not be supported by default. It's possible that Mint's **Driver Manager** may have a driver available for your card. If so, install it and you should be good to go after a reboot. If the Driver Manager doesn't have what you need, manual troubleshooting may be required.

In a nutshell, manually troubleshooting the inability to use your network card is done by first identifying the model of the card and then conducting a Google search for clues. This may seem like a silly approach, but it's surprisingly effective. If you have a problem with your hardware, it's unlikely that you would be the first person to encounter a problem. A typical Google search for Linux compatibility with specific hardware may include results from someone who has already solved the problem. To find your model number, execute the following command:

```
lscpci | grep Net
```

The output of this command will look similar to the following command:

```
00:19.0 Ethernet controller: Intel Corporation 82579LM Gigabit Network
Connection (rev 04)
```

```
03:00.0 Network controller: Intel Corporation Centrino Advanced-N 6205
[Taylor Peak] (rev 34)
```

In the preceding example output, you see two network cards: the first is the wired card, and the second is the wireless card. We know this because of the **Advanced-N** designation in the output. The model number of the wired card in this example machine is **Intel 82579LM** and that of the wireless card is **Intel 6205**. Therefore, we can conduct a Google search with key terms such as `Intel 6205 Linux support` or `82579LM Linux Support` to look for results that may point to clues. As mentioned earlier, if you're using a recently released version of Mint, you most likely won't experience issues.

An introduction to SSH

SSH is one of those technologies where once you get accustomed to using it, you'll wonder how you ever lived without it. The Linux shell is very powerful, and the power is magnified when you're able to access a system remotely. With remote access software, the user will typically see the mouse cursor move around the screen as you access the machine, causing them to stop working until you're finished with your connection. With SSH, you can actually connect to a system and not disturb the person sitting in front of it. To further illustrate the benefit of SSH, imagine that a family member or friend asks you to install FileZilla on their machine so that they can access an FTP site. You can get up, walk over to the machine, disturb the person, and install FileZilla, or you can obtain remote shell access and enter `sudo apt-get install filezilla` on their machine command in the background, without disturbing them. This is especially useful if you're not in the same physical location.

In an enterprise network, using SSH is a very important style of administration. For example, if you have servers in a data center that you're responsible for taking care of, you'll likely use SSH to connect to them rather than walking into the data center and connecting a keyboard and display. In fact, most corporations that utilize Linux on servers or even on desktops often enable SSH by default, so that the administrators can benefit from the ease of administration.

When accessing a machine via SSH, you first open up a terminal window and then type the following command:

```
ssh jdoe@192.168.0.1
```

As you can see, accessing a machine via SSH is simple. You execute the `ssh` command followed by the username you would like to use for the connection (the user account must exist on the target computer), and then you're prompted for the password. After entering the password, your terminal switches to the one attached to the target system. You can then enter commands such as installing programs as if you were there with the machine.

Before continuing with the next activity, you may want to verify whether or not your firewall allows SSH, which typically uses port 22. Some networks include a dedicated firewall, and small and home office routers also typically include a firewall. Either one of these may prevent you from connecting between machines. It's a good idea to ensure that SSH (port 22) is allowed in your environment before continuing.

Accessing your system via SSH

By default, the `ssh` command is available in Linux Mint without the need to install any extra packages. You can connect to other machines via SSH using your Linux Mint computer right away. However, only the package that enables you to connect to other machines is installed and not what's required to connect to your own machine from a different computer. If you would like to access your own computer via SSH, the `openssh-server` package must be installed. To do so, first run the following command:

```
sudo apt-get install openssh-server
```

You're still not done. Once the `openssh-server` package is installed, you must designate which user accounts are allowed to access your system remotely. To do this, we need to edit a configuration file, and this file is the `sshd_config` file that is located in the `/etc/ssh` directory.

However, before editing it, it's a good idea to make a backup copy should you make a mistake. To do so, execute the following command line:

```
sudo cp /etc/ssh/sshd_config /etc/ssh/sshd_config.bak
```

To edit the `sshd_config` file, run the following command:

```
sudo nano /etc/ssh/sshd_config
```

Once the file is open in the `nano` text editor, scroll to the very bottom and press *Enter* to create a new line beginning with `AllowUsers`, followed by the usernames to which you would like to provide access. (The `AllowUsers` clause is the one that allows access into your system.) If you would like to use the machine remotely as yourself, enter your own username. For example, if you wanted to give a user **jdoe** access to your machine via SSH, you would add the following line to the end of the file:

```
AllowUsers jdoe
```

If you would like to give more than one user access to the system, type their username(s) in the same line as shown in the following line of code:

```
AllowUsers jdoe bsmith bdole
```

 Another entry in the `sshd_config` file that you may want to consider looking at is the port that the SSH service listens on. This is typically located at the top of the `sshd_config` file. If port 22 isn't allowed in your environment, you may wish to change this.

Then, save the file by pressing *Ctrl + O*. You can then press *Enter* to confirm and then *Ctrl + X* to exit the editor. Now that you have edited the `sshd_config` file with the required changes, you must restart the SSH service in order for it to recognize the changes. To do so, enter the following command:

```
sudo service ssh restart
```

As long as there are no errors, your system is now ready for SSH access. If the restart command complains about something you entered into the `sshd_config` file, edit the file again to correct the problem, and then try restarting SSH again.

Now that SSH is enabled and you've set up SSH access on your system, try connecting to it from another machine on your network. If you only have one computer running Linux, you can download the **PuTTY** program to access your Linux computer from Windows. (Mac OS X computers should be able to access other computers via SSH by default.) To download PuTTY for Windows, navigate to the following URL via your browser:

```
http://www.chiark.greenend.org.uk/~sgtatham/putty/download.html
```

With a Linux computer, you can access another Linux computer via SSH using the ssh command as mentioned in the previous section. However, to summarize, assume that the command is in the following format:

```
ssh user@192.168.0.1
```

In the preceding line, just replace user with the required username and the IP address with the actual IP address of the system you would like to connect to.

> By default, SSH will use the username you're currently using for the connection. In the previous example, prefixing the command with user@ tells SSH to use a specific user account on the target system. If the username is the same on both machines, you can leave this part out. Also, if port 22 is blocked in your environment and you want to set it to listen on a different port, append the -p option along with the port number to the command.

Once you get connected via SSH, you are able to remotely administer the target system as if you were sitting in front of it.

Accessing FTP servers

If you need to access **FTP** servers, Mint has you covered. Included in Mint by default is the **Upload Manager** tool. You can use this tool to access FTP servers. The following screenshot shows Mint's **Upload Manager** application:

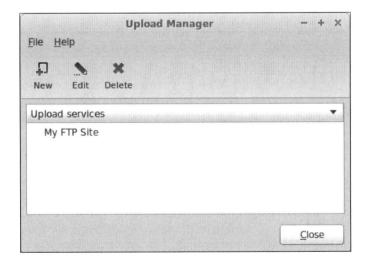

To use this tool, click on the **New** button, and a configuration dialog will appear. This dialog will allow you to enter the required values for the connection. Use the parameters that the FTP provider has given you for the connection and then click on **OK**. The following screenshot shows how to set up an FTP connection in the **Upload Manager**:

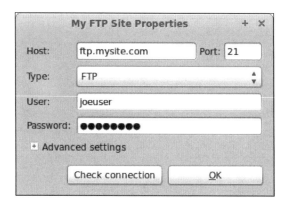

Once your FTP site is configured, a small window will appear to allow you to drag-and-drop files into it. These files will be uploaded. However, when a casual use of FTP is required, **FileZilla** is recommended instead, as it gives you more features and is the industry standard for FTP. With FileZilla, it's much easier to see what's already stored on the FTP server and modify the files stored there.

To install FileZilla, execute the following command:

```
sudo apt-get install filezilla
```

One of the major benefits of FileZilla, other than the many features and its easy-to-use interface, is that it is cross platform. If you have a mix of computers across various platforms, there's a good chance that FileZilla will be available on each, as there are versions available for Windows and OS X, in addition to Linux.

The following is a screenshot of FileZilla—a cross-platform FTP client:

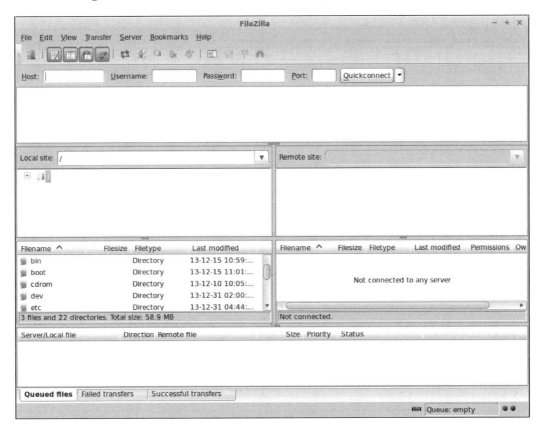

The easiest way to connect to an FTP site with FileZilla is to enter in the required values at the top of the program window (**Host**, **Username**, **Password**, and **Port**) and then click on **Quickconnect** to open up a connection. Additionally, if you expect that you will connect to a site on a regular basis, it may benefit you to add the site to FileZilla's **Site Manager**.

To do so, click on the icon at the very top-left corner of the FileZilla window. Doing this will open the **Site Manager**. There, you can enter the values required for your FTP site so that you can have faster access to it the next time you need to connect to it. The following screenshot shows FileZilla's **Site Manager**, with sample values filled in:

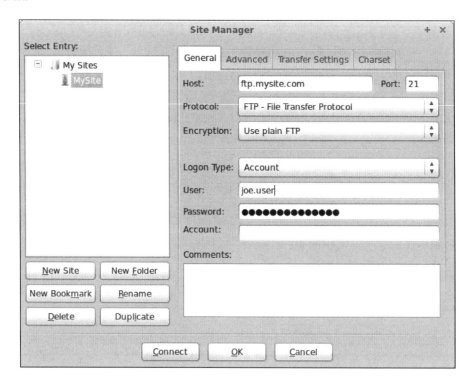

Once you're connected to a site in FileZilla, you're ready to transfer files as well as manage the existing files stored there. On the left-hand side of the FileZilla window, you can browse the filesystem on your local PC. The right-hand section shows the filesystem of your FTP site. You can easily drag files from your filesystem to the FTP server and also manage files, for example, delete and rename files. When finished, simply close FileZilla.

Sharing files with Samba

When sharing files with Linux over your network, there are primarily two main options to pick from. You can choose to share files via **Samba** or **NFS**, and both have their own strengths and weaknesses. The decision about which one you use primarily depends on which types of computers you would like to share files with.

With Samba, the network shares you create will be accessible by any Windows computer, as well as any Linux computer that has the Samba client installed. (Most distributions, including Mint, include this by default.) Being able to share files between both Linux and Windows computers may sound like a match made in heaven. However, Samba doesn't support Linux file and directory permissions without a lot of configuration and planning (which is beyond the scope of this book), to the point that it's generally not recommended for use if you have specific Linux permissions you would like to maintain, though it is technically possible.

NFS, on the other hand, is only supported by very specific versions of Windows and only if you install the NFS feature in the Windows control panel. Microsoft limits the services for NFS functionality to only the Ultimate and Enterprise versions of Windows 7 and the Professional and Enterprise editions of Windows 8. So, the choice basically comes down to whether or not you are going to be interfacing with Windows machines. If you are, use Samba; if not, use NFS.

 As mentioned earlier, firewalls may get in the way when trying to communicate between computers. In the case of Samba, Windows systems also include a software firewall that may block it by default. Before continuing, it may be a good idea to ensure that the system you're wishing to connect to, allows file sharing.

A complete walk-through of how to configure Samba is beyond the scope of this book, as there is a great deal of configuration options in its configuration file (/etc/samba/smb.conf), to the point that entire books have been written on the subject. However, there is a very easy way to get started, and that is with the system-config-samba command. By default, this command is not recognized in Mint. To use it, you'll need to install the associated package using the following command line:

```
sudo apt-get install system-config-samba
```

Once it is installed, you can access this handy package with the `sudo system-config-samba` command or look for the Samba application icon created in your programs menu after installation. The following screenshot shows the **Samba Server Configuration** window:

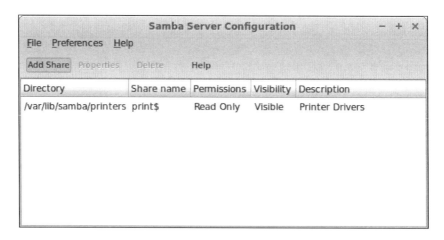

Essentially, the `system-config-samba` application will edit the `/etc/samba/smb.conf` file on your behalf. This is much easier for those who have never configured Samba before. For those who are of the inquisitive type, you can see the difference by looking at the `/etc/samba/smb.conf` file (run the `cat /etc/samba/smb.conf` command) before and after adding a share with `system-config-samba`.

To add a new share, click on the **Add Share** button at the top-left of corner the system-config-samba window. The **Create Samba Share** configuration dialog will appear as follows.

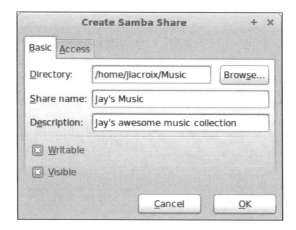

There are several fields to fill out in order to share a directory on your network. First, the **Directory** entry is where you select the path on your filesystem you would like to share. The **Share name** entry is where you can give the share a name, which is what others will see when browsing network shares on your machine. The **Description** entry is shown alongside the name when browsing shares, depending on the file manager that is being used to list your available shares. The two checkboxes at the bottom allow you to choose whether or not others can make changes to the files contained in that directory, and whether or not the share is visible to others.

> Including an option to essentially make a share hidden may seem contradictory to the idea of sharing files. However, situations may arise where you may want to make your files accessible to others, but you may not necessarily want to broadcast the share. To access such a hidden share, you would have to know the network path and type it in manually on the other machine.

Finally, on the **Access** tab, you can select whether to grant access to specific users or everyone. After adding the share, you should see it on other machines by browsing the list of available network places. If the share doesn't show up, you may need to restart the samba service by executing the following command:

```
sudo service samba restart
```

Sharing files with NFS

As mentioned earlier, NFS is another method of sharing files on a Linux machine. NFS is a very worthy choice, especially if all your computers are running on Linux. If you have a mixed environment, Samba would be the preferred choice. To get started, you'll need to install the `nfs-kernel-server` package. You can do this via the following command:

```
sudo apt-get install nfs-kernel-server
```

Once it is installed, you're ready to configure NFS. However, unlike Samba, we'll need to use shell commands in order to get NFS going. The configuration file responsible for NFS shares in Linux is the `/etc/exports` file, which we'll need to edit by opening it using the following command line:

```
sudo nano /etc/exports
```

To share a folder on your system, enter a line similar to the following one at the end of the file:

```
/home/jdoe/MyShare 192.168.1.0/255.255.255.0(rw,sync,no_subtree_check)
```

Now, we'll walk through that line so that you'll be able to deduce how to translate it to fit in with your own system. First, /home/jdoe/MyShare is the folder that we want to share on the network via NFS. Change this to the path of the folder you want to share on your own system. Next, we have an IP address of 192.168.1.0. Notice how the IP address ends in a zero; this is not typical. The zero signifies that we want to allow any computer on the 192.168.1.x network to access the share. You'll need to change this to the IP addressing that's being used on your network (use the ifconfig command if at all you are unsure). Next, we add rw to clarify that we want to allow others to read and write to the file. We would have used ro if we wanted a read-only access. Next, we add the sync option, which, in short, helps prevent file corruption, should the server go down before a file has finished being written to the disk. Finally, we have the no_subtree_check option, which helps reduce problems when files are being renamed.

 If you plan on using NFS, it's recommended that you peruse the man pages for some additional reading for a better understanding of its options, as a tutorial on every available NFS parameter is beyond the scope of this book. To read more about NFS and its options, consider executing the man exports command.

Now that you have configured a share via NFS, the next step is to access this share with another computer. As mentioned earlier, NFS is primarily targeted to the Linux and UNIX systems, as Windows computers cannot access these shares by default without installing the service for the NFS package, which is limited to certain editions of Windows. To mount an NFS share in Linux, first ensure that the nfs-common package is installed on the system using the following command line:

```
sudo apt-get install nfs-common
```

Then, we'll need a folder to mount the share. You can use an existing (preferably empty) folder or create a new one. You can mount an NFS share virtually wherever you have the permission to access it. To mount an NFS share, use the following sample command as a guide:

```
sudo mount -o rw 192.168.1.100:/home/jdoe/MyShare /mnt/MyShare
```

In the preceding command line, the IP address of the machine hosting the NFS share is `192.168.1.100`, so you'll need to replace this with the IP address of your machine. Then, we have a colon followed by the path to the share on the hosting machine. Finally, we have a space and then the path of the filesystem's location on the local computer where we want to access the share. In this example, a folder named `MyShare` was created in the `/mnt` folder, so the files contained in `/home/jdoe/MyShare` on the hosting machine will appear in the `/mnt/MyShare` folder on the local machine. Once you're finished with the share, you can unmount it to disconnect it from your system using the following command line:

```
sudo umount /mnt/MyShare
```

Summary

This chapter was all about networking. We started out by going over both wired and wireless networking, as well as some basic networking troubleshooting, should any problem arise. We also configured a static IP address using the tray icon utility included with Mint. SSH was covered; it is a very useful tool for remote access and administration, an indispensable utility used by many in the world of Linux administration. Accessing FTP servers by both Mint's included **Upload Manager** as well as FileZilla was covered. We also covered how to share files with both Samba and NFS and which situations each is best suited for.

In the next chapter, we'll explore **Security** and **Disaster Recovery**. You'll learn concepts relating to choosing strong passwords, encrypting your home folder, configuring the iptables firewall, blocking access to specific websites, and much more. Stay tuned!

10
Securing Linux Mint

By default, your Linux Mint installation is quite stable, benefiting from the latest security updates and a secure open source kernel. As Linux is inherently secure, the state of its security depends solely on the person using it. If you leave your system open, intruders will be able to dive right in, regardless of how secure your underlying environment is. Practicing safe security, including choosing secure passwords, configuring your firewall, and hardening your system are just some of the many techniques you can utilize to strengthen the security of your system. While an entire course on computer security could be a book on its own, this chapter will get you started on the path to taking security seriously.

In this chapter, we will discuss the following topics:

- Choosing strong passwords
- Encrypting your home folder
- Configuring and testing the iptables firewall
- Installing and configuring ClamAV
- Blocking access to specific websites
- Backing up and restoring important data
- Creating and restoring snapshots
- Hardening your system

Choosing secure passwords

Many believe that Linux is inherently more secure than the other platforms. While there is an endless debate on either side of this argument, no inherent security can save you if you use weak passwords on your system. What it all comes down to is that having a simple password based on a simple dictionary word would be broken by a cracker in just a few minutes, regardless of how secure your kernel is. A longer password with special characters and differing capitalization may be more difficult to type, but it would be harder for someone to guess it by launching a brute-force attack.

One useful tool that checks the strength of your password is the **Password Haystacks** tool found on the **Gibson Research Corporation** website. While it is not specific to Mint or even Linux, it's a very useful tool you can use to check the strength of your password. There, you can type in the password you're considering to see how conceivably strong it is against different attack scenarios such as an attempted online crack or offline crack. As you type characters into the text box on the site, you'll see how each character affects the probability of the password being crackable. You may be surprised to find that your password might not be quite as secure as you may have initially thought. The following screenshot shows GRC's Password Haystacks tool in action:

To find the Password Haystacks tool easily, simply look for it on Google. If the site shows up as having `grc.com` in the URL, you've got the right tool. The complete URL is omitted here, in case it changes.

For basic password security, it's important to not use the same password on more than one service. Having a consistent password across many sites may be convenient (only one password to remember), but it's also dangerous, as a stolen password would give an attacker access to every site that you use. This may seem like common knowledge, but you would be surprised at how vulnerable you might be if a popular service suffers a compromise of its entire password database. Thankfully, there are tools such as **LastPass** that can assist you with this burden. These tools will remember passwords for various sites, and even give you an option to randomly generate strong, secure passwords. LastPass is a browser plugin; so naturally, it works in Firefox (which is included with Mint) as well as Google Chrome (which you can download for Linux from the Google website).

One useful tip is choosing a password mostly made up of letters that cannot be easily typed without looking at your keyboard. Since you'll type your password quite a few times until the next time you change it, you can also become a better typist by practicing weak keys at the same time.

Encrypting your home folder

While it's true that protecting your computer accounts with a password will help prevent someone from logging in to your PC and using your operating environment without your knowledge, this alone will not prevent others from accessing your files when you are offline. As you recall, Linux Mint features a live CD that includes a fully usable operating environment, complete with a web browser and file manager. In fact, most Linux distributions feature live CDs nowadays, which are useful for much more than just booting an operating environment.

With a live CD, you can directly access the underlying hard drive of the computer, regardless of the operating system installed on it. Even if your user account is password protected, a live CD would bypass all the permissions on the underlying filesystem and allow the files to be freely viewed. This means that if your computer were to ever get stolen or fall into the wrong hands, your files would be easily accessible to anyone. Without encryption, an attacker could simply boot a live CD of their own on your computer and access whatever they like.

Thankfully, Linux Mint provides you with an option to encrypt your home folder during its installation. If you do so, an attacker would not be able to read your files without knowing the encryption key. If encrypted, your home directory would only be decrypted when you log in using your password. Without this password, the files would be invisible to anyone else. This means that if your machine is ever stolen or accessed offline, you can be reasonably confident that your files would be safe. The following screenshot shows the option to encrypt your home folder during its installation:

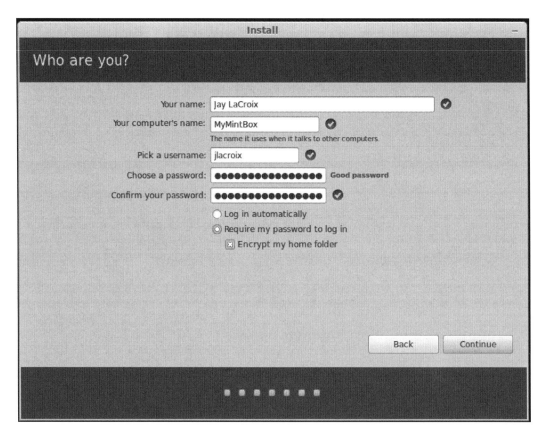

Unfortunately, encrypting your home folder in Linux Mint does come with a downside that you need to consider. As mentioned earlier in this book, Linux Mint does not include an upgrade option, so you aren't able to switch from one version of the distribution to another without doing a full installation again. This means that if you want to reinstall Mint but also retain your data, you would need to use a separate home partition and make sure not to format it when installing the new version.

However, if this home partition was encrypted, you wouldn't be able to easily retain it from one installation of Mint to the other, as the encryption key would have changed. Therefore, you would need to back up all your files outside of your computer, install the new version of Mint, and then copy your files back.

Although this decision may be tough, it is an important one when planning out your Linux Mint installation. If you choose not to encrypt your home directory, it will be much easier to later migrate to a new version of Linux Mint, though your files would be easily accessible to an offline live CD attack. If you do encrypt your home folder, you will need to transfer your files out of your system during the installation and then back into it after the installation is complete; with encryption, your system will be much more protected. If you're using Linux Mint with corporate data or even financial records, it is definitely a good idea to encrypt your home folder.

It's also possible to encrypt your home directory, or even create other encrypted folders on your system using tools such as **TrueCrypt**. In addition, you can encrypt your home folder after your installation is complete, but doing so anywhere else during the installation process is not supported and is at your own risk. As always, back up your data before you encrypt it, just in case the encryption process fails.

Configuring and testing the iptables firewall

Firewalls are another aspect of security worth considering. If your computer is connected to a router with a built-in firewall (most routers contain firewalls by default), then you are already reasonably protected from the outside world. However, a firewall in your router doesn't protect you from hacking attempts from inside your local network.

Although activating a firewall helps on a portable device used on public networks, it's still not a substitute for using a VPN service to pass your Internet traffic through an encrypted tunnel. If you use a laptop in a public place such as a Net Cafe, consider using a VPN service to protect your machine from packet sniffing tools used by someone around you. Sometimes, the biggest hacking threat may even be in the same room as you, without you knowing it.

Linux Mint comes with a preinstalled firewall known as **iptable**s. The iptables firewall is very common in the Linux world and is installed by default in many distributions. However, simply having this firewall installed is not enough; it needs to be configured in order to be effective. Although Mint includes it by default, it's not configured and is easily accessible. For a visual example of this, consider the following command:

```
sudo iptables -L | grep policy
```

After executing the previous command, you'll see that the policies that are in place for INPUT, OUTPUT, and FORWARD are all set to ACCEPT. This basically means that anything that is incoming, outgoing, as well as forwarded, is all accepted without question. Essentially, it's the same as the firewall not being present at all. Configuring iptables involves setting the default policy to DROP or REJECT and then selectively allowing the traffic that you want. A bit of work is required to configure iptables, since as soon as you set the default policy to DROP or REJECT, literally all the network connections will cease until you allow each service that you wish to use. For example, if you set a default policy to DROP, none of your browsers would be able to contact any website, and all the existing connections on your machine will cease working until you enable the services that you want. From a completely disabled firewall, you would then enable each component you want access to, one by one.

 There is an important difference between DROP and REJECT with regard to iptables. With REJECT, the traffic is denied, and the source computer is notified about the rejected traffic. With DROP, the traffic is simply deleted and a confirmation is not sent to the source computer. In most cases, DROP is preferred. Unless you have a specific obligation to keep the source computer in the loop about what you want and don't want to do, there's no reason to inform the source of the rejection.

Setting up an iptables policy via shell commands is beyond the scope of this book and may be a frustrating endeavor for someone who has never configured iptables before. In the earlier versions of Linux Mint (Version 15 and earlier), a graphical configuration tool was included to help you configure iptables simply and easily. For some reason or the other, the Firewall configuration tool was dropped in Linux Mint Version 16. Thankfully, there is a third-party graphical tool that we can install to allow us to configure iptables just as easily. You can install the **Gufw** package using the following command:

```
sudo apt-get install gufw
```

Once the package is installed, **Firewall Configuration** will be listed in your **Applications** menu and will give you a very friendly graphical interface through which one can configure iptables. The following screenshot shows the main application window for the Gufw firewall configuration utility:

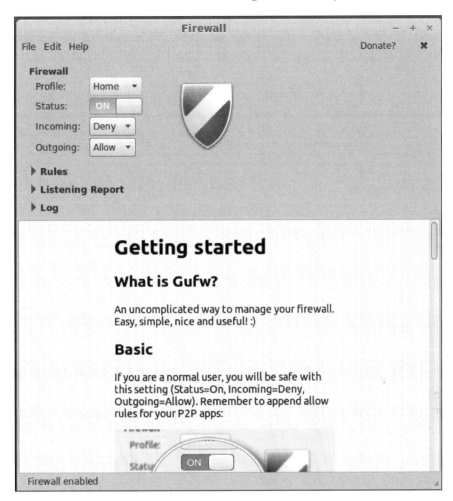

With Gufw, you can configure your policy based on preinstalled profiles (**Home**, **Office**, and **Public**) and set your policies for incoming and outgoing traffic. While the default configuration should satisfy most of the users, you can set individual rules if you wish for a more advanced configuration.

To test how effective your firewall is, consider the following experiment. The GRC website was mentioned earlier in this chapter, for its Password Haystacks tool. There is another useful tool on the GRC website known as **ShieldsUP!!**. You can use this tool to test the port security on your system. To do this, perform an Internet search for ShieldsUP!!, and you should be able to find the grc.com page that links to the tool in the search results. Once there, click on the **Proceed** button and then the **All Service Ports** link to begin a scan. The tool will see which ports it's able to communicate with on your machine, and report the information to you. The following screenshot shows the main selection for GRC's **ShieldsUP!!** tool:

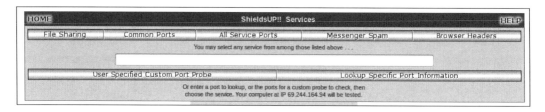

If the **ShieldsUp!!** tool is able to communicate with a port on your machine, then that means others would be able to as well. If a port is open on your machine, consider closing it using an iptables rule (which you can configure using Gufw). To further test the effectiveness of your firewall, consider plugging your computer directly into your Internet modem without a router in between and run another scan. If the **ShieldsUp!!** tool is not able to communicate with any port on your machine, you'll see a response showing **PASSED**, such as the one shown in the following screenshot:

Installing and configuring ClamAV

One aspect that many Linux users will often brag about is how Linux is virus proof and unaffected by malware that plagues many Windows systems. The truth of the matter is that no platform is truly virus proof, as a platform's ability to suffer a virus outbreak is dependent on the skills of the writers of malicious software to produce strong code.

However, at the time of writing this book, there are a few Linux viruses that exist out there. This doesn't necessarily mean that Linux viruses can't exist or won't ever exist; it's just not an issue that Linux users are forced to deal with, at least at the time of writing this book. Could this change tomorrow, next month, or next year? It's impossible to know in advance.

As there aren't many (if any) Linux viruses at the moment, then why include a section about installing an antivirus solution in a Linux book? The reason is because even though Linux has few viruses right now, it's still capable of spreading a virus to a Windows system. Think about it this way—if a friend of yours sends you a file that's infected with a virus and you open it on your Linux computer, you may not notice anything strange about the file at all. However, if you didn't verify the file before passing it along to another friend, they may catch a virus. This type of issue may be more common in a situation where you use a Linux computer as a file server, and the users of various platforms save files onto it. The Linux server itself doesn't care what you store on its disk. However, it's possible that the users of other platforms may spread viruses amongst each other without you ever knowing.

Although Mint doesn't include an antivirus solution by default, installing one is easy and free. **ClamAV** is the tool of choice for Linux users and is even used by some system administrators to remove viruses from Windows machines. To install ClamAV on your machine, enter the following command:

```
sudo apt-get install clamav
```

Once it is installed, it's a good idea to update ClamAV's antivirus definitions with the following command:

```
sudo freshclam
```

Once ClamAV is installed and updated, you're ready to use it. To scan a directory for malware, use the clamscan command with the -r flag and the path of the directory you wish to scan, as shown in the following command:

```
sudo clamscan -r /home/jdoe/my_folder
```

Once the scan is complete, you'll see a status window displaying the results of the scan, as shown in the following screenshot:

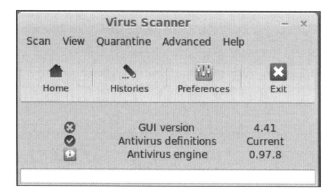

Although ClamAV is a scanner that runs in the Linux shell, it is also possible to install a GUI frontend known as **ClamTk** for the application, if you wish. To do so, execute the following command:

```
sudo apt-get install clamtk
```

Once it is installed, ClamTk will be available in your **Applications** menu. ClamTk is more akin to commercial antivirus packages, providing you with a menu-driven interface to select the style of scan, configure updates, and view items in quarantine. The following screenshot shows the frontend of ClamTk:

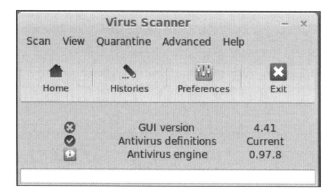

 Unlike most virus-scanning applications, ClamAV is targeted at on-demand scanning. When you install it, it will not watch your traffic to detect the presence of malicious software in real time. ClamAV's main purpose is to catch Windows viruses and not exactly looking for security threats to your Linux system itself.

Blocking access to specific websites

If you plan on allowing others to use your Linux Mint machine, the **Domain Blocker** application may be of use to you. Also known as the Mint Nanny, Domain Blocker allows you to prevent specific websites from loading. Domain Blocker is extremely easy to use, allowing just the basic functionality of adding a domain to block and removing a blocked domain. To add a new domain, click on the **Add** button and type in the URL. To undo the block, click on the domain name you wish to unblock and then click on **Remove**. The following screenshot shows the Mint Nanny application, with one domain blocked:

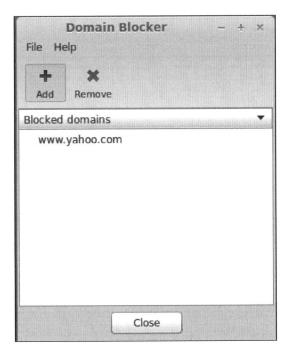

While Mint Nanny can certainly be useful in blocking domains you do not want to visit on your computer, it also has some fairly sizeable weaknesses. First, anyone with the `sudo` access to your machine will easily be able to undo the domains that you block. In addition, aliases for a domain may not be blocked. For example, if you block `www.yahoo.com`, the `www.ymail.com` domain will still work, thus working around the block. For those of you who need a simple tool to block a domain quickly, Mint Nanny may be considered as an appropriate tool.

One of the better solutions for domain blocking is not a Linux solution at all. **OpenDNS** is one such service worth taking a look at. OpenDNS is installed into your router by removing the DNS servers that your ISP provides you with and installing the OpenDNS servers instead. Therefore, someone with the sudo access to your computer would not be able to log in to your OpenDNS account and disable the service. For a walk-through of installing OpenDNS that is specific to your router, have a look at the OpenDNS website for specific instructions.

When you block a domain with Mint Nanny, it's simply adding an entry to your /etc/hosts file. To see this for yourself, consider blocking a domain while checking the contents of the /etc/hosts file before and after adding the block, to see the difference. If you wish, you can actually add the block to the /etc/hosts file yourself without using Mint Nanny, though Mint Nanny may be preferred, as it's not advised to edit your /etc/hosts file unless you have specific reason to do so.

Backing up and restoring important data

Backups are the most important part of a disaster-recovery strategy. Often, people may not consider the importance of backups until they have lost everything. An urgent point to remember is that all hard drives fail eventually. It's a question of when, not if. I have seen some hard drives last 10 years and others last less than a year (even the brand new ones). Under no circumstances should you trust that your hard drive will work when you wake up the next morning. Though there is a good chance the hard drive in your computer will last an average of three years, this is not guaranteed. If you have important files on your machine, it is imperative that you back them up.

Thankfully, Linux Mint, our Swiss Army knife, has you covered with a basic backup utility to get you started. Simply called the **Backup Tool**, you can use it to back up and restore not only your data, but your installed applications as well. The following screenshot shows Mint's **Backup Tool**:

To create a backup, click on the **Backup files** button. For the source, navigate to the directory that you would like to back up (for example, your home directory). Then, you'll be given a chance to exclude files from the backup, should you wish to do so. After clicking on the button, click on **Apply**.

There are some curious things to note about the **Backup Tool**. First, the **Backup Tool** runs as root. When you click on it from the **Applications** menu, it will ask you for your sudo password. In fact, even if you enter mintbackup without prefixing it with sudo on the shell in order to try and bypass the password requirement, it will still ask you for your sudo password. This is a very important thing to note, because when selecting a folder to back up and a target directory to place the backup in, the sudo requirement causes the **Backup Tool** to default to the root folders and not to your folders. For this reason, it's important to click on **Other** in the **Source** dropdown and manually navigate to your home folder. Then, under the **Destination** dropdown, click on **Other** again and manually browse to where you would like to place the backup (which can even be an external hard drive, if you wish).

A second aspect that's important to point out is that by default, your backup will contain a folder structure that is exactly the same as the source. Specifically, this means that the backup isn't placed in a compressed archive by default. Instead, it's just the files and folders themselves. This might be fine for you, but you may want to create a folder to place the backup in before starting the backup, so you don't end up with all your files on the root of the backup target.

However, the Mint **Backup Tool** does actually include an option to place your backup into a compressed archive. On the **Backup files** section of the backup wizard, you'll see a selection for **Output**, which defaults to **Preserve structure**. If you click on this prior to starting your backup, you'll see several options to create a compressed archive instead. In most cases, this is recommended. For example, you can include the date in the filename of the compressed archive, to allow you to organize your backups in a better manner.

Restoring files is easy; simply reverse the steps of creating an archive after clicking on **Restore files**.

 Since the **Backup Tool** runs as root, you'll also need root privileges to delete your backups as a result, as backups created by root are naturally owned by root.

The **Backup software selection** option of the Mint **Backup Tool** is also especially useful. With it, you can create a list of packages that you've installed since you installed Mint on your computer. The list that's created via this tool is in a special format that it recognizes, so if you need to reinstall Mint, you can simply import this list to have the tool reinstall all the packages that you've installed. This is very handy, considering the fact that Mint doesn't include an upgrade option to move from one release to another. You can back up your files, then back up a list of your installed applications, reinstall Mint, and then restore both the backups. This way, you'll have all your favorite applications and your data moved over to the new release. To create a backup, click on the **Backup software selection** button, and then choose a place to save the file. Keep in mind that this tool runs as root, so make sure you select a path from **Other** and then manually browse to where you would like the backup to be placed. To restore it, open the **Backup Tool**, then click on **Restore software selection**, and go through the prompts to select your saved backup.

There's one last note about backups before we move on. Another type of backup you should consider is an **offsite** backup strategy. If you keep all of your backups in one place, you may be at risk of losing your data anyway. For example, a fire or flood could render your backups and your source computer useless, destroying all your data in the process. An offsite backup is ideal; preferably, the one that watches over your files and automatically uploads changes. **SpiderOak** and **CrashPlan** are both good examples, among others. SpiderOak is a very secure backup service, and CrashPlan features optional encryption settings that can be enabled. SpiderOak features device synchronization (so, you can create the same files on multiple devices), and while CrashPlan doesn't offer sync, it's cheaper when storing data over 100GB. Although both are paid services, they feature Linux versions of their backup clients, with which you would benefit from the peace of mind in having an offsite backup.

Creating and restoring snapshots

Although Mint comes with a standard handy backup tool, there are no built-in **snapshot** tools that use a graphical interface. This is actually fine, as there are many solutions available for snapshotting a system; one of which is discussed here.

So what are snapshots and backups? A backup is a collection of your important files, while a snapshot is a backup of your entire machine, from the top to bottom. Snapshots are often referred to as images. The idea is that you can save a backup of your entire machine, right down to your configuration files. When restoring a snapshot, your machine will look and act exactly as it did at the point the snapshot was taken, because it literally is a clone of the machine at that point in time.

There are various ways of performing snapshots in Linux, and the method detailed in this section isn't even exclusive to Mint. One of the many benefits of Linux is that very little is hidden from you, to the point where you could essentially just copy your entire filesystem into a compressed archive and have that serve as your snapshot. In fact, this is exactly what we're going to do with our first approach.

The command that we're going to use is **tar**. The tar command is a very old command, which is still used by many today. It stands for **tape archive** and was once the primary method of saving files onto backup tapes. However, it is still used today to create archives of files as well as complete filesystems.

To get started, it's best to place the commands that we're going to use into a script, so we can easily reuse it later. To create the script, open any text editor. It really doesn't matter which one you use. You can use gedit that comes with Mint, nano that you can use within the Linux shell, or even others such as geany or scite that you can install. Once you have a text editor open, let's type in the first part of our script, which is shown as follows:

```
#!/bin/bash

DATE=$(date +%Y%m%d)
```

So, what did we do so far? If you've already read *Chapter 4, An Introduction to the Terminal*, then the first line should be immediately apparent to you. This is our **hash bang**, which is what we start all bash scripts with. We added a blank line simply for readability (the blank line in between the hashbang and the date line is not required), and then we have a variable.

Variables in Bash scripting are not something we've gone over yet, so what follows is a brief explanation. A variable is simply a name given to something you want to store and reference later. In the DATE=$(date +%Y%m%d) line, we're creating a variable named DATE, and we're setting it equal to the current date stored in our system clock. In the line, Y references the year, m references the month, and d references the day. So, if today was August 4, 2014, the variable would then store 20140804.

Now, let's add some more text to our script, as shown in the following command:

```
sudo tar -cpzf /tmp/`hostname`_$DATE.tar.gz \
```

```
--exclude=/dev \
```

```
--exclude=/lost+found \
```

```
--exclude=/media \
```

```
--exclude=/mnt \
```

```
--exclude=/proc \
```

```
--exclude=/run \
```

```
--exclude=/sys \
```

```
--exclude=/tmp \
```

```
--exclude=*.gvfs \
```

Although the preceding section may look long, it's really only one command. On each line, we use \ so that we can continue typing on the next line. This is only done for readability and is not required. On the first line of the new batch of text, we have the following statement:

```
sudo tar -cpzf /tmp/`hostname`_$DATE.tar.gz \
```

We start the command off with sudo. This is because we're making a full system backup. We need to make sure that we have access to everything. If we get a "permission-denied" response from something we're trying to back up, then that item would be missing from the backup.

Next, we have the tar command. You can look up the tar man page (man tar) for more information on how it works, but in this case, we're using the -cpzf flags with the command. The -c flag clarifies that we would like to create a new archive. The -p flag references that we would like to preserve the permissions of each file included in the archive. This is essential when taking a snapshot. Next, we have the -z flag, which means we want to compress the archive in order to save space. Finally, we have the -f flag, which clarifies that we want to use an archive file. When we type all the flags together, we get -cpzf.

In the next part of the command, we see `/tmp/`hostname`_$DATE.tar.gz`. The short explanation is that this is the path and filename where we want to store the archive, but several parts of this portion of the command deserve more explanation. The `hostname` portion refers to the name of your machine. When you run the script, `hostname` will be replaced by whatever the name of your computer is. If your computer is named `MyBox` then `hostname` is automatically changed to `MyBox` when the file is written. It's also important to note that the hostname is not enclosed in single quotes, but backticks—this is an important distinction. The backtick is located on the same key as the tilde symbol (~), which is typically the key directly underneath Escape.

Next, you see `$DATE` as part of the command. In Linux, when you create a variable, you don't include the `$` symbol, but you do so when you recall it. Earlier, we saved a variable named `DATE`, and now that we have this variable, we're calling it by referencing it as `$DATE`. Thus, `$DATE` will be replaced by today's date in the format we mentioned earlier. If you put the command together with this understanding, and we assume that your computer's name is `MyBox` and the date is May 23, 2014, the command will be as follows:

```
tar -cpzf /tmp/MyBox_20140523.tar.gz
```

Thus, we're saving an archive file in the `/tmp` folder with the name `MyBox_20140523.tar.gz`. As mentioned earlier, the forward slash at the end allows us to keep typing, so the rest of the lines are technically all in the same command. With each additional line, we have an exclude cause, typed as `--exclude=`, with a path typed directly after it. Excluding is important when creating a snapshot, because there are some folders, and it is generally not a good idea to back them up. You may even have other folders that you don't want as part of your snapshot. For example, if you already have a backup of your music collection, there's probably no point including it here. It would just make the archive file extremely large, so feel free to add additional excludes as you see fit.

Take a quick look at the files we're excluding, to get a sense of the logic that this script uses. For example, take into consideration the fact that the `/media` folder is excluded. The reason for this is because if you have a flash drive inserted into your computer and it's mounted under `/media`, then this flash drive would be copied into your archive. This is probably not what you want, especially if you're planning on storing your snapshot on a flash drive. The `/dev` folder is omitted, because it only contains virtual device files; something that is not relevant to your backup as these would be regenerated anyway.

Next, we'll want a more permanent place for our snapshot. The script is saving the snapshot in /tmp. This is good because /tmp is excluded (so essentially, the script won't back up its own archive), but this is not a good place to leave it. In the final line of your script, move your resulting archive file somewhere else. For example, if you wanted the archive moved to /home/jdoe/Backups (assuming, of course, that the directory exists), then enter the mv command with sudo at the end of the script, shown as follows:

```
sudo mv /tmp/`hostname`_$DATE.tar.gz /home/jdoe/Backups
```

Finally, we need to make the script executable; otherwise, we won't be able to run it. To do so, run the following statement:

```
chmod +x nameofscript
```

So, now that we have a snapshot, what do we do with it? First, it's recommended that you copy it somewhere outside of your computer (such as a flash drive or external hard drive). However, the reason we created this script in the first place was to have something we could restore from in case of a disaster. So, how do we restore this snapshot?

There are several ways, but perhaps, the easiest way is to first reinstall Linux Mint on your computer's hard drive. After you've installed the distribution, and with your archive stored on a flash drive that is inserted into your computer now, unzip the archive over the top of your new Mint installation with the following command:

```
tar xvpfz backup.tgz -C /
```

As you can see, we're restoring the saved archive over the top of our entire filesystem, as we referenced / as the target. The options we used this time are xvpfz; x means that we're extracting the archive instead of creating one. The v flag stands for verbose, and this means that we want to see what it's doing. The p flag clarifies that we want to work with absolute names. The f flag, as mentioned earlier, suggests that we're working with an archive. Finally, the z flag, in this case, means we want to uncompress the file.

While you can theoretically use this method to deploy a single image to many machines, this script would only work if you restored it on the same machine you took it from, because the universally unique identifier of your partition(s) are not the same from machine to machine. There is a way to work around this, but it is outside the scope of this book, and you would be better off using a solution such as **Clonezilla** for mass deployments.

Hardening your system

Although Linux is a very secure platform, further hardening can be performed to make the security even stronger. The first and most important rule of security is that if you are not using a particular service, turn it off. Every unused service you disable makes your attack surface that much smaller.

To view a list of open ports on your computer and the applications that are listening to them, install the **nmap** package with the following shell command:

```
sudo apt-get install nmap
```

Then, execute the following shell command to list your open ports:

```
sudo nmap -sS -O localhost
```

Note that in the previous command, we're including the letter o and not a zero. After executing it, you'll see some text appear in your terminal. This text will include a list of ports and also the service that is listening on that port. By default, you may not have many ports open and listening, other than NetBIOS and a few others, and this is perfectly fine. However, if you've installed extra packages that provide a service, you may see others listed. If you aren't using them, remove the package that is responsible for them to lower your attack surface a bit.

In addition, browser plugins can theoretically cause issues with not only security but stability as well. If there is a package installed on your system that runs in your browser and it's not something that you use, you can simply remove it to lower your browser's attack surface. One common example of this is Java. While Java was very commonly used on websites at one time, its usage has been declining. Unfortunately, Java is also a very common attack target for crackers on Windows and Mac platforms, and it's theoretically possible that attacks that take advantage of Java may start being engineered toward the Linux platform. If you don't need it, you can uninstall it.

In Firefox, Mint's default browser, it's easy to see which plugins are in use. To do so, open a new tab and then type about:plugins in the address bar. You'll be taken to a hidden page, where you can see which plugins are in use on your system. To remove a plugin, you'll need to uninstall the package that corresponds to that plugin. To do so, try searching for the name of the plugin in Synaptic, where you can easily remove the package responsible for it.

By default, Mint ships with an SSH client, so that you can connect to other machines via SSH. If you want to allow other machines to connect to you, you'll have to install the **openssh-server** package in order to add the necessary daemon (service) that allows other machines to connect. If you don't need to allow other systems to connect to you, make sure to remove the openssh-server package. If you do need the package, consider editing the `sshd_config` file located in `/etc/ssh` to harden SSH a bit, using the following statement:

```
sudo nano /etc/ssh/sshd_config
```

There are some clauses inside the `sshd_config` file that you should look out for. For example, consider the following entry within the file:

```
PermitRootLogin yes
```

This line is effectively stating that direct logins to root are allowed. Although the root account is disabled, disabling this option will go an extra step to help minimize the risk of someone finding a backdoor to the root account anyway. This is done using the following statement:

```
PermitRootLogin no
```

Port 22 is the default port that is assumed whenever you use the `ssh` command to connect to a machine. As this port is assumed, crackers would try port 22 before any other port. If you want to make it a bit tougher for crackers to guess, consider changing the port number. At the top of the file, you'll see the following line:

```
Port 22
```

Change the port number to something else, preferably above 1024 and below 65000. Then, when connecting to the machine from another one, you'll need to clarify the port. This is done using the following statement:

```
ssh jdoe@192.168.1.2 -p 45632
```

As you changed the port, the following command (without the `-p` flag) would be denied a connection:

```
ssh jdoe@192.168.1.2
```

After making changes to the `sshd_config` file, you will need to restart the SSH daemon for the changes to take effect, using the following statement:

```
sudo service ssh restart
```

Summary

Security is an ever-changing field, and new ways of attacking systems are discovered all the time. The purpose of this chapter is to help you begin computing in a secure way. Linux is one of the most secure platforms around, but it's not bulletproof. Therefore, some extra steps can be taken to help ensure security.

We began this chapter with a section on choosing secure passwords. An easy-to-type password may be more convenient but would also be the first to be broken. We also discussed configuring the iptables firewall with Gufw, a graphical frontend to iptables that simplifies its creation. Then, we took a look at Mint's Domain Blocker tool (also known as Mint Nanny) to help you block websites from being accessed on your machine. We ended this chapter by talking about backups, snapshots, and hardening your system.

In the next chapter, *Advanced Administration Techniques*, we'll take a look at ways to monitor system resources, kill processes, keep an eye on your system, and more ways to manage your system. We'll take a look at managing resources using the shell, killing misbehaving processes, setting up aliases to make commands easier to type, Bash variables, and even monitoring the temperature of your CPU.

11
Advanced Administration Techniques

At this point, you should have a deep understanding of Linux Mint, be able to install and configure it, as well as perform common tasks such as browsing the Web, creating/editing documents, listening to music, watching videos, backing up important files, installing and removing software, executing shell commands via Mint's terminal, and much more. By now, you've probably installed Mint on several of your own machines and may have even showed it off to your friends. In this chapter as well as the next, we're going to round out your knowledge and take your skills to the next level. First, in this chapter, we'll go over all the advanced stuff that isn't required for your day-to-day usage but will help make you a Linux warrior. In *Chapter 12, Troubleshooting Linux Mint*, we'll go over what to do when things go wrong, and help you recover from disasters.

In this chapter, we will discuss the following topics:

- Creating command aliases
- Making aliases persistent
- Killing processes
- Setting up cron jobs
- Preparing to move to a new release
- Exporting and importing package lists
- Using Variables and Conditional statements in Bash
- Monitoring resource usage
- Monitoring CPU temperatures
- Sending system reports via e-mail

Creating command aliases

As you may have noticed, some of the strings of command lines in the Linux shell can be long, and after a while, become a pain to type. While using the shell, you can press the up and down arrows to recall previous commands and even paste commands that you may have saved in a cheat-sheet document. These features certainly help, but there are also features that appeal to the more lazy users out there. **Aliases** are one of those things that when you start using them, you'll wonder how you ever lived without them.

To illustrate the value of command aliases, consider the following command:

```
sudo apt-get update && sudo apt-get dist-upgrade
```

The previous command will first update your cached package sources and then install any updates that may be available for the packages installed on your system. To be fair, this command isn't the longest one in the world; it's just two commands strung together (using `&&` in between them). However, it is long enough, and you could benefit from simplifying it. Wouldn't it be great if there was a way to simply type `update` instead of `sudo apt-get update && sudo apt-get dist-upgrade` and have the same effect? There is such a simple way, and this is where command aliases come into the picture.

To alias the previous command, first execute the `alias` command in the following syntax:

```
alias update='sudo apt-get update && sudo apt-get dist-upgrade'
```

After executing the `alias` command given in the previous example, you can now simply type `update`, and you would instead be executing the full `sudo apt-get update && sudo apt-get dist-upgrade` command. In a nutshell, to create a new alias, you start out by first typing `alias`, then the name of the alias you wish to create, followed by an equal (=) sign, and then the aliased command in single or double quotes. It doesn't matter what you name your alias, as long as it's not a command that already exists on your system. For example, instead of naming your alias `update`, you could have named it `ninja` if you wanted to, and it would work just the same. In our example, we used `update` because it made sense. Now, to download the latest versions of installed packages as well as security updates, simply type `update`.

Another benefit of creating aliases is that you can essentially create your own command and make the alias do the same thing on multiple computers. Consider the fact that distributions such as Fedora, Arch, and Debian use different package managers, so the command to download the latest updates is different on each. You could create an alias named update on computers installed with various flavors of Linux to run the local update command for that computer. For example, you could alias yum update (Fedora's update command) to update as well and have the same end result. This is especially valuable in an enterprise, where consistency always helps.

So, now that we've created an alias, how do we remove it? That's easy — we can use the unalias command. The syntax of the command is simple; all you have to do is type unalias followed by the name of the alias you want to remove. Considering our example update command, you would type the following statement to get rid of it:

```
unalias update
```

With this, the update command would be wiped out. Feel free to practice the alias command and simplify your most used commands.

Making aliases persistent

There is one considerable downside to aliases. If you were to log out of your machine, all the custom aliases you've created would be wiped out. Aliases that you create do not survive once your session has ended. Therefore, if you would like to make an alias or two (or many) permanent, there's another step in the process.

There are many ways to make aliases permanent, but the generally accepted method (which is possibly the easiest) is to edit your .bashrc file and add the aliases to it.

Before we continue with the concept of making aliases permanent, the concept of Bash configuration files should be explained. The .bashrc file is one of several files used by Bash (the Linux shell) for you to store various customizations. There are several of these configuration files, each with a specific purpose, and each is read by the system at a specific time.

In your home directory, one or several of these configuration files may be present. To see which ones you have in your home directory, consider the following variation of the ls command:

```
ls -la ~ | grep bash
```

With the previous command, we're executing the `ls` command with the `-la` flag against the home directory as designated with the `~` character. The `-l` flag means we want a long list (this is not required; it is just easier to read), and the `-a` flag means that we want to see all the files, even those that are hidden (as these configuration files typically are). Next, we pipe the output of the `ls` command (using the `|` character) to the `grep` command, clarifying that we want to see only the output that includes the word `bash`. Put it all together, and you will see all the files containing `bash` in their names stored in the root of your home directory.

At first you'll probably only see the `.bash_logout` and `bash_history` files. By default, Linux Mint does not create the `.bashrc` file in your home directory. However, if you create it yourself, it will be recognized and used by your system.

> The `.bash_history` file shows a history of all the commands you've typed, though it is not relevant to this section. Still, it may be worth checking out, so feel free to take a look at its contents.

The `.bashrc` file is known as a non-login configuration file. This means that it is not read when you log in to your desktop environment. Instead, it's read each time you open a terminal shell. This is perfect for our needs to make aliases permanent, because this means that each time we open a shell, any alias-creation commands we place in the `.bashrc` file will essentially be run for each shell window.

To get started, first let's edit the `.bashrc` file. You can do so with a graphical text editor or even in the shell itself. If you don't have a `.bashrc` file in your home directory (there's a good chance you won't), go ahead and create it. You can use the following command for creating and editing it at the same time:

```
nano ~/.bashrc
```

Depending on whether the `.bashrc` file already existed or not, you may either end up with an empty window, or it may contain text. Either way, add your alias commands to the end of the file, one per line. When you have done this, save the file. In the case of `nano`, you can save the file by pressing *Ctrl + O* and then *Ctrl + X*. If the `.bashrc` file didn't exist when you went to edit it, you should make the file executable as well using the following command:

```
chmod +x ~/.bashrc
```

Assuming you didn't make any typos, all of the aliases you created will survive between sessions from this point forward. However, as we created the `.bashrc` in our local home directory, these changes apply only to our user account. If someone else were to log in to the system, they wouldn't benefit from these aliases. This may be exactly what you want, but there is a way to activate aliases for all users. If you are configuring Linux workstations or servers in a corporate environment, this may be ideal. To create aliases for all the users instead of only for yourself, edit the `/etc/bashrc` file instead of `~/.bashrc`, using the following command:

```
sudo nano /etc/bashrc
```

As with the `.bashrc` file we edited earlier, the `/etc/bashrc` file is unlikely to exist on your system. However, the same direction still applies. Simply add your alias-creation command lines to the end of the file, save it, and make it executable if it didn't already exist. The main difference here is that we need to use `sudo`, since this is a system-wide file. Once you've added your aliases to the file, all the users on the system will be able to benefit from them.

Killing processes

Processes, also known as **daemons**, are programs that run on your system in the background, providing a service or allowing a particular function to work. In order to view how running processes affect your system, you can use Mint's **System Monitor** or the `top` command to get a look at what's running on your system. Most likely, you will not know what the majority of them are for, and this is okay, since you're not expected to. However, if your system starts running slowly or your system's temperature starts increasing (which you'll recognize by the increasing speed of the system's fan), a running process may be to blame. If you see a process using 100 percent of your CPU, there's a good chance that it may be to blame for sluggish performance.

Developers do their best to make sure that the programs and daemons don't negatively impact the system, but the unfortunate reality is that bugs can and do sometimes happen. This is not even specific to Linux, as sometimes, bugs may affect all platforms. For example, your author has experienced an issue in Gmail once that caused the CPU usage of a single core to spike from 90 percent to 100 percent for no apparent reason. When the bug was reported, even those using Mac OS X and Windows saw the same unfortunate behavior. When this happened, it was easy to pinpoint that the web browser was the source of the erratic CPU usage, as the `top` command would show the browser eating an abnormal amount of CPU.

Due to the inherent imperfection of computing, it's always a good idea to watch for strange behavior and to monitor resources when an unusual behavior is observed. The top command is one way of doing this, but Linux Mint also includes the **System Monitor**, available in the **Applications** menu, which suits the same purpose, although graphically. After opening the **System Monitor**, take a look at the **Resources** tab to see if any of your resources show abnormal usage (such as high CPU or memory usage) and also take a look at the **Processes** tab to see what's running on your system. The following screenshot shows Mint's **System Monitor** in the Cinnamon edition:

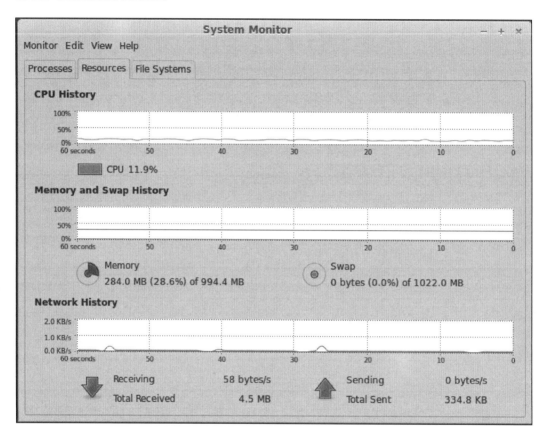

On the **Processes** tab, you can sort the running processes by the resources they are using. For example, if you click on **CPU**, then you will sort the process list by showing these processes that use the largest amount of CPU first. This way, you can easily pinpoint which process is stealing away your resources.

You don't have to check your resources unless there is an issue. Typical warning signs include your computer's fan speeding up and staying on for an unusual amount of time, your system running slower than normal, applications misbehaving, or your machine seeming to feel warmer than normal.

When you right-click on a running process, you'll have an option to kill the process. Should the related application not respond to close events (clicking on the **x** in the top-right corner of the window), killing an application through the **System Monitor** is another option that you may try. The following screenshot shows the **Processes** tab of the **System Monitor**, with the right-click menu:

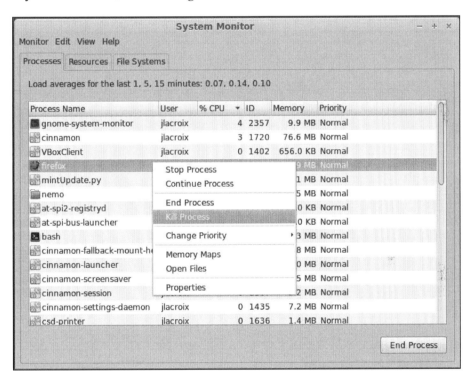

Killing applications through the **System Monitor** isn't the only way to close events. If you're currently using the shell, you can kill an application in one of the several ways that are mentioned in this section. First, you can use the `killall` command. For example, to kill the Firefox web browser, you can use the following command line:

```
killall firefox
```

Killing an application with the `killall` command is not advised unless the application cannot be closed any other way. Applications may save data when you close them. This would not occur if you kill the application. If an application has completely frozen, the `killall` command may save the day. To kill all instances of an application, consider prefixing the `killall` command with `sudo`. If this still doesn't work, it may be easier to restart the system at that point.

If you're working in the shell and not a graphical environment at all, the **System Monitor** would be of no use to you, since it's a graphical application. The `top` command, as mentioned earlier, is a very popular method to see what's running on a system outside of a graphical environment. With it, you can see what's running and what resources processes are taking up. Press the letter *Q* on your keyboard when you have finished using `top`. The following screenshot shows the `top` command running inside a terminal:

```
                              Terminal                          − + ×
top - 13:47:49 up 0 min,  2 users,  load average: 0.56, 0.18, 0.06
Tasks: 130 total,   2 running, 128 sleeping,   0 stopped,   0 zombie
%Cpu(s):   1.0 us,   2.7 sy,   0.0 ni, 96.3 id,   0.0 wa,   0.0 hi,   0.0 si,   0.0 st
KiB Mem:    1018312 total,    746664 used,    271648 free,     64760 buffers
KiB Swap:   1046524 total,         0 used,   1046524 free,    424136 cached

  PID USER      PR  NI  VIRT  RES  SHR S  %CPU %MEM    TIME+  COMMAND
 1287 root      20   0  352m  38m  12m S   1.7  3.9  0:01.09 Xorg
 1617 jlacroix  20   0 1442m  79m  31m S   1.7  8.0  0:02.95 cinnamon
 1417 jlacroix  20   0  105m 1520  964 S   0.7  0.1  0:00.14 VBoxClient
   11 root      20   0     0    0    0 R   0.3  0.0  0:00.15 rcuos/0
 1140 root      20   0  574m 3984 2924 S   0.3  0.4  0:00.02 console-kit-dae
 1473 root      20   0  227m 4532 3520 S   0.3  0.4  0:00.03 upowerd
 1915 jlacroix  20   0 20504 1540 1116 R   0.3  0.2  0:00.05 top
    1 root      20   0 27080 2836 1448 S   0.0  0.3  0:00.82 init
    2 root      20   0     0    0    0 S   0.0  0.0  0:00.00 kthreadd
    3 root      20   0     0    0    0 S   0.0  0.0  0:00.02 ksoftirqd/0
    4 root      20   0     0    0    0 S   0.0  0.0  0:00.00 kworker/0:0
    5 root       0 -20     0    0    0 S   0.0  0.0  0:00.00 kworker/0:0H
    6 root      20   0     0    0    0 S   0.0  0.0  0:00.07 kworker/u2:0
    7 root      rt   0     0    0    0 S   0.0  0.0  0:00.00 migration/0
    8 root      20   0     0    0    0 S   0.0  0.0  0:00.00 rcu_bh
    9 root      20   0     0    0    0 S   0.0  0.0  0:00.00 rcuob/0
   10 root      20   0     0    0    0 S   0.0  0.0  0:00.35 rcu_sched
```

In addition to `top`, there is also the `ps` command. The `ps` command is simpler. It only prints a list of all the running processes on your system. Unlike the `top` command, the `ps` command doesn't continually get updated; it simply prints a quick list of all your running processes and then returns you to the shell prompt. Go ahead and execute the following command on your system for a quick example:

```
ps -ax
```

Immediately, you'll see a list of running processes. On the left-hand side, you'll see the **PID** (process ID), which is a unique number given to each process. Although it may be easier to use the `killall` command against an application's name, you can also use the kill command against the process ID in much the same way. For example, to kill process `26218` using the kill command, all you have to do is type `kill` and then `26218`, as shown in the following statement:

```
kill 26218
```

If the process still won't close, there is another, last-resort command you can try. The command is as follows:

```
kill -9
```

The `-9` flag causes the program to close without an opportunity for cleanup. For example, consider the following statement:

```
kill -9 26218
```

If `kill -9` doesn't help you, force close a program; try to run the command line as the root user, or you can just restart your system.

Setting up cron jobs

There may come a time when you might want a task to run automatically at particular intervals, without your involvement being needed. Linux features **cron**, a utility for doing just that. A cron task is called a **job**, so you may hear the combined term, **cron job**, in the Linux community. Cron may seem rather complex at first, but it's surprisingly simple once it is broken down.

The first thing to note is that each user has his or her **crontab**, which is the term used for the configuration file that contains one or more cron jobs. By default, no user has any jobs created; thus, each user has an empty cron job. Inside a user's crontab, you place cron jobs in their own separate line, with a specific command to be run. This means that each user may have their own tasks to be automatically completed at specific times. For system administration purposes, administrators will often use the root user or a dedicated service account to run cron jobs.

To get started with this concept, try the following command under your own user account:

```
crontab -e
```

If this is the first time that you are running the preceding command, it may ask you to choose a text editor. For those just starting out, `nano` is probably the safest bet. Then, you should see `nano` open an empty cron file for you to edit. Although the file is considered empty, you may still see a bit of text in the file. Upon further inspection, you'll notice that each line begins with a hash character (#), which means that it's a comment that is ignored by cron. As each line begins with a hash, every line in the file is ignored. The included lines are simply pieces of instructional text that provide you with some important information regarding how cron works. Feel free to read it; then, we'll summarize it here.

First, notice the sample command provided in the file. This is a sample cron job line but is commented out like the other lines, so it won't be used by cron. However, it is a good example to start with. The line from a sample Mint PC used for the creation of this book is shown as follows:

```
0    5    *    *    1    tar -zcf /var/backups/home.tgz /home/
```

In the preceding example, we see a series of characters that are separated, followed by a command. The first section of a cron job, a `0` in this example, refers to the minute that the job will happen. Since `0` is used here, the minutes section is `:00`. The next section is the hour; `5` in this case. Therefore, we can gather so far that the command will be run at 5:00 a.m. (cron uses military time). The third section refers to the day of the month, but we have an asterisk (*) here. The asterisk, in this case, means that it doesn't matter what day of the month it is; just run it. Next, we have a section for the month; this is another asterisk. In this example, it means we don't care which month it is. So far, we have a command we want to run at 5:00 a.m., regardless of the date. The fifth field is set to `1` in our example, and this field represents the day of the week. Since we have `1` here, it means that we want to run the command on Mondays. (Sunday would have been `0`). Finally, the command that we want to execute is listed. If we put it all together, this line means we want to run the following command every Monday at 5:00 a.m:

```
tar -zcf /var/backups/home.tgz /home/
```

As another example, if we wanted to run the `emailstatus` command (a made-up command for our example) every Friday at 11:30 p.m., we would use the following command line:

```
30    23    *    *    5    /usr/local/bin/emailstatus
```

Notice how we wanted to run the `emailstatus` command, but the second example shows the entire path to the `emailstatus` command. This is important. While using the command by itself may work fine, there is no guarantee that it will. Typing out the entire path for the command as well as its name is considered to be the best practice with practice when using cron. If you don't know the entire path to the command you want to use, try the `which` command to find out. For example, you wanted to find the entire path for the following `apt` command:

```
which apt
```

The output from `which apt` would be as follows:

```
/usr/local/bin/apt
```

Therefore, `apt` is located in the `/usr/local/bin` folder, and the output includes the full path for `apt`, which you would be advised to include should you want to include it in your cron job. This rule also includes scripts, meaning that if you want to use a script in your cron job (and you certainly can) you should include the full path to the script, as well as full paths inside your script. The reason for this is because some distributions may not recognize the same paths as others, which may cause your cron job to fail.

To create a cron job, simply type it out on its own line after using the `crontab -e` command to open the file. When finished, save the file. In the case of `nano`, you can save the file by pressing *Ctrl + O* and then you can exit the editor by pressing *Ctrl + X*.

> You can actually edit the crontab manually without using the `crontab` command, but that's considered a bad practice and may not be respected by cron when it runs. The `crontab` command is the preferred interface between you and adding new cron jobs.

Our examples so far have been to add a job to run as your own user account. Perhaps, instead, you may want to run a command as the root. To do so, you would use the `crontab -e` command, but prefix it with `sudo`. If you run the `crontab -e` command with `sudo`, you're essentially running it as root. This would therefore result in your editing root's crontab, instead of your own.

To list your cron jobs, the `crontab` command becomes `crontab -l`. With the `-l` flag, the contents of your crontab will be presented on screen, allowing you to view the file for errors or simply see which jobs you have scheduled to run. If you prefix `crontab -l` with `sudo`, you'll see root's crontab instead.

Be very careful when using the root for your crontab. If you can help it, consider creating a dedicated user to run the command, and give sudo privileges for that specific command to this user account, bypassing the password. If the cron user account you create ever becomes compromised, you can reset its password without affecting the root.

Running cron jobs on your system can help you automate many things, such as package updates, temporary file cleanup, backups, or even sending automated e-mails that contain important information about the system, such as available hard disk space, to administrators.

Preparing to move to a new release

At some point, there will come a time when you will need to upgrade your installation of Linux Mint to a newer version. You may do so as soon as a new version is released, so that you can benefit from exciting new features, though the primary reason for upgrading is due to the support of your currently installed version coming to an end. Each normal version of Linux Mint is supported for up to 9 months. After the support for your installed version ends, installing a newer (and supported) version is ideal. Your current version will not suddenly stop working, but you will stop getting security updates, so it is definitely important to stay as current as possible.

As mentioned earlier in this book, Linux Mint does not feature an upgrade utility to move from one version of the distribution to another. This means that the only way to move to a new release of Mint is to do a fresh install. Many may see this as a substantial downside, but it's important to consider that upgrades often fail and may not go as planned and clean installations are more likely to be a smooth experience.

When it comes to other platforms such as Windows, upgrading to a new OS version via a clean installation can certainly be a chore. A clean installation for a Windows user may include reinstalling programs, one disc at a time, which can take many hours to complete. Then, the user may need to go into each of their most used programs and recreate all the settings by opening up each application and setting them up one at a time. It could certainly frustrate someone to have to undergo the same process every nine months.

Thankfully, with Mint (as well as most other Linux distributions), a clean installation is rarely a great deal of work. With proper planning, the process of moving from one release to a newer one will not be a big deterrence. As most applications you use are available in the repositories, you can export a list of installed packages and then import that list into your new installation. Mint's package manager will fetch all of the applications and then install them for you without you having to fetch a single disc. In addition, all of your customization is included in your home directory, so with a proper backup of your files, restoring your files will restore all your settings as well.

If the nine-month support cycle of Mint throws you off, consider using an **LTS** (**Long Term Support**) release instead. LTS releases are published around every 2 years or so, and are supported for at least 3 years from the date of release. For those who are using Linux in a corporate environment, LTS releases are more attractive, as it's difficult to find the staff required to reinstall everyone's operating system every nine months.

Another possible solution to consider is installing Mint with a separate partition for the home directory. If you've done so, you can install a new version of Mint by formatting only the / partition (which contains the distribution), making sure you choose *not* to format the partition that stores /home. During the installation, you can choose to use your home partition as the home partition again, leaving the format checkbox unchecked. Then, you'll benefit from the latest release of Mint without having to recopy all of your files. You'll retain your configuration as well, so your programs (once you get them reinstalled) should behave the same way.

Even if you place your /home directory in its own partition, you should still make sure that you have a complete backup before reinstalling it, just in case you make a mistake. I once tried to retain a partition during a clean installation and accidentally formatted it anyway, forcing a complete data loss. It happens to the best of us. Make sure you back up!

Preparing for an upgrade to a new release of Mint should involve the following steps:

- Completely back up the home directory for each user, including the hidden files
- Export a list of installed packages
- Take a snapshot of the system in case the new version has issues with your hardware
- Copy a list of any cron jobs and related custom scripts, if any
- Review important release notes from the Linux Mint blog to look for possible known issues

Exporting and importing package lists

In the previous section, we discussed the preparation needed to move to a new release of Mint, and exporting/importing package lists was mentioned. In this section, we'll move on to a new release of Mint.

To create or import a package list, you can use Mint's **Backup Tool** to accomplish the task. The **Backup Tool** was covered in *Chapter 10, Securing Linux Mint*, and its ability to back up software selections was briefly mentioned. When you open the **Backup Tool**, you'll first be prompted with your password, as the utility runs as the root. Once it is opened, **Backup software selection** is listed as one of the buttons on the very first screen. If you click on it, you'll first need to set the destination for the file to be created. Here, it's important to note that since the **Backup Tool** runs as the root, the home directory option listed is not your home directory, but that of the root. Therefore, you should select **Other** and then browse manually to where you want the list of software to be exported, followed by clicking on **Next**.

The next screen will allow you to preview the list, which lists only the software you've installed yourself (not the software that are provided by Mint by default). On this screen, you can uncheck a program to make sure it's not present in the exported list. This may be useful if you no longer wish to use a specific application and would like to omit it from being imported. Once you're comfortable with the selections, click on **Next**, and the list will be created and saved in the path you've chosen. The following screenshot shows the **Software selection section** window of the **Backup Tool**:

Now that you have a list, you can move it somewhere safe, preferably outside of your computer. This way, you can always import it if you need to reinstall Mint, or you can even import it on other machines if you wish to install the same packages there. In addition, having a software selection saved will make rolling out new machines even easier.

Restoring applications through the **Backup Tool** is very similar to saving a package list, though you start with the **Restore software selection** button instead, and then select your exported package list when prompted to do so. Mint will then install the packages included in the package list that are not currently present on the system. The following screenshot shows how to restore an exported package list in the **Backup Tool**:

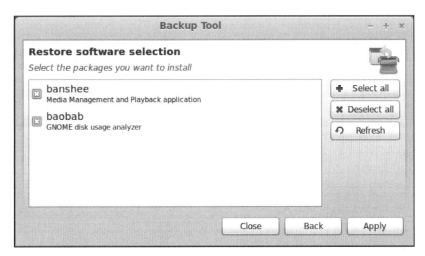

Using variables and conditional statements in Bash

We covered a brief introduction to Bash scripting at the end of *Chapter 4, An Introduction to the Terminal*. In the previous section, we created a simple script that monitors the temperature of your computer's CPU in almost real time. While useful, this script, in particular, won't save you a lot of time, since you can use the `sensors` command to do the same thing with almost the same amount of time. Bash really shines because of the fact that it has all the features you'd expect from an actual programming language, including `if` statements and variables. Bash scripting is used by many administrators to simplify and automate tasks. Paired with cron, you can easily create scripts to automatically run, and with enough skill, completely set up a Linux computer from a bare installation of a distribution to a fully functioning system for a specific purpose.

Before we continue, recall two very important requirements for scripting. First, the script must be executable. After creating a script (which is essentially just a text file), make it executable with the following chmod command:

```
chmod +x nameofscript
```

Another requirement, as mentioned in *Chapter 4, An Introduction to the Terminal*, is the **hashbang** as the very first line of the file. This is shown in the following command:

```
#!/bin/bash
```

Then, after the hash bang, you can enter any shell commands you would like to be executed, one per line. In addition to shell commands, your script can contain if statements and variables. In *Chapter10, Securing Linux Mint*, variables were introduced, but in the context of a script for creating a snapshot. We'll go through a little refresher here before continuing.

In short, a variable is a string of text meant to represent some sort of value. The value it represents can be a number or even text. For example, execute the following command lines either in a script or inside the terminal itself, one after the other:

```
hellomessage='Hello World'
mynumber=5
```

With these command lines, you created two variables. Notice that there was no output; you were simply brought back to the prompt. Don't let this fool you though; the commands definitely did something.

To see the results, try the following two commands:

```
echo $hellomessage
echo $mynumber
```

 If you close your terminal window, the values of any variables you created will be instantly forgotten. To make variables reinitialize each time you open a terminal window, recall the previous section on making aliases permanent. You can add variables, and not just aliases, to the .bashrc file.

As you can see, the values you typed were recalled. So, what exactly happened? First, we declared two variables. The first was a **string** (a line of text). Notice that we didn't include a space on either side of the equal sign. If we did so, the command to create a variable would have failed. The first variable was created with a string of text in quotes, but the second one didn't include quotes. This is because the term "hello world" included a space. If we're going to include a space, we need to enclose the contents of our variable in quotes. As the number 5 didn't include a space, we left the quotes out.

The next two commands used the `echo` command followed by our variable names. The `echo` command simply prints out whatever we tell it to. We could have typed the following command to get the same result as the first `echo` command:

```
echo "Hello World"
```

The `echo` command can also give us the contents of a variable. Consider the following example:

```
echo $HOSTNAME
```

The `$HOSTNAME` variable is built in; we didn't declare it. This variable includes the name of our PC. So, when we executed `echo $hellomessage`, we told `echo` that we want to view the contents of the `$hellomessage` variable, which we set to "`Hello World`" earlier. Notice that when recalling a variable, we prefixed the variable name with a dollar sign, but when creating the variable, we did not.

Next, let's take a look at conditional statements, also known as branching. In scripts that are useful, it's rare that simply one command after another will suffice. We may want to run a command only if a specific condition is true. For this, we would use an `if` statement. Let's take a look at the following example:

```
#!/bin/bash

myvar=5
if [ $myvar = 5 ]
then
  echo "The variable equals 5."
else
  echo "The variable doesn't equal 5."
fi
```

To run the script, save it in a text file and then make it executable. You can run the script by opening a terminal, navigating to where you saved it, and then type the name of the script prefixed with `./`, and it will run.

In the script, we first declared a variable named `myvar` to equal 5. The next line down, we started an `if` statement. Notice that there is a space in between the opening and closing brackets; this is required and may seem out of place, as variable declarations cannot have spaces, though the `if` statement in this example needs the spaces. Inside the brackets, we used the equals sign to compare whether or not the `myvar` variable is equal to 5.

Next, we typed `then`, which is required in an `if` statement. The statement directly after `then` is executed if the condition of the `if` statement is true. The line after `else` is executed only if the previous line did not prove `true`.

However, the `if` statement included is just a sample of how the syntax worked, as the script would be completely useless in real life. With further reading on Bash scripting, you can perform tasks such as installing a package if it's not currently installed, creating users, and much more—pretty much anything you can set your mind to.

Monitoring resource usage

In this section and the next, we'll work through monitoring system resources for problems, and then we'll even create a script to send us a handy message containing the results of our resources. This message is a handy monitoring tool.

Earlier in this chapter, the `top` command was mentioned briefly. The `top` command is one of the most useful commands to know, and simply typing `top` is enough for quite a few situations, to see what is currently happening on the system. The `top` command itself has a little bit more to it than just statically viewing resources. You can also change the sorting, view a single PID, or even kill a PID if you would like to do so.

When you first run the `top` command, the resources are sorted by the CPU percentage. This may be what you want if you were looking at finding out which process was consuming the largest amount of CPU. However, perhaps, you would like to sort the summary window by something else, such as memory consumption, should you find that your available memory seems to be lower than you would like. To sort by memory usage instead, press *Shift* + *M* on your keyboard. To sort by the PID, press *Shift* + *N*. To return to sorting by CPU usage, press *Shift* + *P*.

Additionally, you can kill processes as well. To kill a process, press *K* on the keyboard while `top` is open, and you will be prompted to type the PID number of the process you would like to kill.

Also, you can even change the time interval in which `top` updates the summary area. By default, the content in `top` updates every 3 seconds. You can actually change how often this updates by passing the `-d` flag and then a number of seconds, when first executing the `top` command. For example, consider the following statement:

```
top -d 1.5
```

With this example, `top` would update every 1.5 seconds. You could even set it to 0.5 seconds if you wanted to, in order to make it update even faster. The `top` utility is a very useful command, and one that you will likely find indispensable when attempting to pinpoint how much resources are being used up on your system and which process is the greediest one.

Monitoring CPU temperatures

The more you work the processor in your computer, the warmer it gets. You may have noticed that laptops tend to feel warmer when you run extensive tasks on them. Entire companies are dedicated to making products to keep computers cool, such as laptop desks with built-in USB-powered fans, stronger thermal compounds, and even water-powered heat sinks. In reality, computers are manufactured to keep themselves underneath the maximum temperature they are able to withstand, so these products are rarely necessary unless you are pushing your processor beyond its manufactured limits. However, it's still important to look at your temperatures every now and then, to make sure that your cooling system isn't starting to fail.

The command used in Linux to monitor system temperatures is `sensors`. The `sensors` command prints the current temperatures recorded in your system, and then brings you back to the shell prompt. If you prefer to have the temperatures reported in Fahrenheit instead of Celsius, add the `-f` flag at the end of the `sensors` command.

> Not all computer motherboards provide an interface through which you can check the temperature. If the `sensors` command is unable to detect any sensors, you may be out of luck. If you are unable to monitor your temps with the `sensors` command, consider searching on Google, with key words pertaining to the model of your chipset, to look for clues from others that may have gotten it working. Nowadays, most Intel chipsets seem to support temperature monitoring. If everything else fails, you can try the `sensors-detect` command as the root to see if it is able to find an appropriate driver.

At first, the temperatures may seem alarming. For example, a temperature of 140F may seem like a lot, but you should only be concerned if a temperature is near or over the maximum threshold. When you run `sensors`, it will usually report the temperature that is considered high and the temperature that is considered critical. On the machine this book is being written on, 188.6F is considered high and 221.0F is considered critical. The temperature of the CPU recorded as this paragraph is being written was 114F.

So, what do you do if the temperature is abnormally high? First and foremost, look for a running process that is consuming a fair amount of CPU. The most common culprit nowadays seems to be web browsers, especially if YouTube videos are in the process of being viewed. If a process shows a large amount of CPU being consumed, there's your problem. However, if your system doesn't show much memory or CPU usage but is still running quite warm, you're likely experiencing a hardware issue. In such a case, you should ensure that your files are properly backed up and then either investigate the cooling system or contact the manufacturer for assistance.

Sending system reports via e-mail

To wrap up this chapter, we'll work through an example of having the system e-mail you information at various intervals. This is very useful if you want to be updated periodically about any specific resource, such as installed packages or even backups. In our example, we're going to set up a report that will contain a list of all the packages installed on our system.

In order to create e-mail alerts, you first need an e-mail account from which you can send the alert. It's recommended that you do not use your personal e-mail account when dealing with scripts. Instead, either create an e-mail account for this purpose, or if you work in a corporate environment, ask the e-mail administrator to set you up with an alert account to use. Next, you'll need the **sendEmail** package installed, so let's take care of this with the following command:

```
sudo apt-get install sendemail
```

The `sendEmail` utility runs in the shell, so you won't see it in your **Applications** menu. The purpose of the `sendEmail` command is to provide you with an interface through which you can send e-mails through a script. However, before we dive in, let's take a look at the following example of the syntax used for the `sendEmail` command:

```
sendEmail -f <from_address> -t <send_to_address> -u "Subject of Email"
-o message-file=message.txt -s <SMTP server address> -xu <Email account
username> -xp <Email account password>
```

The `sendEmail` command example is definitely the longest we've used so far, so let's break it down. First, we type the `sendEmail` command; there is no surprise here. Then, we pass a number of flags to the `sendEmail` command. After the `-f` flag, we type the e-mail address that should appear in the "from" field of the e-mail. The `-t` flag is where we supply the "to" address. The `-u` flag is where we type the subject of the message, and the `-o` flag is where we include an attachment to put into the body of the e-mail. Next, we have `-s` where we supply the address of the SMTP server, and then we have the `-xu` flag where we provide the user account used for the e-mail server, followed by `-xup` and then the password for the account.

Another sample with the flags filled in with more relevant examples is shown as follows:

```
sendEmail -f server@mycompany.com -t admin@myemail.com -u "Important
Alert!" -o message-file=/tmp/reporttext.txt -s smtp.server.net -xu jdoe
-xp SecretPassword
```

 Notice how the password is shown in clear text. This is why it's a good idea to use a dedicated account, and not one that's actually important. Even with using a dedicated account, keep the script in a secure place, so bots can't find it and start sending malware using your company's e-mail server.

Notice the message file attachment set to `/tmp/reporttext.txt`. This file does not have to be named `reporttext.txt`, nor does it need to be stored in the `/tmp` directory; this may be a good place to store it though, since you only need the output file long enough to send the e-mail.

So, how do you generate the output used in the `reporttext.txt` file? You can redirect the output of any command you want to report on into a text file. In this example, we want to create and e-mail a list of installed packages. The following command will print a list of installed packages on the system:

```
dpkg –get-selections
```

Unfortunately, the command merely prints the list directly to the standard output (what you see in the terminal window) so this won't help us, but the following statement will:

```
dpkg –get-selections > /tmp/reporttext.txt
```

Now, we have something we can use. We basically took the output of the dpkg –get-selections command and threw it into a text file. Now, we can include this text file in our e-mail. In fact, the beauty of this is that you can send pretty much anything you want. As long as you can get it into a text file, you can send it, so you can report on anything you want. Now, all we have to do is send the file. We can use the following sample command to include the reporttext.txt file and send the contents off in an e-mail.

When you put all of this together in a script, it looks something like the following:

```
#!/bin/bash

dpkg –get-selections > /tmp/reporttext.txt

sendEmail -f server@mycompany.com -t admin@myemail.com -u "Important
Alert!" -o message-file=/tmp/reporttext.txt -s smtp.server.net -xu jdoe
-xp SecretPassword
```

In order for this script to work, you'll have to replace each flag with actual values for a real e-mail server. In order to find out what those values are, you'll have to check the help menu for your e-mail service or ask the individual who manages your e-mail server. Typically though, the values are the same as the values your e-mail service uses to send e-mails from a client program, such as Outlook or Thunderbird.

Now that you have a script, you can move it into the /usr/local/bin folder, using the following command line, so that it is recognized throughout the Linux shell:

```
sudo mv myemailscript /usr/local/bin
```

Then, make sure it's marked as executable using the following statement:

```
sudo chmod +x /usr/local/bin/myemailscript
```

Once this is complete, you can also add the script as a job in cron, so that it automatically sends you the report at various intervals. Feel free to create as many reports as you want and then use the section on adding a cron job as a guide to make the report run automatically. Also, feel free to experiment and see what kind of reports you can create. Another good example is disk space, which you can capture with the following command:

```
df -h > /tmp/hdusage.txt
```

Summary

In this chapter, we covered more advanced system administration topics. We first covered command aliases, which we can use to shorten long commands that are easier to type. Then, we went over how to make aliases stick between sessions, since they are normally wiped out when the shell is closed. From there, we worked through how to kill processes and how to create cron jobs to automate common tasks. We also covered best practices when dealing with moving to a new distribution release, as well as how to back up a list of packages installed on our system for import later. Our coverage in this chapter also included diving deeper into bash scripting and even creating reports, so we can get e-mail messages containing important details about our system that we would like to be kept up to date about.

In the next chapter, we're going to take a look at what to do when things go wrong. For example, we will look at as diagnosing boot issues, recovering data, testing RAM, pinpointing issues with audio, and more!

12
Troubleshooting Linux Mint

As smart as computers are and with as many amazing advancements as we've had in recent years, we're still unable to build computers and software that are not prone to failure. Nowadays, we rely quite a bit on our computers, and when they fail, it can be devastating. Thankfully, Linux Mint is a very stable operating system, but it too has its share of faults. When something happens that prevents us from using our computers, it's important to get it back up and running as quick as we can. In this final chapter, we will take a look at some common issues that can occur and what we can do about them.

In this chapter, we will discuss the following topics:

- Performing the initial triage
- Troubleshooting in the Software Rendering Mode
- Diagnosing boot issues
- Recovering data
- Perusing system logs
- Reinstalling GRUB
- Testing the RAM
- Pinpointing audio issues
- Solving problems with networking
- Solving slow frame rates in games
- Getting help from the community

Performing the initial triage

Before we go over some common issues and their solutions, there are some important, catch-all steps that can be performed in the face of a problem. You never know, one of these steps might just work.

For starters, if you run into a software-related issue on your Linux Mint computer, there's always a chance that the issue you're experiencing may not have anything to do with your computer or your installation at all; you may be experiencing a software bug. For this reason, you'd be surprised at how updating all of your packages often may solve issues. The reason is that perhaps the developers of the application you're having trouble with noticed the issue already and submitted a fix for it. If you use a newer version of the package, it may include a patch that fixes the problem you're having. Even if your graphical environment fails to load, you can still update your system using the shell with the following command:

```
sudo apt-get update && sudo apt-get dist-upgrade
```

Before you confirm any changes, take a gander at the output to see what the package manager wants to update before agreeing to it. If the application you're having an issue with is listed, it may be exactly what you need. Proceed with the updates and then restart the offending application. The `apt-get` command, mentioned earlier, will work on any Mint system even if the graphical environment doesn't load. If you normally use Wi-Fi for your network connection, you may need to connect an Ethernet cable to your computer in order to obtain a connection, in case your graphical environment fails.

Although it may seem like common knowledge, sometimes restarting your entire system may help if you experience issues. While this doesn't fix issues very often, you never know. In other cases, sometimes killing a service and then restarting it may get things rolling again.

Another important tactic to learn is to use Google. This too may seem like silly common knowledge, but the fact is that there's a small statistical chance that you'll end up being the first and/or only person to encounter a specific issue. If you search Google for the issues you are facing, you may stumble upon an online forum posting with someone mentioning your exact problem; this can result in a solution after the community weighs in on the problem. In other instances, you may instead find a bug report that will at least tell you whether or not your issue is beyond something you can fix and is being looked at by those responsible for it. If you need to, you can also post a forum message yourself on sites such as `linuxquestions.org` or on Mint's own forums. However, be forewarned; members of Linux communities have a very uncanny ability to easily sniff out those that have done very little research on their own before asking for help. Do the best you can, and then ask for assistance if you need to.

Troubleshooting in Software Rendering Mode

The **Software Rendering Mod**e is specifically related to the Cinnamon edition of Linux Mint, and it is a mode in which you run the system when there's some sort of a problem with Cinnamon being able to directly access your video card, or acquire the resources it needs in order to run efficiently. When this occurs, you'll see a message after you log in, informing you that there was a problem and that Cinnamon has resorted to the Software Rendering Mode. This mode of Cinnamon gives you the opportunity to still be able to use your computer while you troubleshoot the underlying cause. Unfortunately, while the Software Rendering Mode gives you access to your programs and files, it's likely to be missing features you may be accustomed to. The following screenshot shows the Software Rendering Mode notification, which appears when there's a problem:

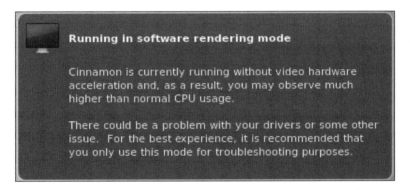

In most cases, issues that cause Cinnamon to resort to the Software Rendering Mode are typically due to drivers or your video card not having enough power to support Cinnamon. Most computers sold today, even those without dedicated graphics, should not have an issue running Cinnamon. Problems with hardware support typically arise when someone tries to use a very old computer with the Cinnamon edition of Mint (such as those that initially shipped with Windows XP). Computers from the XP era, including some from the Vista era, may be unable to run Cinnamon. If you have an older computer, you should consider a different version of Mint, such as the Xfce edition or the Mate edition.

Assuming that your computer is new enough to run Cinnamon, your video card may require proprietary drivers. You may want to open the **Driver Manager** and see if a proprietary driver is available for your computer. Although proprietary drivers are not preferred (developers don't have direct access to their code in order to fix bugs), the performance benefit may be just what you need. If you're already using the proprietary driver for your card, consider going back to the open source driver for your hardware, as these are typically better supported.

Another pain point with video drivers is switchable graphics, which some computers ship with today. Switchable graphics essentially utilize an integrated card (such as Intel) and then switch to dedicated graphics when the need arises (for example, you start performing a graphics-intensive task). One example of switchable graphics is NVIDIA's **Optimus** technology, which switches from Intel graphics to NVIDIA graphics when extra performance is needed.

While this technology saves power and handles resources more efficiently, support for switchable graphics in Linux is not perfect at the time of writing this book. Mint 16, for example, ships with Linux kernel 3.11. Switchable graphics was introduced in kernel 3.12. This was finalized after Mint 16 was released, but since Mint 16 doesn't ship with kernel 3.12, you won't benefit from this change until a newer version of Mint is published. In addition, since support for switchable graphics was only just recently introduced, it may not be completely stable in Linux yet, even if you were running kernel 3.12. If all else fails, you may consider changing the settings of your PC to disable switchable graphics, either enabling only your integrated graphics card or your dedicated graphics card.

 Enabling dedicated graphics as your primary card will increase your average system temperature, and not all systems that ship with switchable graphics will allow you to change the settings.

If you still have no luck, consider searching online for others who may be experiencing a similar issue, to see how they might have fixed it. However, first, you'll have to gather important information. For starters, if you don't already know which type of video card you have, you should run the following command to find out:

```
inxi -G
```

It will be helpful if you include information regarding your video card, model, and what steps you've performed to try to solve the problem if you are creating a forum post. In addition, searching for the model number of your computer along with the symptom will usually fetch useful results. For example, searching for `Thinkpad T430 Software Rendering Mode` may retrieve relevant results on Google.

Diagnosing boot issues

Issues related to booting your Linux computer may happen due to any one of several reasons. However, most startup issues seem to be caused by Windows. If you dual-boot Windows and Linux, it's not uncommon to have issues with booting Linux at some point. When upgrading from one version of Windows to another, Windows will typically not respect the fact that you dual-boot into Linux and may even wipe out your Linux boot sector. To solve this particular issue, see the *Reinstalling GRUB* section later in this chapter. Typically, when you reinstall GRUB, it will discover that you also have Windows installed and create an option to boot it along with Linux. Windows, on the other hand, will wipe out your Linux boot options when its boot loader (NTLDR) is reinstalled.

Other issues that can cause your computer to cease booting normally include hard drive corruption, faulty RAM, UUID changes, and invalid GRUB configuration. In the case of faulty RAM, this chapter includes the *Testing the RAM* section, which will walk you through diagnosing whether or not your system has memory issues. An invalid GRUB configuration, even for reasons outside of Windows overwriting the boot configuration, is solved by reinstalling GRUB.

However, **UUID** issues can be tricky. In fact, UUIDs are both a blessing and a curse. Before UUIDs were in common use, the naming convention of `/dev/sda1`, `/dev/sdc3`, and so on were used system-wide, even for removable devices. The problem was that if the order of the device connections was swapped around inside your case, the system may become confused and initialize the media in the wrong order. UUIDs have solved this problem by generating a UUID value unique to each device, therefore referencing them by something predictable instead of something that is dynamically applied. In fact, most (if not all) Linux distributions shipped today use UUIDs.

The downside of the UUID methodology is that they make it harder to deploy a single Linux snapshot across several computers of varying makes and models. Worse, if the UUID doesn't match what the boot loader expects, the system will refuse to boot. In order to fix issues such as these, you can either find the new UUID and change it in all the related files, or you may find it less of a pain to reinstall GRUB.

If you wish to update the UUID value to what it's supposed to be, follow these steps. First, we need to know which partitions are on our system. Unfortunately, we can't boot the system, because that's not working. For reasons such as these, it's important to keep a live CD or DVD handy. Mint's install disc is live media, so you can boot from the same disc you used to install the distribution. Once loaded, you will have a fully functional environment and will be able to work toward repairing the issue.

First, you'll need to mount your hard drive. The easiest way to do this is to open it through the file manager, such as Nemo in the Mint edition. Then, execute the following command to get a list of partitions on your hard disk(s):

```
sudo fdisk -l
```

The output of the previous command will list all the partitions on your system. Pay attention to your primary hard disk (or any hard disk on which Linux is installed) and write down the device names. You can usually deduce which one corresponds to which mountpoint. If you need clues, look at the content of the `/etc/fstab` file (located in the `/etc` folder of your disk, *NOT* the live media). It typically has some comments regarding which partition is matched to which mountpoint. Next, we need to find our current UUIDs. The following command will display the current UUIDs:

```
sudo blkid
```

Now, you are armed with the information that you need. You have your partition layout, the UUIDs of your partitions, and the `/etc/fstab` file as a guide to what goes where. The following files are the ones you will need to update with the correct UUID. Keep in mind that the paths listed are relative to your hard disk, not to the file system of the live media. For example, if your hard disk is mounted under the `/media/jdoe/MyDisk` directory in the file manager, the path to the `/etc/fstab` file, for example, would then be `/media/jdoe/MyDisk/etc/fstab`.

The following is the list of files that contain the UUID and would need to be updated:

* `/etc/fstab`
* `/boot/grub/grub.cfg`

If your next boot also fails, make sure that you have edited your UUID in every occurrence. For example, consider the following command:

```
cat /boot/grub/grub.cfg | grep UUID
```

The preceding command will search a text file for every occurrence of UUID, therefore displaying all the values as well. You can compare these values to what the values should be.

Recovering data

Recovering data from a failed drive is actually a simpler process than it may seem, assuming that the damage is not so severe that data cannot actually be recovered at all. It's important to keep in mind that all hard drives break eventually; it's a matter of when, not if. If a hard drive has gone past the point of no return (for example, you hear a constant audible clicking noise, and the drive isn't recognized by the computer), then there may not be much you can do aside from sending in the drive to an expensive data recovery firm.

If the drive is at least recognized by your computer (for example, it shows up in the BIOS), then there is still hope. As the Linux Mint installation media doubles as a live operating environment, you can access your hard drive directly from within the live media and attempt data recovery from the GUI that you already know. The first (and perhaps easiest) method is to attach a USB flash drive or external hard drive, and then browse your internal hard drive through the file manager, copying files to your USB drive as you come across them.

In more severe corruption cases, the hard drive may not be accessible even to the live media. If this is the case, you can try more advanced tools, such as **SpinRite** (a third-party product available for purchase), which includes its own operating system and can aid in data recovery by repeatedly accessing faulty sectors until it is able to read the data and move it to the sectors known to be good. In many cases, you still won't be able to trust the drive, but SpinRite may be able to allow it to be read one last time, long enough for you to retrieve data.

If you have successfully recovered your data, you can consider running the manufacturer's diagnostic tools to troubleshoot and check whether the drive is actually defective. If the error seems to be a problem with the partition tables or the installation itself, your drive is likely to be fine, and a reinstallation of Mint may get it up and running again. To be safe, it doesn't hurt to run the manufacturer's diagnostic tools to double-check the quality of the drive. Each of the manufacturers (such as Samsung, Seagate, Western Digital, and Toshiba) has their own diagnostic tool available for download on their respective websites. This tool is in an ISO format that you can burn to a disc. With several of these tools, you have to set your hard drive access mode to **Legacy** (also known as IDE) in the BIOS in order for the tools to be able to access the drive, as most of the tools are based on older technologies and run within an open source DOS clone. If your drive gets a clean bill of health, chances are that it's fine, but still keep a backup, just in case. Sometimes, a **Pass** result from a diagnostic tool may not always be reliable.

Perusing system logs

As your Linux system runs, it captures logs of basically everything that goes on. You'd be surprised to know how much information Linux keeps in its logs, everything from logins, website look-ups, and even when USB devices are inserted and/or removed. This is great considering that if you run into problems, chances are that something in the logs may help you pinpoint where the error originated. This is especially true if an error shows up while booting but goes away quickly before you have a chance to read it.

Logs are kept in the /var/log directory. If you navigate to this directory and then list its storage, you'll see quite a few logfiles, each with their own purpose. The logfiles contained in this directory of interest in regards to troubleshooting include kern.log, dmesg, auth.log, boot.log, and syslog (these are explained later in this section). To read a log, type the cat command followed by the name of the log. Depending on the permissions of the log, you may need to use sudo, so keep this in mind in case you receive a permissions error when attempting to read a log.

When you use the cat command against a logfile, the content of the logfile will fly across your screen. This is fine if the log is small, but larger logs can be so large that not everything will fit on your screen. The less command, when used with cat, can make things much easier to read. Basically, you can pipe your command into the less command. This allows you to scroll the output by pressing *Enter*, so you can read at your own pace. Press *Q* on your keyboard to return to the prompt. Consider the following command line for an example of how to pipe the contents of a logfile into the less command:

```
cat /var/log/syslog | less
```

The most important tip when perusing logs is the use of the grep command, which is basically essential here. Many Linux logfiles become quite large, and scrolling through them line by line or even by page may take you a while. If you have an idea of what you're looking for, you can use grep with the output of the cat command.

For example, say you are having an issue with your network card, which is established as eth0. To see messages specifically related to eth0 contained in the syslog, consider the following command line:

```
cat /var/log/syslog | grep eth0
```

The same logic can be applied to any logfile. If you generally know which component is responsible for your issue and you want to see pertinent information specific to that hardware, you simply use the `cat` command to display the logfile, but pipe the output into `grep` with a keyword so that you'll see anything that includes that keyword. The same logic can even be used when auditing security. For example, consider the `auth.log` file, which keeps the records of sessions as they are opened and closed. If you were searching for entries containing a specific username, you could type the following command line:

```
cat /var/log/auth.log | grep jdoe
```

The following are some specific logs to consider:

- `kern.log`: This contains messages specific to the kernel. This is a great place to start your search if you're having trouble with a piece of hardware.

- `dmesg`: This log isn't really a log at all, though you can use it as if it were one. It's actually a utility, and the `dmesg` command is recognized by the Linux shell even outside of the `/var/log` directory. The information that `dmesg` provides is useful for diagnosing hardware as well as errors during the boot process.

- `auth.log`: This log answers questions such as "Who is logging in to your system" and "Who has attempted to use `sudo` or access the root account". In corporate environments, it may be useful to periodically peruse this log to see if any suspicious activity is occurring.

- `boot.log`: If you see an error flash by on your screen while booting, but it goes away so fast that you can't read it, the `boot.log` file is useful, because it contains boot messages.

- `syslog`: This file contains a wealth of information. If you face a problem, this is a good log for you to look through.

Another useful trick to have at your disposal is the `tail` command. With `tail`, you can view the tail end of the file. By default, the `tail` command will show you the last ten lines of a file. The `tail` command is used in the following manner:

```
tail /var/log/syslog
```

However, you're able to view a different number of the last lines using the `-n` option. For example, to view the last 25 lines of the `syslog` file, you can type the following command line:

```
tail -n 25 /var/log/syslog
```

From here, `tail` only gets more awesome. The `tail` command also features a `follow` mode, which continuously scrolls a file as it grows. You can use the `follow` mode with the `-f` option as shown in the following command line. As the logfile grows with more information, your terminal will be updated, allowing you to watch a logfile in almost real time as it gets updated (press *Ctrl + C* to stop):

```
tail -f /var/log/syslog
```

While administering Linux machines, the `tail` command's `follow` mode can be indispensable. While troubleshooting an issue, you can watch a logfile with `tail` and try to reproduce the issue at the same time, watching the logfile react to your actions. To see this in action, try executing the following command, and while it is running, insert and remove a flash drive or network cable:

```
tail -f /var/log/dmesg
```

 The `head` command is very similar to `tail`, although it defaults to showing you the first 25 lines of a text file instead of the last 25.

Reinstalling GRUB

GRUB, which stands for **Grand Unified Bootloader**, is the program that is responsible for booting Linux Mint. If, for some reason, it becomes damaged, you won't be able to boot your machine and will get errors. This could be for any number of reasons, such as Windows overwriting the **Master Boot Record (MBR)**, a failed cloning attempt, or even nonfailure incidents such as simply wanting to make something bootable, such as a flash drive.

If you want to install GRUB on a different disk, the `grub-install` command, shown in the following command line, should be all that you need:

```
sudo grub-install <device>
```

For `<device>`, simply type the device on which you're attempting to install GRUB. If you want to reinstall GRUB on your main drive, `<device>` will typically be `/dev/sda`, but you should always verify your devices before installing or reinstalling GRUB. The following command will list your drives:

```
sudo fdisk -l
```

Take note that when you install or reinstall GRUB, you don't specify a partition. This is because the boot sector is written before the partition table, so in order for GRUB to be bootable on a device, it must live at the beginning of the drive. Thus, you'd type /dev/sda instead of using /dev/sda1 for the device when working with GRUB.

However, what if you were unable to boot at all? One of the most common reasons why someone may reinstall GRUB is due to a booting issue. If you can't boot, you can't issue the grub-install command required to make it boot again. Actually, there is a way of doing this. If you boot from live media (such as the installation disc you created for Mint), you can access your installation and repair it. As mentioned several times in this book, keep a live disc handy at all times; you never know when you might need it. Linux live discs are even useful for recovering Windows systems, among other uses.

To repair GRUB from a live DVD, first insert it and start your computer. In the case of Mint's live media, you'll have a fully functional graphical environment to work with. This graphical environment will also allow you access to the system's hard disk and Linux installation. The first step is to mount the hard drive that contains the installation you would like to repair. The simplest way to do this is to open the Nemo file manager, and click on your system's hard drive. Doing so will automatically mount it just before it shows you the contents. If a graphical environment won't load, you can mount your main hard drive with the following command:

```
sudo mount /dev/sda1 /mnt
```

 The previous command assumes that your root partition is /dev/sda1. To be sure, issue sudo fdisk -l to get a listing of your partitions.

After executing the mount command, the contents of your root partition will now be located in /mnt. Feel free to navigate to the /mnt folder, and check the contents to be sure that you've mounted the appropriate device.

Next, you can reinstall GRUB. The following command will do the trick:

```
sudo grub-install –root-directory=/mnt/dev/sda1
```

Again, adjust /dev/sda1 to the device on your system. After the command executes, reboot your system (type reboot in the terminal window, or click on **Reboot** through the desktop environment's **Quit** menu), remove the disc when prompted, and see if your machine now boots as expected. As long as you typed the commands properly and used the proper values, there shouldn't be any issues with GRUB.

Testing the RAM

RAM can and does fail, and sometimes, it can be difficult to troubleshoot, as the symptoms are rarely consistent. Sometimes, you may get memory errors, which is a clear indication that you should run a diagnostic scan on your machine. Other times, you won't see any errors at all but may be facing issues and not realize that your memory is bad until you rule out everything else. Thankfully, memory is quite easy to test. In fact, Linux Mint includes **Memtest86**, a popular memory-testing utility, built right into the installation media. After Mint is installed on your machine, the Memtest86 is installed as well and is available from Mint's GRUB menu.

To access the memory-testing utility from the live media, look for the screen after you boot from the disc that reads `Automatic boot in X seconds...`, and press any key on your keyboard before the number of seconds elapses. You'll see an option, **Memory test**, which will be the fourth option. The following screenshot shows Linux Mint's boot menu from a bootable DVD, showing the **Memory test** option:

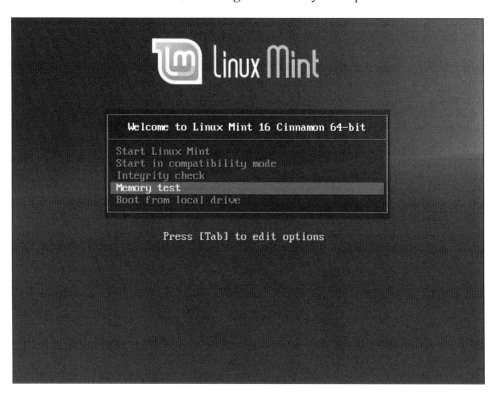

If Linux Mint is already installed on your computer, you can access the memory test by holding *Shift* while the system starts up, just after the BIOS screen, which will bring you to a boot menu with a selectable option for the memory-test utility. The following screenshot shows the GRUB boot menu in Linux Mint, showing the **Memory test** option:

Once the option is selected, the memory test will run. In fact, the memory test will run repeatedly, so if you don't see any errors after a while, you can be confident that your memory is not defective. The following screenshot shows the memory-test utility (**Memtest86**) running on a machine:

```
     Memtest86+ v4.20          | Pass  2%
Intel Core Gen2 2856 MHz       | Test 23% ########
L1 Cache:   32K 114239 MB/s    | Test #3  [Moving inversions, 8 bit pattern]
L2 Cache: 6144K  50999 MB/s    | Testing:   196K - 2048M 2048M
L3 Cache:       None           | Pattern:   bf bf bf bf
Memory  : 2048M  17521 MB/s    |
IMC :           Intel(R) Core(TM) i7-3520M CPU @ 2.90GHz  / BCLK :   0 MHz
Settings: RAM :   0 MHz (DDR3-   0) / CAS : 0-2-0-232 / Dual Channel

WallTime   Cached  RsvdMem   MemMap   Cache  ECC  Test  Pass  Errors ECC Errs
--------   ------  -------   ------   -----  ---  ----  ----  ------ --------
 0:00:10    2048M      0K    e820      on    off  Std    0       0



(ESC)Reboot   (c)configuration   (SP)scroll_lock   (CR)scroll_unlock
```

If the memory test were to fail, you would see errors listed in the bottom-half section of the Memtest86 window. In the preceding screenshot, you'll see that the bottom half is all blue, with no text at all. If errors were to be encountered, they would be highlighted in red, so it would be hard to miss them.

> If Memtest86 finds errors with your RAM, don't immediately run to your computer store for a replacement kit. First, try reseating your memory modules (with the power cord unplugged and battery removed) to see if this solves your issue. Especially with laptops, memory modules can get loose if the laptop gets bumped well enough.

Pinpointing audio issues

With most computers, audio generally works without any configuration at all. Sometimes, you may run into a computer with a problematic sound card. When faced with sound issues, and you've already tried the obvious (turning up the volume), you should first check to see if your sound card has any compatibility issues. The following website lists audio hardware and whether or not they are compatible with Linux:

```
http://www.alsa-project.org/main/index.php/Matrix:Main
```

Keep note that the list in the preceding website is incomplete and may or may not include information regarding your sound card. If you aren't sure of the make and model of your sound card, the following command should point it out for you:

```
aplay -l
```

For the most part, integrated sound cards seem to work the best in Linux, and your author rarely ever experiences a problem with onboard sound. Third-party sound cards, which you can purchase in computer stores, may or may not support Linux, and it's important to check before you purchase one. Also, most sound cards that are compatible with Linux will not advertise, for example, on the back of the books, so it would be best if you look for reviews online. In the case of newegg.com, reviews for hardware products will often include a review or two from individuals using a device with Linux, and you'll get to read about their accounts. Some cards are supported well in Linux, others not so much, and some not at all.

There are two useful utilities for troubleshooting sound in Mint. The first is found by opening **System Settings**, then searching for **Audio** where you'll find Cinnamon's audio configuration utility. There, you can do some basic triage, such as making sure that the correct sound card is selected for use, just in case your system detects more than one. In addition, you can click on the **Test Sound** button to diagnose if your sound is not working at all or if the application itself is having issues.

The following screenshot shows Mint's sound settings utility:

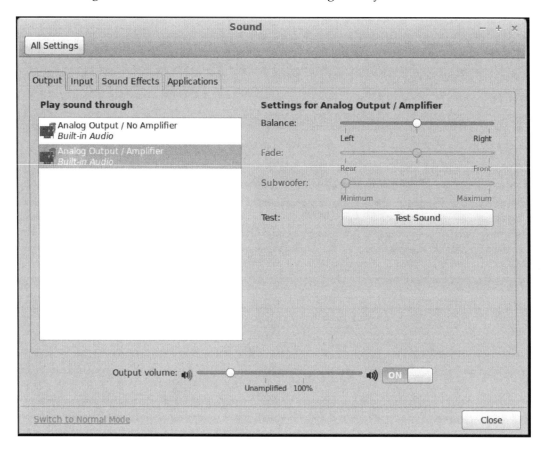

Although useful, your options in Cinnamon's sound settings utility may be limited. Another useful utility that you may wish to install is called **PulseAudio Volume Control** and is installable via the following command:

```
sudo apt-get install pavucontrol
```

After installing the pavucontrol package, you'll find the PulseAudio **Volume Control** in your **Applications** menu if you search for it. With this utility, you'll have many features that are the same as Cinnamon's **Sound** utility but also a few more. For example, on the **Configuration** tab, you can set your profile to **Analog Stereo Output** instead of the default. This sometimes solves audio playback issues. The following screenshot shows the PulseAudio **Volume Control** utility:

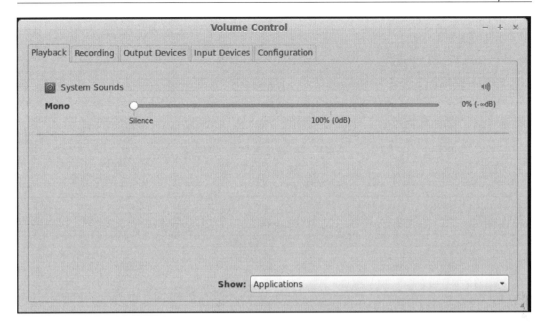

In addition to helping you configure your audio output, you can also use the PulseAudio utility to configure input such as microphones. Many Linux recording applications will simply accept input from your default mic, which is almost always set to that of your integrated microphone, if you have one. The integrated mic in typical computers is usually of very low quality, so if recording audio is important to you, you can opt for a dedicated third-party microphone. If you do so, you can select the microphone to use in the PulseAudio utility.

In the case that you are still unable to get the audio working, or if the `aplay -l` command shows no output as if it thinks you have no sound card, the best that you can do is to search the Web for clues for your specific machine. In some rare cases, not being able to play audio may be due to a bug in the kernel itself, so consider choosing a different kernel to boot from by holding *Shift* right after your BIOS screen appears, during the boot process. Since Mint doesn't remove outdated kernels as it updates them, you can try your luck with an earlier version.

Solving problems with networking

What if you're not able to connect to the Internet at all? Thankfully, networking issues are rare in Linux nowadays, but in case you do experience an issue connecting, there are some things you can do in order to pinpoint the problem.

First, check to see if you have an IP address. To do so, execute the `ifconfig` command, and look for either `eth0` (which represents your Ethernet card) or `wlan0` (which represents your wireless card). The naming convention can be different, so don't worry if you see neither declaration. The following screenshot shows the output from the `ifconfig` command:

```
                              Terminal                             - + x
mint@mint ~ $ ifconfig
eth0      Link encap:Ethernet  HWaddr 08:00:27:e8:b5:9d
          inet addr:172.16.254.203  Bcast:172.16.254.255  Mask:255.255.255.0
          inet6 addr: fe80::a00:27ff:fee8:b59d/64 Scope:Link
          UP BROADCAST RUNNING MULTICAST  MTU:1500  Metric:1
          RX packets:1024 errors:0 dropped:0 overruns:0 frame:0
          TX packets:219 errors:0 dropped:0 overruns:0 carrier:0
          collisions:0 txqueuelen:1000
          RX bytes:237620 (237.6 KB)  TX bytes:23994 (23.9 KB)

lo        Link encap:Local Loopback
          inet addr:127.0.0.1  Mask:255.0.0.0
          inet6 addr: ::1/128 Scope:Host
          UP LOOPBACK RUNNING  MTU:65536  Metric:1
          RX packets:28 errors:0 dropped:0 overruns:0 frame:0
          TX packets:28 errors:0 dropped:0 overruns:0 carrier:0
          collisions:0 txqueuelen:0
          RX bytes:3515 (3.5 KB)  TX bytes:3515 (3.5 KB)

mint@mint ~ $ []
```

If you see an IP address listed, you should be connected. However, if you don't, you may want to check your `/var/log/dmesg` log for messages specific to `eth0` or `wlan0` depending on what you're connecting with. If you see log entries mentioning timeouts when trying to acquire an IP address from your DHCP server, your issue may simply be that your clock is wrong. If you click on the clock in the bottom-right corner of the screen, does it show the correct time? If the time is correct, does it show the proper date? It may sound trivial, but if your date/time is wrong, your computer cannot sync with a DHCP server.

If you need to correct the date/time, execute the following command:

```
sudo date MMDDHHMMYYYY.SS
```

Let's walk through the command, since you'll need to replace the letters after the word "date" with the proper values. The first variable, MM, is the month. So, if it's currently August, you'd replace MM with 08. The variable, DD, represents the day of the month, so if it is currently 16, you'd replace DD with 16. Next, we have HH that stands for hour. Then, we have MM again, but this time, it represents the minute portion. Then, we have YYYY, so you would put the year here. Finally, there's a period followed by SS that you'll replace with the seconds. For example, to set the time to something specific, you might type the following command line:

```
sudo date 081611302014.32
```

After correcting the date and/or time, try connecting again. You just might be able to connect. Unfortunately, if you're unable to connect, you may have an issue with your router (such as running out of IP addresses), or perhaps, your network card is not supported. If this is the case, you may want to try connecting elsewhere to see if the issue is related to your location, or in the case of a lack of hardware support, you can research bug reports and community articles to search for possible known issues and work-arounds specific to your computer.

Solving slow frame rates in games

Another issue that may come up is slow frame rates when playing games on Linux. An extremely common cause for frame rate issues in Linux games is due to something called desktop effects, also known as compositing. Many desktop environments, Cinnamon included (but also others, such as KDE), use special effects to make GUI actions look more stylish, such as animating when you minimize windows or showing a transparency effect in menus. These features certainly make the desktop look more appealing, but they come at a cost; they steal resources from your video card.

The typically accepted solution that most developers seem to try to include into desktop environments is the act of automatically disabling desktop effects when full-screen applications are being run. In fact, many developers claim that desktop effects are disabled for full-screen windows (games typically run on full screen) by default and that this should no longer be an issue. However, your author plays games on Linux daily and can confirm this issue is anything but fixed on any desktop environment at the time of writing this book.

The manual work-around is to disable desktop effects yourself prior to playing a game, then re-enable desktop effects (if you wish to keep them) after you finish playing. To temporarily or permanently disable desktop effects in Cinnamon, access **System Settings** and then click on **Effect**s. There is a checkbox in the top-left corner of this window; it reads **Enable desktop effects**. Disable this checkbox, and then try your game again. You may find that the game runs much better.

Getting help from the community

As mentioned earlier in this section, you can always seek help from online communities should problems that you're unable to solve arise. One of the biggest benefits of Linux is its helpful communities, with entire sites dedicated to helping users overcome their problems or to answer questions.

When creating support requests, such as posts in a forum, always include as much pertinent information as you can. Community volunteers are often very helpful, but their time is not infinite. The more information you provide, the better equipped they would be to assist you. Consider including information such as sections of relevant logfiles, exact error messages, computer make and model, exact edition of Mint (Cinnamon, MATE, and so on), exact steps to reproduce the issue, as well as what you've tried to solve the problem so that others don't duplicate your efforts.

Many great sites exist for finding help, a few of which are as follows:

- The Linux Mint forums (`http://forums.linuxmint.com/`):

  The Linux Mint forums are a great place to go, because no one knows Mint more than its own community. While Mint's forums are certainly not the largest in existence, they are specifically targeted toward Mint, so it's a great place to start.

- LinuxQuestions.org (`http://www.linuxquestions.org/`)

  Although not specific to Mint, LinuxQuestions.org does feature a dedicated section to Mint, so feel free to check out this forum for answers. In addition, if you ever venture to other distributions outside of Mint, LinuxQuestions. org has sections for most popular distributions, so you can also get help with other distributions as well.

- Ubuntu Forums (`http://ubuntuforums.org`)

  Although not for Mint, Mint is based on Ubuntu, and the Ubuntu Forums actually hosts a section specifically for talking about other distributions, so you can also post Mint questions there.

In addition, you can also request live help via **IRC**. **Xchat** is included with Mint, and by default, a Linux Mint chat room opens when you open the application. IRC chat is very old but still a very fun way of interacting with other people. If you plan on using IRC (and you should consider doing so), you may want to spend some time researching some IRC commands. However, on its own, simply opening Xchat is easy enough, since it immediately connects you with the community, and all you need to do for basic usage is type messages and press *Enter*.

Summary

The final chapter of our Linux Mint adventure was based on discussing some basic troubleshooting and where to go in order to find help. The most valuable skill you'll ever learn in Linux is how to find assistance when you need it and where to go whenever you run into trouble. Finding information via search engines is a very important skill, as you'll likely be able to find articles regarding just about anything you'd ever want to do. Mastering Linux, after you have learned the basics, is all about reading and searching for answers. The more questions you ask, the more answers you can find.

In this chapter, we discussed testing memory, reinstalling GRUB, perusing logs, data recovery, and requesting assistance from other users. Your adventure has only just begun here and will get even more exciting. Will you run Linux on a server? Will you set up a home theater PC on your television? Will you develop your own awesome Linux apps? Will you become a community guru, or even get a job as a Linux administrator? The possibilities are endless.

A
Reinstalling Mint while Retaining Data

As Linux Mint doesn't feature an upgrade utility, the only option for someone to move from one version to another is to reinstall the entire distribution. New versions of Linux Mint are released every 6-7 months, and most releases are only supported for 9 months. This means that in order to keep updated, you may need to reinstall it twice a year. Linux Mint does feature **Long Term Support** (**LTS**) releases, which are published around every 2 years. However, LTS releases may lack the hardware support necessary for their installation on current machines. As non-LTS releases are published more frequently, it's only natural for them to include newer kernels, which in turn support newer hardware. So, what do you do? This appendix is dedicated to helping you overcome this limitation by learning how to retain your home directory and packages between installations.

In this appendix, we will discuss the following topics:

- Considering LTS releases
- Why an upgrade utility isn't included
- Preparing for the migration
- Installing Linux Mint while retaining /home
- Importing a list of packages for reinstallation

Considering LTS releases

Before we get into the process of installing Linux Mint while retaining data, it's important to first mention the LTS releases that are available in Mint. LTS releases are supported for 3 years, unlike the 9-month period of non-LTS releases. If reinstalling Mint is an inconvenience for you, you can consider the LTS releases instead. The main downsides of LTS releases are that the kernel is usually out of date (and therefore, the latest computers may not work well with them) and applications are also not the newest versions. If this is not an issue for you, using LTS releases would mean that you would need to redo your installation less often. The process of retaining data between installations, discussed in this appendix, is compatible with the LTS releases as well. So, you'll still be able to use the same method to keep your installation updated.

 Linux Mint is considering basing all future versions on Ubuntu LTS releases, though the final decision hasn't been made by the time this book went to press.

Why an upgrade utility isn't included

Detractors of Linux Mint will often cite the fact that there is no official upgrade procedure to be a downside that warrants considering other distributions. In enterprise environments, system administrators surely wouldn't want to reinstall Mint on everyone's computer every 9 months, especially if it's a company that has 100 or more computers. To be fair, the lack of an official upgrade procedure is definitely an inconvenience. However, in order to understand why things are this way in Mint, one must look at the bigger picture.

First, upgrading from one operating system to another is almost never a smooth experience. To put it in perspective, with 30,000 or so packages in the repositories, there's literally no way to test how an upgrade procedure contends with every possible combination of packages that may be installed on one's system. When developing a distribution, a clean installation would be the most tested process and would have a greater chance of succeeding. With one system being upgraded to another, all it would take is one package to conflict with another and the entire upgrade process would come tumbling down. If the process of upgrading from one system to another fails, you'll end up in a much worse shape. This problem isn't specific to Linux, as I've seen many Windows upgrades fail in much the same way, and even the ones that succeed, later end up having problems. A clean slate is the best approach.

Second, LTS releases that are supported for 5 years are recommended in business and enterprise environments. If a system administrator works for a company that adopts Linux Mint on their computers, using a non-LTS release would be a bad idea, as they would be creating a lot of unnecessary work in regards to mass reinstallations when a version is obsolete. LTS releases are geared toward environments that need something proven and stable to last a while, with minimal work. For an administrator, creating a deployment image of an LTS release of Mint with preinstalled packages geared toward the overall function of the business would be the best course of action.

Third, consider the subject of compatibility. For example, let's say there was another way to upgrade, and someone used an official utility in order to do so. The person goes through the process and then reboots the PC hoping that it will be up and running on the new system. Unfortunately, the system won't boot, and nothing works anymore. If the new version of Mint was incompatible with your computer or contained problems that prevented it from working, you would know as soon as you boot the live media and test it. With an upgrade utility, the program would simply upgrade your system, and you wouldn't know how your system is going to react until after the process is finished and you reboot it. With a clean installation from an ISO image, a user would be more likely to run into compatibility issues before the upgrade process even begins.

Don't let the lack of an official upgrade procedure scare you, though. The process that we'll use in this appendix is surprisingly simple and achieves almost exactly the same result as if there was an official upgrade method. In addition, this method is the most reliable way to go.

Preparing for the migration

The key to being able to effectively manage your Linux Mint installation is planning it properly right from the start. In order to retain your home directory between installations, you at least must have originally installed Mint with the home directory attached to its own partition. If you haven't, the way you'd be able to move from one release to another is to back up your files, reinstall, and completely start over. Giving the home directory its own partition is a highly recommended practice.

Installing Mint with a separate home partition has several benefits, including the following:

- You can retain your data across different installations
- You can switch from one distribution to another without recopying user data

- If your Mint installation fails, your data is less likely to be at risk

- User applications store data in /home; therefore, the settings will be preserved

 If you chose to encrypt your home directory during the installation of Linux Mint, you will not be able to maintain your data between installs easily, as the encryption key would become different. There's always a way to work around issues such as these, but doing so is not supported. If you encrypt your home directory, your best bet is to back up your data manually. If you prefer to encrypt your data, consider the LTS release instead, as you'd need to reinstall Linux Mint less frequently.

The benefits of using a separate home partition cannot be overstated. With this configuration, it will be much easier to maintain your installation. Sure, not having an upgrade option is certainly a drag, but if you're properly prepared, it won't impede you. In addition to retaining your home directory, you can also back up and restore a list of the installed applications, so you won't have to remember what you've installed. Armed with a persistent home directory and a backup list of your packages, you're essentially upgrading anyway, regardless of Mint not supporting this process itself.

Before we begin the upgrade procedure, we should make sure that we're actually prepared for it. First, we should always make sure that we have a backup of our data in case we make a mistake. Even though we're going to be preserving our home directory in the new installation, this is no substitute for a good backup. For example, what if we accidentally click on the format option even though we didn't mean to? This would be a very bad situation if we didn't have a backup. Consider third-party cloud backup solutions such as **SpiderOak** and **CrashPlan** to automate the backup process.

In *Chapter 11, Advanced Administration Techniques*, we went over creating a list of installed packages via Mint's **Backup Tool**. Make sure that you have the text file it created during the process as well, especially if you want to install a large list of packages that you like.

Installing Linux Mint while retaining /home

In this section, we'll walk through installing Linux Mint as we did earlier, but this time, we're going to assume that we want to maintain the home directory partition. This way, you'll see how the installation procedure differs when you also want to retain your data. To get started, you first boot your computer with the Linux Mint installation DVD or flash drive that you would have created earlier in this book, and start the installer by double-clicking on the **Install Linux Mint** icon on the desktop.

For the first several screens of the installer, we'll go through the process the same as we did the first time. On the first **Welcome** screen, we'll choose our local language and then click on **Next**. On the next screen, we'll click on **Preparing to install Linux Mint** and click on **Next**.

The third screen of the installation procedure, **Installation type**, is where we'll start diverging from how we installed Mint the first time around. There, we'll first choose **Something else** instead of the default option and click on **Continue**. The following screenshot shows the **Installation type** screen during the reinstallation process, with the appropriate item chosen:

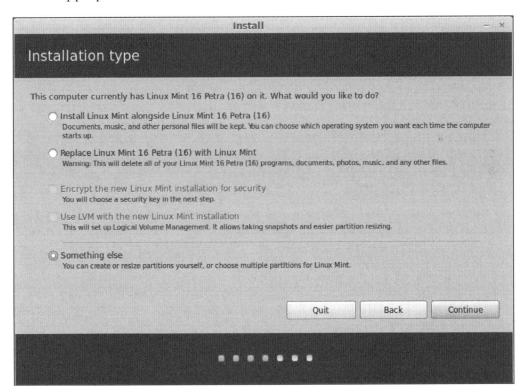

The next screen (also called **Installation type**) is where we'll need to pay very special attention. When you first arrive on this screen, you'll see your current partitions listed. The following screenshot shows the partitioning screen during the installation, without any changes:

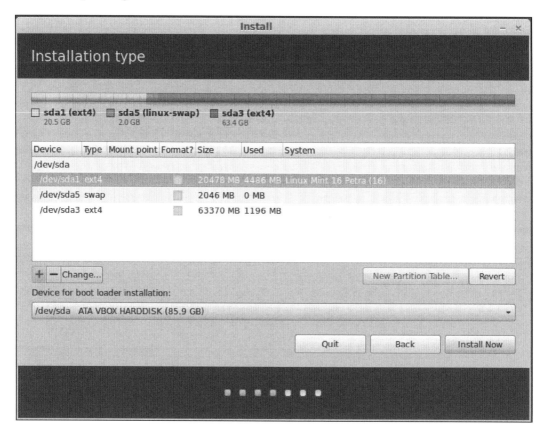

On this screen, we'll need to edit our partitions in a specific way. First, double-click on the first item that represents your root directory (the label of this partition will read **Linux Mint** and then your version number). After this, an **Edit partition** window will appear. Leave the **Size** option as it is, and set **Use as** to **EXT4 journaling file system**. Check the box that reads **Format the partition** and set the **Mount point** option to **/** (a single forward slash). As the / partition contains the distribution itself, we want to format it. Since we want to do a fresh installation, the format option will ensure that we're wiping out the old installation. When you are satisfied, click on **OK**. The following screenshot shows how to edit the root partition:

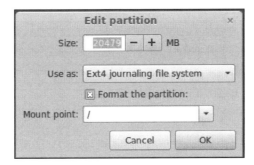

For the swap partition, if you have one, follow the same procedure as you did for the root partition, but change **Use as** to the swap area.

Next, double-click on the last partition. Leave the **Size** option as it is, and set **Use as** to **Ext4 journaling file system**, just as you did earlier. This time, *do not* check the box that reads **Format the partition**, because if you do so, your home partition will be wiped out. Click on **OK** and you'll be returned to the partitioning screen. The following screenshot shows the final partition layout; note that the **Format** checkbox for **/home** is *not* checked:

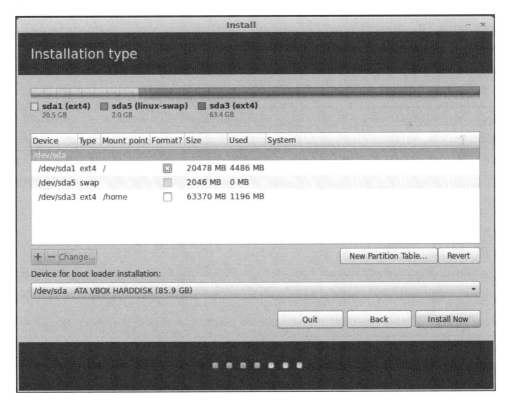

Once you're satisfied with your selections, click on **Install Now**. On the next screen, **Where are you?**, choose your location and then click on **Next**. Then, choose your keyboard layout on the **Keyboard Layout** screen. Finally, on the **Who are you?** screen, fill in your user details, but make sure you create the same username as you did when you installed Mint the first time; otherwise, you'll have issues with file permissions.

From here, Linux Mint will install and not format your home directory. When you first log in, you should see that your desktop is exactly the way you left it. However, you may have shortcut icons that point to programs that are no longer installed, but we'll fix this in the next section.

Importing a list of packages for reinstallation

In *Chapter 11, Advanced Administration Techniques*, we covered Mint's **Backup Tool**, which allows you to save a text file containing a list of all your installed programs. You'll need that file for this section. To recap, you can create this file by opening the **Backup Tool** and clicking on **Backup software selection**. Preferably, save the text file somewhere in your home directory, as the tool defaults to saving the file in the root's home directory.

Once our system is up and running, we can import the software selection list we created. This list will prompt the **Backup Tool** to install all the packages that may not be present on the system. To restore the file, open the **Backup Tool** and enter your password when prompted. Then, click on **Restore software selection**. The following screenshot shows Mint's **Backup Tool**:

On the **Restore software selection** screen, click on **(None)** and then browse to where you saved the backup file containing your packages. The following screenshot shows the first screen of the **Restore software selection** process:

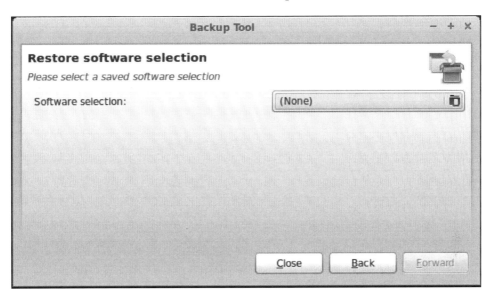

After importing your backup file, a smaller window with a list of all the packages you've installed will appear; basically, it includes any package (that normally isn't a part of Mint) you had installed. Here, you can click on **Apply** to have the tool install the packages for you. If you prefer, you can also peruse the list and uncheck anything that you may not need anymore. The following screenshot shows the **Restore software selection** process, showing the applications we would want to reinstall:

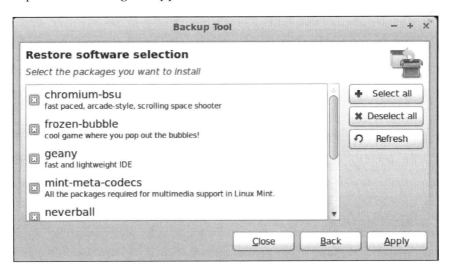

After clicking on **Apply**, the **Backup Tool** will install your packages. The following screenshot shows that the selected software is restored:

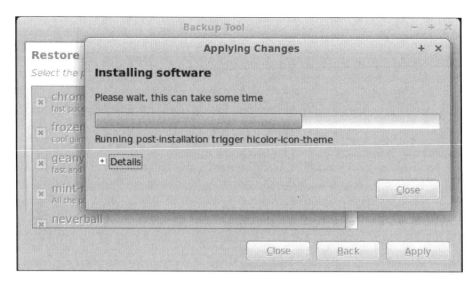

Now that this process is complete, your installation should be as it was the last time, but with a new version of Mint. All your favorite applications should be present; your settings (such as browser favorites and e-mail accounts) should also be preserved, and your personal data should be stored in your home folder.

Summary

It may be considered a reasonable downside that Linux Mint doesn't contain an official method of moving from one release to another. However, in this appendix, we were able to easily work around that. Not only did we get a completely new and fresh installation of Linux Mint, but we were also able to retain our packages and installed applications as well. Essentially, we actually did upgrade from one release to another. While the **Backup Tool** is exclusive to Mint, the idea of retaining a home partition between an old installation and a new one is not. Retaining your home directory while reinstalling your distribution is actually a very common practice in the Linux world; I am yet to see a distribution that doesn't allow you to do this. In fact, you can even move from one distribution to a completely different one and retain your data this way if you choose to.

B
Using the MATE Edition
of Linux Mint

While the Cinnamon edition of Linux Mint is often considered the default (due to its popularity), by no means is it the only edition worth trying out. Cinnamon is a very appealing and functional desktop, but it may not run well on older machines that lack the hardware resources to run a desktop with as much eye candy as Cinnamon. In this appendix, we'll discuss the **MATE** edition of Mint, which runs better on older hardware. Despite the fact that it runs better on older computers, many people will often run the MATE edition on newer computers too, so you may want to give it a try even if your computer is a beast.

In this appendix, we will discuss the following topics:

- Introducing MATE
- Understanding the differences between MATE and Cinnamon
- Launching applications
- Customizing MATE

Introducing MATE

MATE (pronounced Mah-Tay) is a desktop environment available for Linux. Although Mint ships a special release of their distributions which opts for MATE instead of Cinnamon, MATE is by no means limited to Linux Mint. It is what we refer to as a **fork** in the Linux world. Essentially, a fork is where a developer or group of developers takes an existing project and creates a different project from it. In some cases, a forked project may be very similar to the original, but over time, it becomes its own project altogether.

The origin of MATE goes back to when the third major version of GNOME was released. Although GNOME 3.x has come a long way since its inception, a lot of users were less than enthused with the changes in GNOME 3.x over that of GNOME 2.x. MATE is appealing to those who prefer the older 2.x releases of GNOME over the newer 3.x series. In addition, MATE generally runs better on older hardware, and may be appealing to users who don't prefer a great deal of flashy effects with their environment and who want something that puts more focus onto the applications.

You can read more about the MATE project at the following URL:

```
http://mate-desktop.org
```

Understanding the differences between MATE and Cinnamon

At first glance, you may not notice a great deal of difference between MATE and Cinnamon. This is due to the fact that the Mint developers modeled the default layout of MATE to look closer to their other offerings, so as to create a consistent look and feel between versions. If you look at the screenshots on the official MATE website (mentioned earlier), you'll notice that the version included in Mint looks quite a bit different than how MATE does by default. Despite the similarities in how the Mint developers have set it up, MATE is a completely different desktop environment and is unrelated to Cinnamon. The following screenshot shows the MATE desktop environment:

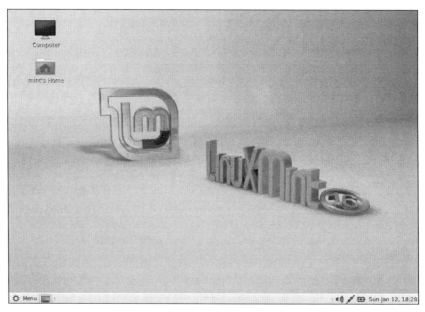

When you click on the **Applications** menu, you'll notice one difference right away; MATE uses a different application launcher. Many consider the application launcher in MATE to be superior for several reasons. For example, there is a text box on the bottom of the **Applications** menu that allows you to search for installed programs (just as Cinnamon allows you to do), but in addition allows you to also search for more than just installed programs. For example, you can type the name of a package into this text box that you don't have installed, and MATE will give you an option to install it, without even opening a package manager! In addition, you can even type a term into this text box, and options will appear that will allow you to look up that term in Wikipedia or to perform a Google search on the topic. The following screenshot shows MATE's application launcher with a generic search term typed in to show the various search options:

Another difference between MATE and Cinnamon is how you configure the environment. While Cinnamon features a **System Settings** application from which you can configure your desktop, MATE features an application known as the **Control Center** which does essentially the same thing but has a different appearance. The following screenshot shows MATE's **Control Center**:

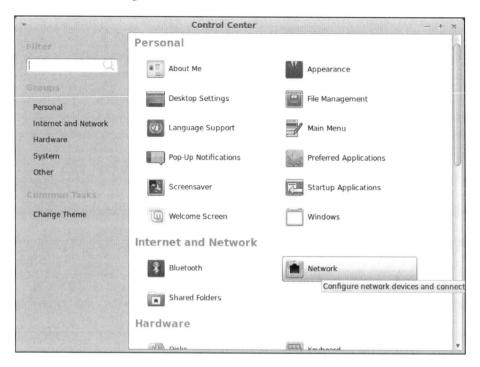

In the **Control Center**, you can configure things such as **Appearance** (the look and feel of the desktop), **Screensaver**, **Printers**, **Users**, and more.

As mentioned, MATE is lighter on resources than Cinnamon, but by no means is it lighter on features. The environment is completely customizable, so it's easy to make it your own. You can easily change the wallpaper, add applets to your panel, add a new panel, add application shortcuts to your panel and your desktop, change the theme, and much more. Just about anything you can configure in Cinnamon is configurable here as well, with one of the few exceptions being Cinnamon's Desklets. The following screenshot shows how to add an applet to the panel in MATE:

Another difference between Cinnamon and MATE is the file manager. While Cinnamon bundles the Nemo file manager, MATE instead opts for a program called **Caja**. Although they are completely different programs, their basic usage is the same. Using Caja, you can easily browse your filesystem, rename files, remove files, and navigate in much the same way as in Nemo. The following screenshot shows the Caja file manager:

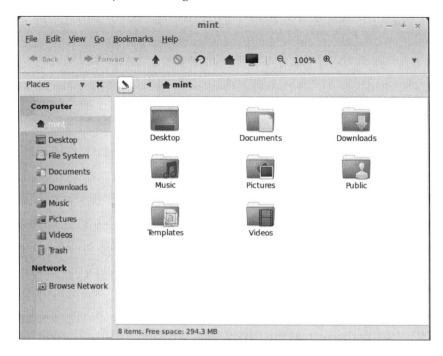

Aside from these differences, the best way for you to get a good feel for the MATE edition is to use it. After you've spent some time with it, you'll be able to determine which one you prefer for your computer.

Launching applications

As discussed earlier, MATE's application launcher is one of the bigger differences between it and Cinnamon. The application launcher consists of four main sections. The first section, **Places**, on the upper-left corner of the window, lists filesystem locations, such as **Computer**, **Home Folder**, **Network**, **Desktop**, and **Trash**. Clicking on any of these items will open the Caja file manager with the contents of the chosen item. Directly underneath the **Places** section is **System**, which gives you quick access to managing your software, accessing the **Control Center**, opening a terminal, and ending your session.

In the middle section of the window, we have a section of the launcher dedicated to **Applications**. Installed applications are categorized into sections such as **Internet**, **Office**, **Sound & Video**, and so on. The topmost category, **All**, displays all of the installed applications in a single list in case you're unsure which category it falls under. As you peruse the categories under **Applications**, the section on the right-hand side of the window will display the applications included in that category. The following screenshot shows MATE's application launcher:

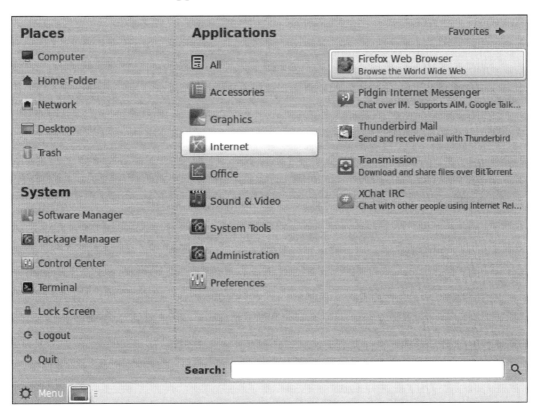

Another feature of MATE's application launcher is the ability to store favorite applications for easy access. On the upper-right corner of the launcher, there's a button you can use to switch between **Applications** and **Favorites**. To add an application as a favorite, first locate it in the menu, right-click on it, and click on **Show in my favorites**. To remove one, switch to the **Favorites** view, right-click on an application, and then select **Remove from favorites**.

Applications will appear and disappear from the panel along the bottom of the screen as they are opened and closed. Running applications are handled in the same manner as in other desktop environments, allowing you to minimize/maximize windows and close applications right from the panel from the right-click menu. The right-most area of the panel will display the date/time and battery charge (if your system has a battery) and will also allow you to adjust the speaker volume. Basically, all the standard features you'd expect from a desktop environment.

The MATE edition of Mint includes many of the same applications discussed throughout this book. Despite the desktop environment being different, you'll still find Mint's staples, such as **Backup Tool**, **Software Sources**, **Software Manager**, **USB Image Writer**, and **USB Stick Formatter**. Also, the default browser is the same for all of the editions of Mint (that is, Firefox). The following are some of the noteworthy applications that are included under the following categories:

- **Graphics**: GIMP, gThumb, Simple Scan, and LibreOffice Draw
- **Internet**: Firefox, Pidgin, Thunderbird, Transmission, and XChat IRC
- **Office**: LibreOffice Base, Calc, Impress, and Writer
- **Sound & Video**: Banshee, Brasero, Videos, and VLC

As you can see, despite the fact that the environment is different, most of the same applications we've used throughout this book are all present, so you'd be able to choose MATE instead of Cinnamon and still follow through all the non-Cinnamon-specific chapters. The software included in this edition is typical in regards to most Linux distributions. For example, quite a few distributions include LibreOffice, Firefox, and Brasero. The familiarity you build with these applications will certainly follow you if you decide to check out other distributions down the road.

Customizing MATE

Customizing your MATE experience is easy and rewarding. Using the components that the MATE edition includes, you can customize pretty much every portion of the desktop. Listed in this section are some of the highlights.

Desktop background

Just like the Cinnamon edition, the MATE edition contains a slew of backgrounds you can use for your desktop. If you don't prefer any of those that are installed by default, you can click on **Add...** and browse to find a picture of your own to use. The following screenshot shows how to select a desktop background:

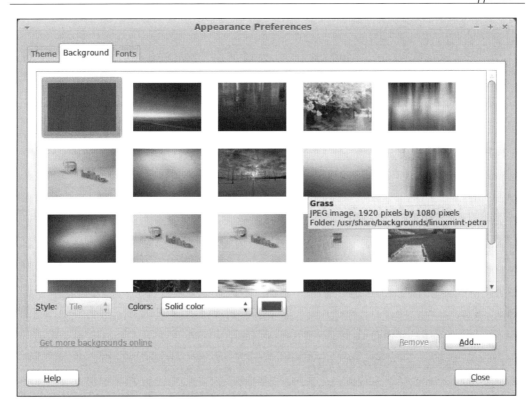

Screensaver

Also located in the **Control Center** is a section where you can change the screensaver that appears during a period of inactivity. In this section, you can choose your favorite screensaver, the length of time until it appears, or disable the screensaver altogether. By default, there are only a few screensavers installed, so this aspect of MATE may be a bit underwhelming.

Panel applets

The panel (the bar along the bottom of the screen) is also customizable using **applets**. To add an applet, first right-click on any empty portion of the panel. On the right-click menu, select **Add to Panel...** and the **Add to Panel** window will appear. From there, a list of available applets will appear along with a short description of each. To add one that interests you, click on it and then click on the **Add** button. You'll notice that the applet will appear on your panel, but likely not where you'd prefer it to be. To move the applet, right-click on it and then click on **Move**. From the right-click menu, you can also select **Remove from Panel** to get rid of it.

Desktop themes

In the **Control Center**, there's a section labeled **Appearance**. There, you can customize your theme. By default, only the **Mint-X** theme is installed. Install the `mate-themes` package, which will add several more themes for you to choose from. If you wish to install more, consider searching on Google for `Mate Themes`, and you may find additional themes with installation instructions. The following screenshot shows MATE's **Appearance Preferences** window with the `mate-themes` package installed:

Once you apply a new theme, you'll notice that the appearance of your panel, window borders, and button controls will completely change.

Summary

MATE is a very efficient desktop environment and a worthy contender to Cinnamon and other environments that are available for Linux. Although primarily recommended to those that have slower computers, MATE benefits everyone. MATE is chosen by users who prefer a desktop environment that is lighter on resources, so their applications will run with as little overhead as possible. The MATE environment is very customizable and easy to make on your own. In this appendix, we walked through many of the features that make MATE different from other environments as well as some of its strengths. Feel free to check out the MATE edition on your own system. In fact, try others as well, and you may find a desktop environment that you like even better.

C

Using the KDE Edition of Linux Mint

Until now, we've discussed some of the other editions of Linux Mint such as the **MATE** and **Xfce** editions, but we have yet to take a look at the **KDE** edition. If you've tried the other versions of Mint, you may have noticed that apart from the inherent differences relative to the various desktop environments, each is made to look and function mostly the same. The Mint developers have ported the Mint-X theme to the Xfce, MATE, and **Debian** editions, so each of them have a very close look and feel. However, the KDE edition is the most unique among the various spins of Mint and is certainly worth taking a look at.

In this appendix, we will discuss the following topics:

- The KDE desktop
- Using Dolphin–KDE's file manager
- Adding Plasmoids to the desktop
- Discovering Mint KDE's default applications
- Utilizing Activities and Workspaces
- Configuring network connections

Understanding the KDE desktop

With all the different desktop environments available for Linux, your options are endless. In the Linux world, we have GNOME, Cinnamon, Xfce, MATE, Pantheon, Unity, Openbox, KDE, and others from which you can choose. The benefit is that if you don't like one interface, you can use another, though finding your favorite can take a bit of research.

The **K Desktop Environment (KDE)** has been around for quite a while and is actually one of the oldest of the Linux graphical environments. It largely competed with the GNOME desktop in the early days, and for the most part, the decision of which user interface to install basically revolved around those two environments. Back then, the GNOME desktop largely resembled the user interface used by Mac while KDE looked closer to Windows. However, today, GNOME doesn't resemble the Macintosh platform anymore, and KDE has also developed an aesthetic of its own. Even today, many debates on the "best" desktop environment often still revolve around GNOME or KDE, though there are, of course, other contenders nowadays, such as Cinnamon.

While initially KDE was an all-inclusive term to describe its desktop environment as a whole, the software has since been componentized. Now, KDE is known as **KDE SC (KDE Software Compilation)** which consists of the **Plasma Workspace** (the desktop/interface layer) and **KDE Applications** (a suite of applications to run on the Plasma Workspace).

 As the terminology has become confusing, most Linux users still refer to the software generally as KDE. It's unlikely that you'll hear KDE SC referred to as anything other than just simply KDE in the wild. Although the official name has changed, it has yet to catch on.

The KDE edition of Linux Mint doesn't adhere to the same Mint-X theme that is used in all other versions of Mint. This means that instead of the green icons and colors you may be used to, the KDE edition takes on a blue color scheme instead. This is in line with how KDE is by default, as the Mint developers haven't changed the look and feel as much as they have with other versions. The reason for this is because KDE is designed around the **Qt** toolkit, which uses a completely different theme style than **GTK**, which is what Cinnamon, Xfce, and MATE use.

In order to port Mint's theme to KDE, it would have required a fair amount of reengineering. So, much of the default KDE theme has been left as it is, though some minor customizations (such as the wallpaper) have been added. Another difference with Mint's implementation of KDE is that you open icons by double-clicking on them rather than a single-click as in most KDE-based distributions. The following screenshot shows Linux Mint KDE's default desktop:

KDE's **Application Launcher**, which is almost always the icon on the far left of the panel, is split into sections such as **Favorites**, **Applications**, **Computer**, and **Recently Used**. To start an application, you move to the **Applications** tab, find the program you want to launch, and click on it. You can also find applications by typing into the search box at the top of the Application Launcher. The following screenshot shows KDE's Application Launcher:

If you want to add an application to **Favorites**, simply right-click on the application and click on **Add to favorites**. From that point forward, that application will be available on the **Favorites** tab (the first section) for easy access. The **Recently Used** tab lists files/locations that you've opened recently. The **Applications** tab shows all the applications available on your system, which are categorized so that you can find them easily.

The Application Launcher icon in Mint's implementation has the letters "lm" over a gear. In most other versions, the Application Launcher is a "K" icon instead. Other than the different icon, the Application Launcher in Mint's implementation is the same as in other KDE distributions.

Moving on, the next item visible in the KDE edition's panel is the Show Desktop icon, which does exactly as its name suggests. If you click on it, all windows are minimized. If you click on it again, the windows that were minimized will reappear. Next, there's an icon to launch **Dolphin**, which we'll get to in the next section.

On the right-hand side of KDE's panel, you'll find icons that display the status of system components (such as networking and audio volume) as well as the date/time. Clicking on **Kmix** (the volume control icon) will allow you to adjust the volume, whereas right-clicking on it will allow you to edit more advanced sound settings. The **Network Manager** icon will display either a wired icon or a wireless icon depending on your network connection, and this will be discussed in greater detail later in this appendix.

In the middle of the panel is where your running applications will be listed. The style of showing applications in KDE is very similar to Windows; so, if you've used Windows, then you'll immediately be familiar with the concept.

Using Dolphin – KDE's file manager

Dolphin is KDE's file manager, and is one of the many applications included in the KDE Applications suite of utilities. Its usage is very similar to other file managers we've discussed earlier in this book (Nemo and Caja), and it integrates well with the rest of the KDE desktop. The following screenshot shows KDE's file manager, **Dolphin**:

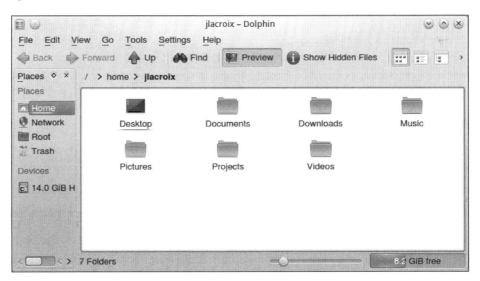

Just as in other file managers, Dolphin features several different views, such as **Icons**, **Default**, and **Compact**. You can switch between these modes using the three icons on the top-right corner of the **Dolphin** window, and you can also adjust the size of the icons by adjusting the slider at the bottom of the window. The view modes won't stick between folders, so you'll notice that as you navigate around the view mode will change. To make your desired view mode stick, click on **Settings** and select **Configure Dolphin**. In the new window that appears, you can make your current view mode the default by clicking on the **General** section, and then select the **Use common properties for all folders** option. While you have this window open, feel free to peruse the available options to customize Dolphin further—the options featured here are quite extensive.

On the left-hand side of the **Dolphin** window, you'll notice a pane featuring shortcut icons to various areas of your filesystem. Removable drives appear under **Devices**, and favorite folders appear under **Places**. To add a new folder as a favorite, simply drag it into the pane and drop it where you'd like it to appear. If you right-click on an existing icon, you'll have a chance to remove it.

Adding Plasmoids to the desktop

One of the features that sets KDE apart from other desktop environments is the concept of **Plasmoids**. Plasmoids are a suite of applets that can be added to your desktop in order to show useful information, provide a service, or perhaps give you something neat to look at. For example, you can add a Plasmoid to control a media player, display a comic strip on the screen, weather information, statuses from social networking accounts, and the list goes on.

To add a new Plasmoid, right-click on an empty portion of the desktop and then click on **Add widgets**. Along the bottom of your screen, a horizontal list of available widgets will be displayed. To add one, drag it onto your desktop. To remove it, hover your mouse pointer over one and click on the **x** icon that appears in the pop-up menu. The following screenshot shows KDE's menu to add widgets:

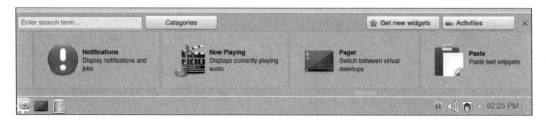

In fact, the entire desktop itself is a Plasmoid, known as a **Layout**. In Mint, KDE's layout is set as **Folder**, which is a layout that closely resembles classic desktop paradigms. For example, with Mint's default **Folder** layout, you can add shortcut icons, folders, and files to your desktop. However, this is not the norm in KDE. By default, KDE normally opts for the **Desktop** layout, which doesn't feature icons at all and is just a canvas for you to place Plasmoids. To select a different layout for your desktop, right-click anywhere on the desktop where there is no icon or Plasmoid and click on **Folder settings**. In the window that appears, you can select a different layout. Feel free to test out the various layouts available to see which ones you like best.

 You can also add a Plasmoid to your panel. To do so, simply drag a Plasmoid onto your panel rather than onto your desktop.

One Plasmoid that is especially useful is **Folder**. The **Folder** Plasmoid displays the contents of a single folder, which is very useful if there is a specific folder you access frequently, such as your home directory. Some users place a **Folder** Plasmoid onto their desktop to provide the same functionality of the **Folder** layout, but constrained to a specific area. This allows one to use the **Desktop** layout but still benefit from desktop icons. The following screenshot shows KDE's **Folder** Plasmoid:

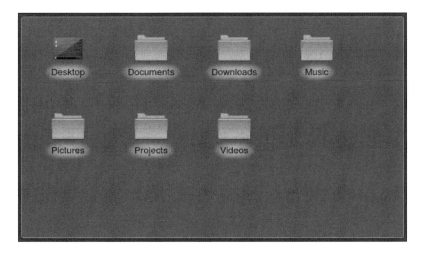

By utilizing the various layouts as well as Plasmoids, you're able to create a desktop design that is truly your own, with all of the items that you find most relevant to the way in which you use your computer available to you. The possibilities are endless, so feel free to experiment.

Discovering Mint KDE's default applications

Quite a few of Mint's custom applications are present in the KDE edition as well. For example, **Update Manager**, **Software Manager**, and **USB Image Writer** are all present. However, there are some applications that are only present by default in the KDE edition.

One of the applications specific to the KDE edition is **Kate**, a powerful text editor. At first glance, Kate may appear to be a generic text editor, but it's actually one of the most popular text editors available for Linux. While it will suit generic purposes of creating text files just fine, its real power becomes apparent in the hands of a software developer. Featuring powerful syntax highlighting and developer tools, it's a great utility to have at your disposal. The following screenshot shows KDE's Kate text editor:

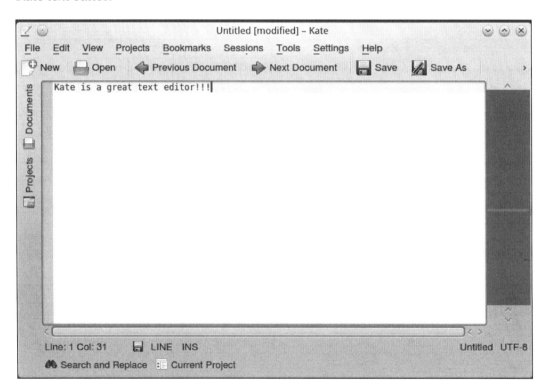

Another application specific to the KDE edition is **Amarok**, a music player and playlist manager. Amarok is another KDE application that is very popular, so much so that it's even installed by many users in non-KDE environments. Its features are near or maybe even greater than **Banshee** (the default music player in other editions), including such things as downloading lyrics and Wikipedia information for the songs in your library. If you're a music fan, it's highly recommended that you give Amarok a spin. The following screenshot shows **Amarok**—a wonderful music player and playlist manager:

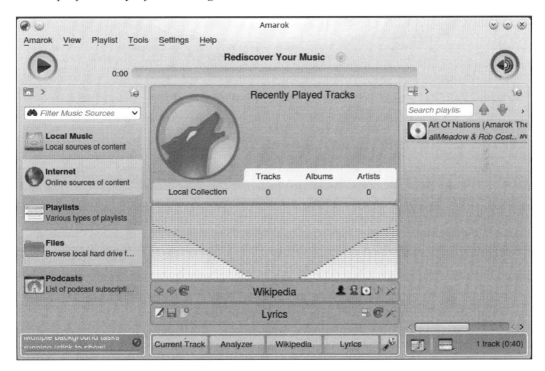

In addition to those applications, there are some other noteworthy changes in the KDE edition's software selection when compared to other editions. For example, the KDE edition features KDE IM Contacts instead of Pidgin for instant messaging, **Kmail** rather than **Thunderbird**, **K3b** instead of **Brasero**, and **Konversation** instead of **XChat**.

Utilizing Activities and Virtual Desktops

Another of KDE's extensive features is known as **Activities**. You may be familiar with **Virtual Desktops** (also known as **Workspaces**), which is a concept used in practically every Linux desktop environment. With Virtual Desktops, you can have completely separate screens running different applications. KDE allows you to utilize Virtual Desktops as well, but the feature is disabled by default. In **System Settings** (KDE's configuration tool), you can click on **Workspace Behavior** and then **Virtual Desktops** and enable Virtual Desktops by changing the number of available desktops to any number greater than 1. To switch between Virtual Desktops, you can add the **Pager** Plasmoid to your panel to easily switch between them. After enabling it, the concept works the same here as it does in other environments. However, KDE actually takes this a step further.

Activities is a concept very similar to Virtual Desktops, but it offers additional features. With Activities, you also have a separate set of running applications per Activity, just as you would with a virtual desktop. However, with Activities, you can select applications to automatically open whenever you switch to that specific Activity. For example, imagine creating a `Music` Activity and having Amarok automatically open when you switch to it, or a `Photo Management` Activity that automatically opens your preferred folder editor.

Both Activities and Virtual Desktops have a specific Plasmoid that helps you to switch between them. For Virtual Desktops, you can add the **Pager** Plasmoid to your panel. For Activities, you can add the **Activities** Plasmoid. Once added, you can easily add a new virtual desktop or Activity and switch between them. Essentially, this allows you to switch between more than one complete workflow, and the concept works best when you design an Activity around a specific task.

Configuring network connections

Just as in other editions of Mint, you're able to configure your various types of network connections in KDE as well. The concept is very similar here, though a different application is used to manage these connections than in other editions. Connecting to a network is easy. To do so, simply click on the **Network Management** icon on the panel near the clock. The actual icon itself changes depending on its status (disconnected, connected, and so on), but once you click on it, you should see a list of wireless networks around you (if you have a wireless card) or your wired connection if you have an Ethernet cable plugged in. The following screenshot shows KDE's Network Management application:

To edit existing connections, click on the wrench icon in the bottom-right corner of this menu. There, you'll have an option to add a network manually (such as a static address) or modify/delete wireless connections. The concept here is very similar to **Network Manager** (used in all other editions). To create a new connection, click on the **Add** button and select the type of connection you wish to add (wired, wireless, VPN, and so on). The **New Connection** window will appear. Switch to the **IPv4** tab and add your desired address, DNS servers, and the search domain with values appropriate for your network. The following screenshot shows KDE's network connection editor:

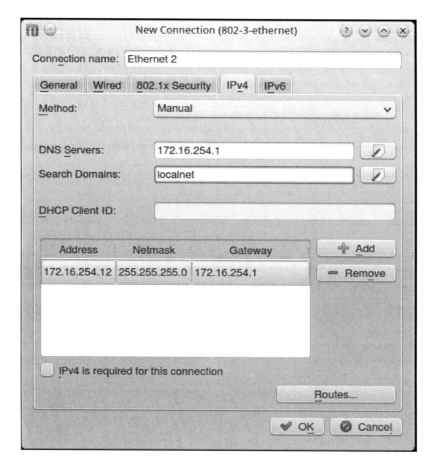

Summary

The KDE edition of Mint is certainly an exciting distribution to try and is far different from other Mint versions. The KDE desktop is a very powerful environment, allowing you the most customization over other desktop environments, complete with differing layout widgets (Plasmoids) and an application suite containing powerful applications such as Kate, Dolphin, and Amarok. KDE is a great choice for those that love to tweak their desktops and create the perfect environment to suit their needs. Technologies such as Activities complement your workflow and help you stay organized. If you try only one other version of Mint, this should be the one. While not as popular as the other editions, the KDE edition is a very well-made distribution and is worth checking out.

Index

F

file management
  with Nemo 58, 59
file permissions
  about 168-172
  modifying 173, 174
files
  managing 83-85
  searching for 89, 90
  sharing, with NFS 191-193
  sharing, with Samba 189-191
filesystem
  navigating 77-83
FileZilla
  about 120, 186
  installing 186
find command 89, 90
Firefox
  about 55
  default search engine, changing 63-65
Firewall Configuration tool 15
flash drives
  formatting 97-99
forum accounts
  creating 18
Frozen Bubble 119
FTP servers
  accessing 185-188

G

games
  slow frame rates, solving 259
gibibytes
  versus gigabytes 107
gigabytes
  versus gibibytes 107
GIMP
  about 56
  photos, editing with 149, 150
GNOME Terminal 73
GNU Image Manipulation
      Program. *See* GIMP
GPL license
  URL 11
Grand Unified Bootloader. *See* GRUB

graphical user interfaces (GUIs) 10
grep command 220, 248
GRUB
  reinstalling 250, 251
grub-install command 250
gThumb 57
Gufw
  installing 200

H

hashbang 93
home directory partition
  maintaining, in Linux Mint
      installation 267-270
home folder
  encrypting 41, 42, 197-199

I

ifconfig command 258
initial triage
  performing 242
installation process 34-40
Install button 119
Install Now button 38
International System of Units (SI) 107
iptables 200
iptables firewall
  configuring 199-202
  testing 199-202

K

Kate text editor 292
KDE 23, 286
KDE desktop 286-289
KDE SC (KDE Software Compilation) 286
K Desktop Environment. *See* KDE
kern.log 249
killall command 224
Konsole 73

L

LastPass 197
launchers
  creating 54

mkfs command 99
mount command 251
MP3 tags
  editing 145, 146
music files
  playing 140, 141
mv command 85

N

nano command 86
nano text editor 86
Nemo
  file management, using with 58, 59
network connections
  configuring 295, 296
networking
  problems, solving with 258, 259
network interface card (NIC) 176
networks
  wired network, connecting to 176-178
  wireless network, connecting to 180-182
new applications
  installing 118, 119
new users
  creating 156-160
NFS
  about 189
  files, sharing with 191-193
nm-tool command 180
notifications, Cinnamon 52

O

OpenDNS
  installing 206

P

package lists
  exporting 230, 231
  importing 230, 231
packages
  importing, for reinstallation 270-272
  managing, in Linux Mint 116
panel applets, MATE 281
partitioning 30-33
passwd command 160

passwords
  changing 160-162
persistence 25
persistent aliases
  creating 219, 220
photos
  editing, with GIMP 149, 150
  viewing 148
Pidgin 56
Plasmoids
  about 290
  adding, to desktop 290, 291
PPA... button 130
PPA (Personal Package Archive) 130
problems
  solving, with networking 258, 259
processes
  killing 221-225
programs
  launching 46-48
  running 164, 165
PulseAudio Volume Control 256
PuTTY program 184
pwd command 76

R

RAM
  testing 252-254
removable media
  accessing 96, 97
Remove button 123
resource usage
  monitoring 234
rm command 84
rm -r command 164

S

Samba
  files, sharing with 189-191
screensaver, MATE 281
scripting 92-94
Search button 124
Search domains 179
secure passwords
  choosing 196, 197

Thank you for buying
Linux Mint Essentials

About Packt Publishing

Packt, pronounced 'packed', published its first book "*Mastering phpMyAdmin for Effective MySQL Management*" in April 2004 and subsequently continued to specialize in publishing highly focused books on specific technologies and solutions.

Our books and publications share the experiences of your fellow IT professionals in adapting and customizing today's systems, applications, and frameworks. Our solution based books give you the knowledge and power to customize the software and technologies you're using to get the job done. Packt books are more specific and less general than the IT books you have seen in the past. Our unique business model allows us to bring you more focused information, giving you more of what you need to know, and less of what you don't.

Packt is a modern, yet unique publishing company, which focuses on producing quality, cutting-edge books for communities of developers, administrators, and newbies alike. For more information, please visit our website: www.packtpub.com.

About Packt Open Source

In 2010, Packt launched two new brands, Packt Open Source and Packt Enterprise, in order to continue its focus on specialization. This book is part of the Packt Open Source brand, home to books published on software built around Open Source licenses, and offering information to anybody from advanced developers to budding web designers. The Open Source brand also runs Packt's Open Source Royalty Scheme, by which Packt gives a royalty to each Open Source project about whose software a book is sold.

Writing for Packt

We welcome all inquiries from people who are interested in authoring. Book proposals should be sent to author@packtpub.com. If your book idea is still at an early stage and you would like to discuss it first before writing a formal book proposal, contact us; one of our commissioning editors will get in touch with you.

We're not just looking for published authors; if you have strong technical skills but no writing experience, our experienced editors can help you develop a writing career, or simply get some additional reward for your expertise.

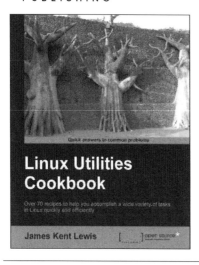

Linux Mint System Administration Beginner's Guide

ISBN: 978-1-84951-960-1   Paperback: 146 pages

A practical guide to learn basic concepts, techniques, and tools to become a Linux Mint system administrator

1. Discover Linux Mint and learn how to install it.

2. Learn basic shell commands and how to deal with user accounts.

3. Find out how to carry out system administrator tasks such as monitoring, backups, and network configuration.

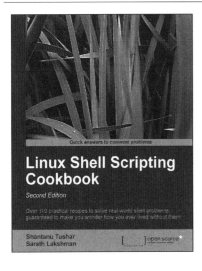

Linux Shell Scripting Cookbook
Second Edition

ISBN: 978-1-78216-274-2   Paperback: 384 pages

Over 110 practical recipes to solve real-world shell problems, guaranteed to make you wonder how you ever lived without them

1. Master the art of crafting one-liner command sequence to perform text processing, digging data from files, backups to sysadmin tools, and a lot more.

2. And if powerful text processing isn't enough, see how to make your scripts interact with the web-services like Twitter, Gmail.

3. Explores the possibilities with the shell in a simple and elegant way - you will see how to effectively solve problems in your day to day life.

Please check **www.PacktPub.com** for information on our titles

Printed in Great Britain
by Amazon